The Collected Works Of William Morris: Journals Of Travel In Iceland. 1871. 1873...

William Morris

William Morris

(March 21. 1877)

THE COLLECTED WORKS
OF WILLIAM MORRIS

WITH INTRODUCTIONS BY
HIS DAUGHTER MAY MORRIS

VOLUME VIII
JOURNALS OF TRAVEL IN ICELAND
1871 1873

LONGMANS GREEN AND COMPANY
PATERNOSTER ROW LONDON
NEW YORK BOMBAY CALCUTTA
MDCCCCXI

CONTENTS

INTRODUCTION

THE visit to Iceland was another land-mark in my father's life. In itself, apart from what it stood for in his work, it was something of an undertaking. A seasoned traveller would have smiled at the adventure of six days in a small steamer and six weeks' riding among friendly people; but my father was not a seasoned traveller. He had a deep love and knowledge of country things, and was country bred, but his every-day life was necessarily a sedentary one: he was going to exchange this, without any training, for six weeks' hard riding over difficult country in a wild climate, cutting himself off from every possible communication with his own folk—no little thing for a man so deeply-rooted in the home-life. So it must be said that he started in a somewhat adventurous spirit that spoke well for the success of the journey.

His courage, however, was nothing to that of Charley Faulkner. My father's old college-friend was not in good health and thought the careless open-air life would benefit him: this partly, but he went chiefly out of sheer affection for my father, interested in, though not sharing his absorbing passion for the things of the North. He suffered untold miseries on any sort of salt water, endured the long days in the saddle the best he might, and during the journey was several times on the verge of illness: moreover, his short-sight almost amounted to blindness, and many a time it must have been only the wisdom of those admirable little ponies that saved him from disaster. Yet with all this, and not living in the magic dream that possessed his friend, he managed to keep going by sheer pluck and enjoyed it, rough times and smooth times and all. He was store-keeper and paymaster to the expedition. With them went Mr. W. H. Evans, of Forde Abbey, Dorsetshire, who had been attracted to Iceland for the shooting and fishing. Mr. Magnússon made up the party of four and was, of course, the organizer of the travelling details: once landed and making for the interior, they would have to travel in primitive fashion with guides and a troop of ponies, carrying tents and food and everything for their needs. There was a great to-do over the buying of outfits and packing of stores; the cooking too had to be considered. Mr. Mackail in his "Life" tells how the Burne-Jones children remembered my father coming one day and building "a little hearth in their garden with loose bricks, over which he cooked a stew in the manner of some pirate or backwoodsman in a story-book." And it was not so long ago that I came upon the rather melancholy rüins of Jenny-and-May's out-door "kitchen" in one of the home-closes at Kelmscott, built in the same way. My father wrote to Faulkner months before, bidding him practise riding. "I began this morning. By Gum the Great we shall have plenty of it there according to our program." But I think it must have been a very desultory and fitful sort of training.

Then and later my father never lost the youthful zest and "picnicky" feeling of travelling in a new place, especially if the little discomforts were merely those attendant on primitive conditions—the inconveniences of missing trains, of dirty hotels, discourteous or grasping traders, unsympathetic officials, closed museum doors, all such as these he bore with different degrees of impatience, sometimes mild enough, sometimes bordering on frenzy.

It was a gay little party that started from Granton Pier that Sunday morning in July for a few precious weeks in the free air. From the very first the voyage was full of keen pleasure for my father; his high spirits and excitement are shown by a letter written from Reykjavík to mother after they had seen the guides and collected the ponies for a start.

Reykjavík, Iceland,
July 16th, 1871.

Well, my dear, here I am safe and quite well; I have written to the littles too, because I thought it would be fun for them: all goes well and we start up the country to-morrow

xvj

with twenty horses, such jolly little fellows the poneys are; they almost look as if they would talk. We had a very good and swift voyage out on the whole; the first day it was very calm, and so was the next morning (we didn't sail till Sunday at 6 a.m.) but after we passed the Orkneys we got a very heavy sea for some hours, and I was sick though not very ill, C. J. F. being pretty much prostrate; that was on Monday; on Tuesday morning about seven we reached Thorshaven in the Faroes, and went ashore for twelve hours; we went a long walk over the hills on the most beautiful of days and it was so calm that evening that the Captain was able to thread the labyrinth of the islands, and a most wonderful sight it was: I have seen nothing out of a dream so strange as our coming out of the last narrow sound into the Atlantic, and leaving the huge walls of rocks astern in the shadowless midnight twilight; nothing I have ever seen has impressed me so much. We saw no land all Wednesday which was a very cold bleak day, though the wind was fair; but on Thursday morning about three Magnússon called me up to see Iceland. I think I told you we were to go to Berufirth in the east first of all; and we were just at the entrance to it now; it is no use trying to describe it, but it was quite up to my utmost expectations as to strangeness: it is just like nothing else in the world; it was a wild morning too, very black out to sea, and very bright sun under a sort of black canopy over Iceland.

We coasted all that day and had fine weather at first, as we passed by the stupendous mass of glaciers they call Vatna Jokul where ice-rivers seem to run fairly into the sea: We sailed by Croefa Jokul too with fair weather; it is the highest mountain in Iceland; after that the clouds settled on the land and it began to rain and blow and the sea soon ran very high, but the wind was fair and the ship went very fast: about nine p.m. we were opposite Njal's country and the clouds lifted a corner there to show a watery copper and green sunset, very splendid; then about two a.m. on Friday we made the Westman Islands, and stopped there to give and take letters; they were some time coming off and we had a good view of that wild collection of rocks, in which there showed great caves, with little beaches to them, a rare matter in the rocky coast we had seen; it was a doleful sight rather to see the poor chaps going back in their walnut shell of a boat with three letters which was all their post.

Next morning we had a good knocking about before we reached Reykjavík but I had got my sea-legs by then, and didn't mind it much: we got to Reykjavík about three in the afternoon this day (Friday) and went ashore soon, and were taken by Magnússon to the house of one of his kinsfolk and are quite comfortable a-nights on the floor [of] a very small clean room, and are abundantly fed; the town itself might be in Canada and is quite common-place, but all the houses seem clean—inside.

We three worked hard at repacking all yesterday—and oh, my dear—do you remember the parcel from the Cooperative Stores that they ought to have taken out of our case and didn't send in time to do it. Well, many a speculation we had as to what it would be; whether good to eat, drink or wear; and I for my part said: perhaps it will be Floriline and hair brushes—excitement there was when we got to it—and—may I never be forgiven if it did not contain these articles:—

     1st 2 doz. bottles of scents,
     then 2 doz. do. of *Floriline*.
     then 1 large box of violet powder.

There! there! there! here is a laugh to end with: we howled so over it that we nearly killed the landlady with curiosity to know what it was all about.

Please, dear Janey, be happy and don't forget the date of letter to me. The boat starts back for England September 1st, so I hope to be at home about the 8th (in London I mean); if you are still at Kelmscott I will come at once to see you. Be happy.

    I am, with all love,
        Your most affectionate,
            William Morris.

The following came at the same time to "the little rascals" Jenny-and-May.

Reykjavik, Iceland.
July 16th, 1871.

Dear little daughters,

Isn't it funny that I am writing to you from Iceland? I got here safe and sound about four o'clock on Friday afternoon; we had a good voyage, and I was not very sick: one day we saw porpoises a long way off and when they saw the ship they swam after it as fast as they could, jumping out of the water so that you could see them all: they soon came up with the ship and played about her, it made one laugh so, because they looked like oiled pigs: We first saw Iceland about 3 o'clock on Thursday morning; that was at a place called Berufirth; it looked very wonderful; for there was a huge mountain like this with clouds all round it. We saw several whales that morning; afterwards we sailed along the coast and saw great ice mountains with rivers of ice looking as if they were running into the sea; this is a funny little town with more poneys than men in it, and we are lodging in such a queer little cottage, but very clean. We have bought twenty ponys for our journey, and we shall begin our journey to-morrow if all goes well; it is a very bright beautiful day to-day and very warm.

I hope you are very good and are kind to Mama and that you are happy at Kelmscott; it is not much like Iceland I can tell you. I send you some wild thyme I plucked this morning in the fields close by here; there are many pretty flowers about, but no trees at all, not even a bush about here, but the mountains are very beautiful.

I send kisses and love, my littles, and good-bye. I am writing to Mama too.

I am,
Your most affectionate Father
William Morris.

The tour was well-planned and was not marred by any serious mishap, nor, except for the apprehension caused by Charley Faulkner being unwell for a few days, hampered by sickness. The more than ordinary sympathy between the party and the people they were visiting made their journey easy and pleasant in a very important respect. They experienced the luxury of travelling in a land where they were plainly and soberly welcomed—a luxury far outweighing discomforts and occasional hardships that were all part of the fortunes of war. That one of them was a native of the island and used to the methods of travel made things easy—I might even say possible—for the three Englishmen whose journey was far more extended than was usual in those days and often covered ground but little explored. The Icelanders soon became interested in the foreigner who knew their history; they were tickled at an Englishman coming out, not to shoot their moors and fish their rivers but to make pilgrimage to the homes of Gunnar and Njal, to muse on the Hill of Laws, to thread his way round the historic steads on the Western firths, to penetrate the desert heaths where their outlaws had lived. Later on he was known to them as "The Skald," the Skald from the country "west over the Sea" which their ancestors in the old days had been wont to visit for trading or warfare, who had been telling their tales in his own tongue. The story of the Island was a living thing to folk who still dwelt in the country-sides made famous by the great families of the early centuries. Local antiquarians showed the travellers at Bergthorsknoll what were surmised to be charred fragments of the Burning: Snorri's bath is still used as in his time: Gudrun's grave—a howe covered with flowers—is still pointed out. Even the empty heaths were peopled by their imagination: I remember my father telling how Jón, one of the guides on their second visit, believed so strongly that the descendants of the outlaws still lived hidden in the desert places that he started out one day, bundle on shoulder, on a voyage of discovery. The whole land teems with the story of the past—mostly unmarked by sign or stone but written in

men's minds and hearts, the story of their forefathers who
had wrested from the

> Land of deep snows and scarce hidden fires

a grim livelihood of hardship and incessant struggle. To
these folk living their frugal life between the firth and the ice
mountain came the modern skald brimming with eagerness
and desire to get at the heart of their story. He was moved
by the Iceland of to-day as well as by the Iceland of the past,
his interest keenly aroused by a place which the current of
commercial life swept by leaving it unchanged, whose arts
and small industries grew simply and naturally out of the
needs and fancies of the people.

My father was especially interested in the handicrafts of
the Island. One result of the remoteness of the country is the
preservation of tradition in the arts; when he was there he
came across silver-work, carved horns, embroideries, etc., all
of a real and fine character; the dress of the Icelandic ladies
too was full of dignity and distinction, their silver ornaments
being often heirlooms of noble fifteenth century character.

The poverty, the incessant privations of the Icelanders,
moved and disturbed him; he would tell us how they went
to the fishings and describe vividly their little cockleshells of
boats not fit to battle with those terrible seas—some of the
poor fellows never coming back, and he would tell us how
the foreigners, the French principally, I think, got all the
abundant harvest of the deep-sea fishing before the Icelanders' very eyes, as it were—they too poor for the necessary equipment.

The merry little train of ponies made away South to the
Njal country, this portion of the journey including a memorable expedition to Thorsmark; returning a little on their
tracks the party went North, stopping some days at the Geysirs, across the wastes of the central watershed; thence they
went down the Northern drain into the valley of Waterdale.
From here they made their way across to the Western firths

and so back down the South-western track, the last camping ground being the Thingmeads. The journal of 1871 was written from two note-books, battered and in places rubbed and illegible, whose appearance is eloquent enough and tells of long journeyings and soakings in that precious little haversack—familiar to everyone who knew my father. He took very full notes, and it is surprising to think of the diligence of this travel-worn Londoner, coming into camp after a long day in the saddle, to the work of pitching the tents, cooking (nearly always entirely left to him), clearing up, and then to have energy enough left to write up a diary! It was found in early days that the Poet was also to be the Cook, because his dinners were so much better than those of the rest of the party.

They were received kindly and hospitably everywhere; occasionally they were allowed to pay modestly for their entertainment, sometimes the farmers would only accept payment for the beasts' food, sometimes they would accept nothing, while of course in many places they were received as guests by people of distinction. But everywhere, at the prosperous homesteads and at the poorer ones, the same idea of hospitality prevailed. It has sometimes struck me that there are certain similarities between travel in the deserts of the East (in Arabia, for instance) and that in Iceland: there are the same conditions that make a rigorous hospitality a necessity; the custom of starting on the journey late in the afternoon with an escort of friends from the city to see the party on their way; the frugality and hardships, the simple and dignified art: again, the tradition of a heroic past with its relentless blood-feuds, the volcanic country with its bursts of green—all with a big difference! I have often thought that if my father could have endured the great heat he would have been much attracted to desert travel in Arabia, had he once begun to taste its alluring charm. C. M. Doughty's "Arabia Deserta," by-the-by, was one of his very favourite books towards the end of his life.

Here is the letter my father sent home by the Danish vessel lying off Stykkisholm, whose skipper asked them to breakfast on board—to the travellers' confusion when they found he had not invited their charming and cultivated host.

August 11th [1871].
Stykkisholm on Broadfirth.
Iceland.

Dearest Janey,

This is a little sort of town by the sea-side, a trading station, and there is come into the haven a Danish schooner from Isafjorde (Icefirth) that will sail for Liverpool in a day or two; he (the merchant) has kindly offered to take letters for us and as there seems a chance of their reaching you before I do, I write.

I have little time however as we go early to-morrow morning; I am tremendous in health and in very good spirits, and enjoy the riding very much; the poneys are delightful little beasts, and their amble is the pleasantest possible means of travelling: everybody has behaved charmingly; even I have not lost my temper often: C. J. F. (from the other side of the table) begs to state that he would have been better-tempered had it not been that riding has not been as enjoyable to him as to me, and that even a black sheepskin has not made his saddle as soft as by rule of three it ought to be. We shan't get through above half our stores, I fancy; people have been so hospitable, there has been but little roughing it, and I find sleeping in a tent very comfortable work even when the weather is very cold; the weather has been cold, and rather broken till the last few days: last Tuesday week we had a very bad day, riding over the wilderness in the teeth of a tremendous storm of snow, rain and wind; it was an eight-hours' job, but I was not a penny the worse for it next morning. You've no idea what a good stew I can make, or how well I can fry bacon under difficulties. I have seen many marvels and some terrible pieces of country; I slept in the home-field of Njal's house, and Gunnar's, and at Herdholt: I have seen Bjarg, and Bathstead and the place where Bolli was killed,

xxiij

and am now half an hour's ride from Holyfell where Gudrun died. I was there yesterday and from its door you see a great sea of terrible inky mountains tossing about: there has been a most wonderful sunset this evening that turned them golden though; the firth we look on here is full of little islands that breed innumerable eider ducks, and a firth we crossed yesterday was full of swans: Give dear love to the little ones and tell them I am going to try to bring them my pretty grey poney home; but if I don't they must not be disappointed for there may be difficulties or he may not turn out well: his name is Falcon, and when he is in good condition he ambles beautifully fast and deliciously soft; he is about 13 hands high. I wish you could see us to understand how jolly it is when we have got a good piece of road, and the whole train of twenty horses is going a good round trot, the tin cups tinkling and the boxes rattling (my word how the shine is taken off them!) I must "premise" however that I am dirtier than you might like to see me: my breeches are a triumph of blackness, but not my boots, by Jove! I may mention in passing that an Icelandic bog is not good riding, and that the loose stones on the edge of a lava-field is like my idea of a half-ruined Paris barricade: that there are no lice in Iceland and that itch is unknown; but Evans deposeth that there are fleas galore,—however, they don't bite me.

Good-bye, my dear, I have so often thought of the sweet fresh garden at Kelmscott and you and the little ones in it, and wished you happy. Please write to mother with my best love. I would have written but time presses strongly.

Good-bye, with all love.

Your loving
William Morris.

I have already told of the chance discovery of Kelmscott (Vol. IV, p. xiij) and of my father's delight in it. He was not too full of Iceland nor too deep in the last details of packing to give a thought to domestic matters before leaving, and to write some detailed directions about repairs of the newly-discovered treasure of a house; he gives an eye to the possibilities of cray-fishing in the stream, too, and bids my mother have Philip the handy-man get a "basket" for them and begin the fishing as soon as they come on.

"I have written a ballad about that story we were talking of on Sunday," he goes on: "I will send it you if I can get it copied in time.... How beautiful the place looked last Monday: I grudged going away so; but I am very happy to think of you all happy there, and the children and you getting well. Ned, Webb and Faulkner dined here yesterday and we were all jolly enough. Yesterday morning I saw Evans off by boat for Edinburgh; such a packing as Charley and I had the day before! twelve blessed packages, however all is well there: I have made all my adieux and am off by the 9.15 p.m. train. We go 3rd class but the train is good and comfortable.

"Now I will say good-bye dear, for the present, with all blessings on you. Kiss the littles and give them my best love. I shall write a line from Edinborough. Live well and happy.

"Your affectionate,
William Morris."

During the six weeks that my father was in Iceland we were at Kelmscott, in fact, I think we spent the whole summer there. The house was taken jointly with Mr. Rossetti, who occupied the Tapestry Room and the bedroom adjoining. He writes to W. B. Scott in mid-July: "I am writing in my delightful sitting-room or studio, the walls of which are hung with tapestries which I suppose have been here since the house was built." He was there all this summer and into the autumn. We saw nothing of him all day unless one of us happened to be sitting to him; he came down to a late breakfast and I often wondered at a person being able to eat so many eggs, forgetting that while we were eating our solid mid-day meal he was shut up at work, taking no other food till the evening family dinner, after which we all sat in the studio with him. Just about dusk he would come down from his work, and go for a solitary walk, wet or fine. My mother would go with him sometimes, not often, as she was never strong, but the impression remains on my mind of the solitariness of those twilight walks. I can see the rather broad figure tramping away doggedly over the flat green meadows, in search of exercise and air enough to keep in health for the day's work; I can see him returning after dark with a burden of weariness upon him—even the young child in pauses of happy playhours felt the loneliness of it. Indeed, we youngsters were more conscious of this element of solitariness in our family life than our elders knew; one incident in particular drove it home to me. My mother and Jenny were away, and after dinner, there being some visitors in the house (among them, I think, a light-hearted model who lacked excitement) we young folk started a game of hide and seek all over the house, romping and skirmishing in the garrets. I was the first to return to the studio and found Mr. Rossetti sitting over the fire—alone. It is difficult even now to shake off the childish pang of self-blame that came over me at the sight, wishing that I at least had not been so thoughtless, and wishing I could tell him how sorry I was. Rossetti was fond of us, and I think we amused him, wild little animals tumbling about among the flowers and declining lessons.[1] He made most of me—by the beautiful law of contraries, I imagine, for Jenny was far the more virtuous and amiable child: the slight aptitude for drawing I was considered to have interested him; I was also a useful model for angels. Anyway our mother told me a few years later, he had wanted to adopt me. It can be imagined how disconcerted mother was at the way I took this. Instead of flinging myself in her arms and exclaiming, "Dearest mother, never let us be parted!" or words to that effect, I turned seraphic eyes on her and asked, "Well, mother, why didn't you? You've got Jenny." I trust I have since made up to my mother for this painful moment of disillusionment!

I enjoyed the long sittings in the studio, and posed well and patiently. When he was in a silent mood there was the tapestry

[1] "The most darling little self-amusing machines that ever existed," he says of us.

xxvj

to look at, and if he happened to place me opposite Samson having his eyes gouged out, or Samson pulling down the gates of the temple, I was absorbed indeed. In another position one could watch the doings of the pigeons on the grey stone slates of the roof of another gable, or I would catch sight of my sister's face at a window at right angles; and there was always plenty to dream about. But sometimes Rossetti would chat as with a "grown up," asking questions and really seeming to listen to what one answered, and that was agreeable.

One day he seriously enquired which I thought the uglier of two ladies of our acquaintance. I considered the matter very gravely and proceeded conscientiously to give my verdict, explaining the why of it. With equal gravity he said, "I think you are right," and we discussed the points of the ladies. This being innocently reported to mother, her severe comment, "It was very, very naughty of Mr. Rossetti," quite surprised me.

I am still telling my story from the child's point of view, and what I remember of our dear traveller and his doings comes back to me always with the child's eyes. Iceland had begun to be one of the familiar fairy-land places in our imagination, and it was with a thrilled curiosity and excitement that we received the letters that came to our little Earthly Paradise that August. I remember with what delight we heard of the pony that would arrive with my father, the little beast with the delightful name of Falki, all virtue and no vice.[1] Of other things we heard vaguely, and then the stir of his coming home, down to Kelmscott, with all that burden of adventure and travel upon him—coming back out of the land of trolls and awful mountains. Then closer knowledge of the strange place came to us through him. The wonder side of it we knew something of already, through the legends of Iceland and through our own Storyteller: we were now to hear something of the actual human life, the charm of the melan-

---

[1] As will be seen, not Falki but another beast turned up—our playmate for many years.

choly little steads, with their flowers and their bright green-lipped streams gracing the edge of the awful volcanic wastes: we heard of the doings of little maids like ourselves, how they span and knitted and sang old ballads and how prettily they played the housewife on occasion; we even wore their silver girdles and their embroidered bodices—we certainly had good material for dreaming ourselves into another life than our own. It is all very long ago, but Iceland, till then a spot on the map that one often forgot to draw in, it was so tiresomely high up, and so far off it didn't matter—Iceland became and has been ever since a real thing, at once overpoweringly beautiful and overpoweringly melancholy.

One of the links between us and that far North was Mouse, the intelligent sure-footed little animal my father rode all through this first journey: "The bravest and best-tempered of little beasts: you should have seen him picking his way in one of those dismal bogs, where if you sneeze, the earth or rather the roots of the grass, trembles violently." [1] Dear old Mouse! gentle and staid but not without his quiet humour and shrewd estimate of human friends. Ambling down peaceful lanes must have been poor sport to him after the grim reality of travel in Iceland, and when I mounted him he occasionally relieved the monotony of our rides by trying to rub me off his broad back against a certain gate-post as we left the home-field. The mild trick created no bad blood between us, though he must have laughed at my horsemanship. Father rode him about the country a good deal at first, and then I rambled around with him, and we also had a little basket-carriage, between the shafts of which he looked incredibly fat and funny. I often thought about him, the lonely little beastie, getting bored and longing for his friends and the frolic and incident and hard life at home, and admiringly recalled all we had been told of the difficult rides which had tested his fine qualities of brain and his endurance. It was long a grief to us children to know that the fate of many of his fellows when sold to the Scottish dealers was to go down

[1] Life, I, p. 274.

into the mines, where they never saw daylight again—the squalor, the desolation of it, after the wild free life between firth and mountain! Mouse would stand at a certain corner of his field, whence he could watch the village road and the great horses coming to the smithy to be shod; he stood there day-long with his head stretched forward, the very type of a philosopher who has known the world. He was no mere animal in the Kelmscott life, but a personality, and we children often exchanged wistful glances with him, wishing the stupid barrier between three playmates might be removed. We grieved at his death, and the home-close wore a blank air for a long time when he had gone.

It must have been a hot pleasant summer that year my father was away North, and while he was riding among the black wastes and crossing the great rivers of that land of wonder, we were basking by our gentle uneventful Thames.

Poor mother manfully tried to make us do lessons—me at least—for Jenny as before mentioned was virtuous, also studious—indeed, it is not known how she learnt to read, as it came to her without pain or tribulation. Those glowing August mornings we sat in the pleasant cool of the Panelled Room trying to learn things about the Roman emperors, and outside the wide mullioned windows the blackbirds were chuckling and feasting among the gooseberries; golden stacks were growing roof-high in the yard outside, and the huge barn was alive with busy men and women. It was all too interesting: the Roman emperors were not to be endured for long, and mother became philosophical over my truancy. I fancy Jenny stuck to them, because so many of my escapades were lonely ones. Among other things I took to roof-riding like Glam at Thorhall-stead, the house with its many gables and the noble farm-buildings being particularly adapted to this pastime. One day, however, the feat did not quite come off—or rather I nearly did: for choosing to explore a specially inaccessible roof, having reached the ridge, there I sat astride and could not move. It is not difficult to imagine my mother's agony at discovering the situation: the poor soul bravely mastered her feelings and encouraged me to hold on, sending old Philip the gardener post haste for the longest ladders the village possessed. The dangers of the river she took more calmly, partly because Philip was usually with us—or supposed to be, and partly because we took to the water instinctively, and could handle a boat or punt without losing our heads.

The manor, or the "Lower House," as it is called in the village, belonged to a yeoman family, whose graves lie in the little churchyard, going back to the sixteenth century. Mr. Turner was dead, but his widow, our landlady, lived with an unmarried sister and brother in her old home down the river. We used to make pleasant visits there, going to see the beasts and watching the cheese-making, and after gigantic teas coming back in the cool of the evening, the boat laden with flowers and fruit—everything the free-handed souls could prevail upon us to take away. A tall frail handsome woman was Mrs. Turner: she left the farm down the river and crossed over to Kelmscott as a bride, and then left the manor and crossed back to her old home—and died there. Perhaps the serene-looking face had lived down some impatience, mastered some vagrant fancies as the long years slipped by, but to picture that quiet journey from home to home and at last to the churchyard that lies embowered among orchards high above the river, is indeed to think of life as a placid dream.

The second journey to Iceland was made in 1873; Mr. Faulkner was my father's only travelling-companion, though on board the "Diana" they met with John Henry Middleton, who went with them as far as the Geysirs. This new acquaintance, known already to Charley Faulkner, was a man of note and distinction. He was an architect and subsequently held the post of Slade Professor and Keeper of the Fitzwilliam Museum, Cambridge. For the last few years of his life he was director of the South Kensington Museum. The meeting was the beginning of a close and lasting friendship. My father had the greatest admiration for Middleton's scholarship and taste; they had many things in common, and out of a wide and practical knowledge of Eastern arts Mr. Middleton was able, in later days of weaving and dyeing experiments to give his friend much valuable help.

I have often wondered why Mr. Middleton ever went to Iceland.[1] He was not particularly bound up in the things of the North, he detested cold as a cat does, yet there he was, utterly unprovided with the ordinary traveller's outfit; he had no comforts, positively nothing, as though he had fallen down from the moon; he is out of the story at the Geysirs, so far as the journey is concerned, but he soon came into our family circle, and later on married a great friend of ours, the daughter of W. J. Stillman, for a long time the American Consul and "Times" correspondent in Rome.

The travellers started from England about July 10, and were away two months. The journey was harder and more adventurous than that of 1871, with many forced rides over unfrequented wastes: after a second visit to the Njal country they set out across the great central desert to the north-east of it, the furthest point reached being Dettifoss on Jokulsá, the tremendous river that runs nearly in a straight line from the Vatna-Jokul, the glacier region of the South-east, to the Arctic Ocean. They stopped at Akreyri, the northern port, and thence began to turn their faces south. They had some very long days and a good deal of rough weather, but seem to have come back all the better for the six or seven weeks of stiff travelling. My mother received the following letter while at Kelmscott.

Reykjavík,
July 18th [1873.]

Dearest Janey,

Here I am safe after having seen some part of the wonders that those see who are fools enough "to exercise their business in the great deep." In fact I have been very sick as was no wonder for we have had several rough days, especially last

---

[1]A friend remarks: "He went 'for to admire and for to see;' he went to Fez for the same purpose, and to many other remote places."

night when we fairly had to turn tail from the last headland and lie-to under the lea of the land till the gale lulled a little; however, no bones are broken and I am quite well now and so is C.J.F.

We are off to-morrow morning to my great satisfaction, except that it keeps me from writing a long letter to you my dear, as I should like to have done. I'm afraid we shall have a coldish season, there is much more snow on the mountains than in '71. However all seems like to go well otherwise.

It is all like a kind of a dream to me, and my real life seems set aside till it is over.

Kiss my dear little ones for me and tell them I positively have no time to write to them, as you would easily know if you saw me now amid the boxes with C.J.F. and another man in the room: I will send a letter to them from Akreyri (in the North) if I find a ship going to Iceland.[1]

My dear how I wish I was back, and how wild and strange everything here is. I am so anxious for you too, it was a grievous parting for us the other day—and this shabby letter! but how can I help it, not knowing whether I am on my head or my heels?

With all love to you and the dear good little ones.
I am, your loving
W. M.

P.S. We start back from here on September 5th, so don't expect me before the 12th.

I am printing the unfinished diary of this second journey almost as it stands. The direct daily record of impressions seems to bring us very near the traveller and his emotions; he saw things keenly and with broad vision, and the eager close account of the volcano-torn country can, I think, be read without feeling discomfort at omissions and want of finish. It takes us—literally with him—through all the desert region that so fired his imagination; we pass the dreadful

[1] Sic: to England, he means. Ed.

xxxij

mountains, sharing his depression at the sight of them, follow him through the flowery little valleys, whose sweetness is the sweeter for the contrast. At last when the faithful daily account becomes abrupt and broken, we feel more than ever the mood that comes on him—the long day, every moment full of the changing panorama, all the excitement of the journey accumulating, the nights of physical fatigue, with their details of camp-life duties—two men to do the work that four had shared before; and we feel how it is that at last, after the endless day's ride hunting after Dettifoss through the cold mists, the diary becomes a mere string of notes, and breaks off altogether a few days after they have started on the return journey.

The return to Iceland touched him even more closely than his first visit had; the strangeness of the land was wearing off, his attention did not need to be so concentrated on everything that happened, and all that first excitement gave place to an exaltation of spirit peculiarly intense, expressed in some degree by the sort of detachment the diary conveys. He was entirely absorbed in the country they went through; it is curious to see how little mention is made of persons. One gets an impression that for the time he had shaken off his human sympathies, that people did not interest him—he had no need for them—and that he had withdrawn into a frame of mind in which he saw the wilderness in its real loneliness, awful, unloveable and remote from human life—the elemental horrors had seized upon him and perhaps he saw sights and heard sounds from another world than that in which he and his fellow-travellers were moving—who knows indeed where the poet wanders when he withdraws into his own country?

"The journey," he writes of it after his return, "has deepened the impression I had of Iceland and increased my love for it. The glorious simplicity of the terrible and tragic, but beautiful land, with its well-remembered stories of brave men, killed all querulous feeling in me, and has made all the dear faces of wife and children and love and friends dearer than ever to me. I feel as if a definite space of my life had passed away now I have seen Iceland for the last time: as I looked up at Charles' wain to-night, all my travel there seemed to come back to me, made solemn and elevated in one moment, till my heart swelled with the wonder of it: surely I have gained a great deal, and it was no idle whim that drew me there, but a true instinct for what I needed."

MR. MAGNÚSSON, the survivor of the first party, has been kind enough to look over the two Journals and to contribute some interesting and useful notes on the travels, for which I take this opportunity of thanking him.

Jón Jónsson, or Jón söðlasmiður ('saddle-smith') as he was generally called, who figures so largely in the second journey as the principal guide, died a few years ago. My father kept up friendly relations with him all through his life, and the letters of greeting that came regularly from Iceland always touched and pleased him in their sincerity and simplicity. The family have interchanged greetings with Jón thereafter each year, until he too departed.

The transcript of the first Journal, given to Lady Burne-Jones, was completed just before starting on the second voyage from diaries kept during travel, as a note at the end of the manuscript says. The second Journal is printed directly from the diary—unfinished and far more hurried towards the end than was the earlier one. The year that the first Iceland journal was written out from the original notes, my father was very full of his " painted books," and in the middle of the manuscript his ordinary firm, clear copying-hand blossoms out into a beautiful and careful script, of which I give an example here (page 98).

Following my usual practice of interfering as little as

¹ Life, I, p. 295.

possible with individual spelling, I have retained my father's occasionally somewhat anglicized forms of Icelandic names, which are, however, easily recognisable. In all cases (except for the points of the compass and for the names of the party) I have marked an expansion of abbreviated names by square brackets, curved brackets being the author's. It will be quite clear, I hope, that variety in spelling is due to careful transcription; everything has been left as it came from the writer's hand—notes and impressions that he might have written out later for his friends' reading, if other matters had not filled his mind.

The charming maps which illustrate the journeys are due to the zeal of Mr. Emery Walker and to the enthusiasm of Mr. H. W. Cribb, who did the actual drawing. But I also have to thank Mr. W. G. Collingwood, who very generously placed at my disposal his collection of water-colour drawings done for "The Saga-steads of Iceland." They have not only helped us over certain difficulties in the map-making, but were invaluable to me in supplementing my father's description of the colour of Iceland, helping me to realize his wonder and pleasure over its strangeness.

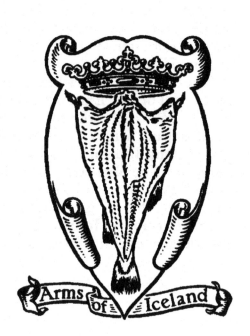

Arms of Iceland

A JOURNAL OF TRAVEL IN ICELAND
1871

CHAPTER I. LONDON TO REYKJAVIK
Thursday, July 6th, 1871.

AFTER a fidgety afternoon C.J.F. and I started from Queen Square in two cabs to meet Magnússon there,[1] Evans having gone on before by steam-boat from London Bridge. Of course I felt as if I had left everything behind, yea, as if I myself should be left behind. We found Brown[2] waiting to see us off, but no Magnússon as yet, so we took our tickets (third class) and C.J.F. bribed the guard to keep other people out of the carriage, telling him we should be five in number, for Magnússon's womankind were expected to come with him.

He was so late that I began to get very fidgety, for though that morning my heart had failed me and I felt as if I should have been glad of any accident that had kept me at home, yet now it would have seemed unbearable to sleep in London another night.

Thursday, July 6th, Newcastle.

At last just a minute before the train was due to start he came in a cab, without his womankind, who could not get off till the next day: he fidgeted me still more by having a quarrel with his cabman, but at last we got him into the carriage, where the guard came to look at us, and pulled a face at first at our being only three; but at last he brightened up on consideration of what he obviously deemed the depth of Faulkner's cunning, and there we were off for Iceland: a third-class railway journey by night (we started at a quarter past nine) is neither eventful nor pleasant; we droned away as usual in such cases, though I for my part was too excited to sleep, though we made ourselves comfortable with two of the huge blankets that were to be our bedding in camp. Day dawned,

[1] At King's Cross Station. Ed.   [2] Ford Madox-Brown. Ed.

Newcastle dull and undramatic as we left York, over about the dullest country in England, striking neither for build of earth, nor for beauty of detail: as we passed between the forges of Darlington the sun fairly rose and got confused strangely with some of the fires of the ugly sheds there: it was one of those landscapes in the sky, the sunrise was, with light clouds floating far in advance of the gleaming white undersky, and a clear green space down low in the horizon. North of Darlington the country gets hilly, and is soon full of character, with sharp valleys cleft by streams everywhere; but it is most haplessly blotched by coal, which gets worse and worse as you get towards Newcastle, so wretched and dispiriting that one wants to get out and back again: Newcastle itself has been a fine old town and very beautifully situated, but is now simply horrible: there is a huge waste of station there, quite worthy of it.

Thursday, July 6th, Berwick.

Leaving Newcastle the country gets cleaner, but is dull enough till we strike the sea at Warkworth with a glimpse of a very beautiful old castle there; thence we go pretty much by the seaside past the poetical-looking bay in which lies Holy Island: a long horn runs far out into the sea there, and near the end of it, all up the hill, is a little town that looks very interesting from a distance: the country is all full of sudden unexpected knolls and dales, but is nowise mountainous; it has plenty of character: so on still along the sea till we come to Berwick: there the Tweed runs into a little harbour, nearly land-locked, and on the north of this lies a picturesque old town on the hillside with long bridge of many pointed arches uniting it to the south bank, the said bridge having its arches increasing in size as they get nearer the north bank instead of in the middle as usual: I suppose because the scour of the water on that side made the water deeper, and therefore bigger arches were wanted for the bigger craft that could pass under them. We are all very tired by now, none of us having slept anything to speak of: Faulkner indeed did get to sleep a little before Berwick, but I woke him up to

2

see it; for which rash act I was rewarded with an instinctive Berwick clout on the head.

So there we were in Scotland, I for the first time: north of the Tweed the country soon got very rich-looking with fair hills and valleys plentifully wooded. I thought it very beautiful: we had left the sea now; but every now and then we would pass little valleys leading down to it that had a most wonderfully poetical character about them; not a bit like one's idea of Scotland, but rather like one's imagination of what the backgrounds to the border ballads ought to be: to compensate, the weather was exceedingly like my idea of Scotland, a cold grey half-mist half-cloud hanging over the earth.

Friday, July 7th, at the Granton hotel.[1]

I MUST make the new day begin here I suppose, at Edinborough, though it has been Friday and broad daylight many hours. As you come up to Edinborough it looks striking enough certainly, and is splendidly set down, with the huge castle-rock rising in the middle of it and on its outskirts the quite wild-looking mountains about Arthur's Seat; underneath lies what is left of Holyrood: once upon a time it must have been an impressive and poetical place, but I should think always very doleful: the dolefulness remains, the poetry is pretty much gone: the station is a trifle more miserable-looking than the worst of such places in England: looking up from it you see high houses going up the sides of the deep gorge it lies in; they are black, they are comfortless-looking and not old now: we went up for a few minutes into the dismal street where people were taking their shutters down, then wandered about the station, felt frowsy, and drank ineffably bad coffee in the refreshment-room till the train started for Granton. When we came there to a particularly wretched little station by the pier, we went to the agent's and found Evans, who had landed about six in the morning, going there too: the agent was vague about the arrival of the

[1] I am supposed to be writing the journal at night after each day's travel for clearness sake.

"Diana," and I began to be afraid I should have my first experience of a Scotch Sabbath: however, I consoled myself with
thinking I should moon the time away somehow: and so we
went to a dismal big inn close to the pier, which has the sole
advantage of having a look-out over the firth and its islands,
the going and coming trains, and the steam-ferry to Burnt
Island that lies on the other side of the firth. Granton is a dull,
dull place with the slip-shod do-nothing air that hangs about
a small port, though I suppose more is going on than seems
to be: except for the steam-ferry aforesaid, which is always
coming and going, the same vessels seem as if they must always be lying in the same places, and the sailors loafing about
look as if they had been "struck so" with their hands in their
pockets. After breakfast we took train into Edinborough
again, and walked ourselves pretty well off our legs buying
odds and ends. I had my hair cut in terror of the dreaded
animal, Faulkner all the while egging on the hair-dresser to
cut it shorter: he and I afterwards drove about a bit in an
open chaise thing with the uncomfortable feeling that one
doesn't know where to tell the driver to drive to, and that he
and everybody else are pointing the finger of scorn at us for
being strangers and sightseers: well, we drove into the Grass-
market and other parts of the old town; there is little left now
that is old in look, and all is dirty and wretched-looking in
the old town, and the new town provincial and pretentious
to the last degree: so at last back we went to Granton and dinner, very well tired: nevertheless we went out afterwards and
wandered about the harbour till dark, well enough amused
in watching little matters about the ships: a timber-ship
amongst others where they had opened two great holes in the
bows, and were running out the timber through them: it
looked queer seeing into the hold of the ship: withal there
stood on a raft outside a Scotchman with a hook, who tried
to catch the timber as they came out to make them fast to the
raft: he fell into the utmost Scotch fury because he kept missing them, to Faulkner's huge contempt: at last he did catch
one and so back we went home: there was a very considerable

4

racket in the coffee-room when we got in, partly from some Granton who are to be our fellow-travellers, partly from German mates and the like dropping in for a drink: but we played at whist amidst it till we could sit up no longer and so went to bed dog-tired.

Saturday, July 8th. On board-ship "Diana" lying in Granton Harbour.

I WOKE up at five this morning to a very bright calm day, and ran to the window to see if "Diana" has come in during the night, for I have a sort of feeling that we shall never get away from Granton, and indeed, it is a place to inspire that feeling: however, there was nothing new there, and I went to bed again till I thought my less impatient friends would be stirring, and then came down to breakfast, in the middle of which Magnússon's womankind came in from the train: then Faulkner and I went out together and walked about the pier watching the smoke of every steamer (a good many they were) that was to be seen in the firth: Evans had gone to see a friend up the country, and I secretly thought him very rash; not really I mean, but from the imaginative point of view. Well, after getting my letters from the agent, we came into the coffee-room again, and still amused ourselves by looking over the firth for our ship, till I saw the smoke of a steamer that seemed coming our way, and presently Magnússon's brother-in-law cried out that he thought it was the "Diana:" so we looked till we could see a vessel making straight for the harbour which we thought was a screw, and then Faulkner and I ran out in great excitement, and on to the pier-head and there she was stem on and certainly a screw, and in a few minutes Magnússon joined us and told us that the agent had just come in with the news that the "Diana" was sighted: she ran up her flag presently, but we couldn't see it because she was meeting the wind; but the rig and look of her was just what the "Diana" had been described as being: she brought up a little way from the harbour because they were signalling to her about where she was to

5

go; but presently came on again, and the captain bellowed to the harbour-master: "Where then?" The harbour-master bellowed back: "What have you got to deliver?" The Captain: "Nothing at all." The harbour-master said something I didn't hear and presently she was into the harbour and broadside on to us and there anchored in the middle of the harbour;[1] she was a long low vessel with three raking masts, and was once a gunboat; she carries the swallow-tailed Danish flag with a crown and post-horn (royal mail) in the corner. Magnússon, Faulkner and I got a boat presently, and boarded her, and saw a fat mild-faced steward, who refused five shillings which I had the bad manners, I don't know why, to offer him: he showed us the berths, and we picked out four unengaged ones: I pretended not to be dismayed at the size of them and the sleeping-cabin—but I was: however, there was a comfortable deck-cabin with sofas[2] to lie on all round; and the look of the boat is satisfactory to me; because yesterday we were told that she was only 140 tons; whereupon Evans pointed out to me a steamer-yacht lying in the harbour, and told me she was 150 tons, and as she was about as big as an up-Thames barge, though I pretended not to care, my flesh crept, for I expected firstly to die of sea-sickness, secondly to be drowned.[3] Well, we made arrangements for getting our luggage on board, for we were told we should sail at eight that evening, and then I went to write my letters in a rather excited frame of mind, having managed to get rid of the feeling that had possessed me since I got to Granton, that we are about come to our journey's *end*. About six p.m. the porters came for our luggage, and Magnússon, Evans and I went down to the boat with it, getting thoroughly wetted on the way by a Scotch shower; (for both this day and the day before the weather had been very violent & uncomfortable after eleven a.m.)

[1] It seems she stuck on a mudbank, and couldn't get to the coaling pier till she floated again at high water which was what delayed us.

[2] The said sofas, however, were berths by night and had a board also that let down above them, so that they were double berths.

[3] We found out afterwards that the "Diana" was 240 tons.

6

"Diana" was amidst of coaling, and was dirty and confused,
and I felt as if we should none of us be allowed to eat or go to
bed all the voyage through: but in spite of the confusion a
red-headed good-tempered mate, who spoke English, and by
the way was very like P.P. Marshall,[1] received us with smiles;
but informed us that she wouldn't sail till six the next morning, as also, which I didn't know before, that we were not going straight to Reykjavík, but should touch at Berufirth in
the East:[2] these were blows to me, who was impatient to an
absurd degree to be fairly on the expedition and in the saddle;
but I bore them well, and we went back to dinner: but just as
we were asking for our bill, came a message from the captain
that he was going to start that evening; so out we all turned
and down to the ship; as we went along the pier a long queer-
looking sailor more or less in liquor came up and began talking Faroese (which to my pride I understood) and it seems
he wanted to get a passage out there in the "Diana;" he suc-
ceeded and I saw him, tarry and beery, shaking hands with a
Faroese lady-passenger on board. Well, there we were on
board without tuck of drum, not so much as Blue Peter hoisted, to Evans' great disgust; in such a muddle! the luggage
undiscoverable, and I quite sure in my mind that it had never
come on board, the decks dirtier than ever; twenty-four passengers on board that bit of a vessel, and where the deuce were
they to sleep[3] and eat: moreover, after all we are not to sail
till to-morrow morning: however we three were in high
spirits and enjoyed ridiculously small things; but Magnússon seemed depressed, and chaff failed to rouse him. The four
of us sat down to whist in the cabin, played a long rubber, the
last, alas! for many a day, and then went up on deck about
midnight for a bit; it was very cold and very bright with the

[1] One of the members of the firm of Morris, Marshall, Faulkner
and Co. Ed.
[2] It was a gain as it happened, as we saw thereby some of the strangest and most striking scenery in Iceland.
[3] They slept (part of them) as in note p. 6 of course: as to the eating,
everybody was not *always* able to sit down to table.

7

light of the dawn already showing in the North-east and presently the moon rising red over the firth. I felt happy and
adventurous, as if all kinds of things were going to happen,
and very glad to be going. So to bed.

Sunday, July 9th. On board-ship "Diana," somewhere in the
Pentland Firth.

WOKE after fair sleep, and a dream of having letters
from home, about a quarter to six, and heard the
steam getting up, so jumped up, and washed and
dressed under difficulties, and going up on deck had presently
the pleasure of seeing them warping the ship's head round,
then the screw began to turn, and we slowly steamed out of
the harbour towards Iceland, unregarded by any living soul,
but with our colours flying for all farewell: it was a sunny
morning but with threatening of rain. Once out of the harbour they began to swab the decks and the little vessel looked
quite clean and tidy now: she is as aforesaid an old gunboat,
long and low, rising somewhat forward, and with bulkheads
across the deck just forward of the deck-cabin, that seemed
to us to forebode plenty of water on board: she has three
masts, the foreward one has two square sails and a fore and aft
sail, the middle one a fore and aft sail, and the after one no sail
at all bent on it: round about the rudder is a little raised platform where we lay about a good deal on the voyage out, then
comes the deck-cabin with a narrow covered passage leading
forward on each side of it, and with a hurricane deck on the
top: then there is a small open space broken by the skylights
of the engine-room between the deck-cabin and the galley
(cooking-place): there is good space for a walk forward of this,
but when there is the least sea on, unless the wind is right
astern it is too wet to be pleasant: over the galley, I forgot to
say, is the bridge where the captain or mate stands to steer the
ship: also our sleeping cabin is reached by stairs from the
deck-cabin, and there is a ladies' cabin on the other side of
ours—ours is a very small place, and almost pitch dark when
the lamps are not lighted; as small as it is we were surprised

8

to find that it really was not very stuffy, for they have managed to ventilate it well.

Well, when we were all fairly up, they gave us coffee and minute tops-and-bottoms, and we ate and drank on deck in comfort enough; the firth being quite smooth; nine o'clock was breakfast proper, by which time we were getting out of the firth and she was beginning to roll, for which she had a great talent; nevertheless I sat down to breakfast with a huge appetite (please don't be too much disgusted): breakfast was beefsteak and onion, smoked salmon, Norway anchovies, hard-boiled eggs, cold meat, cheese and radishes and butter, all very plenteous: this was the regular breakfast, only varied by eggs and bacon instead of beef.[1] Faulkner looked serious as he sat down and presently disappeared; I think the first man on board.

We were soon fairly out and running north along the Scotch coast, a very dull and uninteresting-looking coast too: there is not much sea and the wind is astern, the day very sunny and bright and I enjoyed myself hugely though I was rather squeamish at first: you get lazy and are quite content-ed with watching the sea on board ship when all is going well and the weather is warm: Faulkner is prostrate now but very resigned, and lies without moving on the platform by the wheel: the day clouded over a little towards evening and threatened rain, but throughout the weather was fair; one amusement was seeing the sailors heave the log, which they do every two hours, I think; it consists of throwing a piece of wood and a long line into the sea, and letting it run out and then winding it up again, whereby (not being scientific, I don't know why) they find out how fast the ship is going: the cox-swain saw to this; he was a queer little man with a red beard, and a red nose like a carrot, and bright yellow hair like spun glass: as they wound the line up they would sing a little sea-song that pleased my unmusical taste.

We went under sail all day and made about ten knots an

[1] They victualled us for 3s. 9d. per diem—cheap—but then you see everybody had always to pay, but everybody couldn't always eat.

9

hour, which was good; about nine we saw the last of the Scotch
coast, and I turned in at twelve with no land to be seen anywhere, and we in the Moray firth.

Monday, July 10th. On board-ship "Diana," somewhere between the Orkneys and the Faroes.

I FELT rather ill last night when I turned in, and Faulkner
gave me some chlorodyne to make me sleep; it kept me
awake and made me very nervous, so that I felt as if the
ship were going to the bottom at every lurch, i.e. at every two
seconds, for she rolled heavily; however, I got better of my
qualms, in all despite of the bilge-water—such a sweet smell!
I woke finally about five, went up, and walked barefoot about
the decks as they were swilling them still; it was a grey morning with a very calm sea now, and a cloud rather darker than
the others on our left was the southern isles of the Orkneys:
later on, about 9 a.m., I think, we passed the northernmost
isle quite close, but all we saw was a sandy strip of land with
a lighthouse on it; on the other board was the Fair Isle now,
where Kari stayed with David before he struck the last strokes
in the avenging of Njal[1]; and further northward we can see
Shetland very dimly. Fair Isle and Shetland are both high
conical hills to look at.

We are to run between the Orkneys and the Shetlands, and
were told last night by the mate that we were going to catch
it to-day, as here we first met the roll of the Atlantic meeting,
itself, the races between the islands; his prophecy was speedily fulfilled now, and I was soon sick, but not very ill; I lay
mostly in the deck cabin as quietly as the ship's rolling would
let me, but went out at whiles to be sick and look about me.
It grew a lovely sunny day though with plenty of wind; the
sails were hoisted and we were going at a round pace, while
the great swell came in right abeam of us: once when I went
out as far forward as I could for the wet (for she shipped seas
plentifully), there seemed to be a great glittering green and

[1] The Story of Burnt Njal; by Sir George Dasent, Edinburgh,
1861, II, 322.

white wall on either side of us, and the ship staggering down
the trough between them; the sails flapped and swelled, and
the sea seemed quite close to the low gunwale amidships;
then I went to the little platform astern and lay about there
watching the waves coming up as if they were going to swallow us bodily and disappearing so easily under her: it was all
very exciting and strange to a cockney like me, and I really
enjoyed it in spite of my sickness. As the day wore the wind
fell somewhat, and poor Faulkner, who had been very bad
came up on deck and lay on the stern with me wrapped up in
blankets till about eleven when it was still quite light, when
we went to bed right out in the Atlantic.

Tuesday, July 11th. On board-ship "Diana," the Faroes
astern of us.

I HAVE often noticed in one's expeditions how hard it is
to explain to one's friends afterwards why such and such
a day was particularly delightful, or give them any impression of one's pleasure, and such a trouble besets me
now about the past day.

I woke up later than usual, about half-past six, and went
on deck in a hurry, because I remembered the mate had promised that we should be at Thorshaven in the Faroes by
then, and that we should have sighted the south islands of
them long before: and now there we were sure enough
steaming up the smooth water of a narrow firth, with the
shore close on either board: I confess I shuddered at my first
sight of a really northern land in the grey of a coldish morning:[1] the hills were not high, especially on one side as they
sloped beachless into the clear but grey water; the grass was
grey between greyer ledges of stone that divided the hills in
regular steps; it was not savage but mournfully empty and
barren, the grey clouds dragging over the hill-tops or lying
in the hollows being the only thing that varied the grass,
stone, and sea: yet as we went on the firth opened out on

[1] The Faroes seemed to me such a gentle sweet place when we
saw them again after Iceland.

one side and showed wild strange hills and narrow sounds between the islands that had something, I don't know what, of poetic and attractive about them: and on our side was sign of population in the patches of bright green that showed the homefields of farms on the hillsides, and at last at the bight's end we saw the pleasant-looking little town of Thorshaven, with its green-roofed little houses clustering round a little bay and up a green hillside: thereby we presently cast anchor, the only other craft in the harbour being three fishing-smacks, cutters, who in answer to the hoisting of our flag ran up English colours, and were, we afterwards found out, from Grimsby for Iceland. The shore soon became excited at our arrival and boats put off to us, the friends of our three passengers for the Faroes, and others, and there was a great deal of kissing on deck presently. Then came a smart-looking boat carrying the governor, and having eight oars a side, manned by the queerest old carles, who by way of salute as the boat touched our side shuffled off their Faroish caps in a very undignified manner. These old fellows, like most (or all) of the men, wore an odd sort of Phrygian cap, stockings or knee-breeches loose at the knee, and a coat like a knight's *just-au-corps*, only buttoning in front, and generally open. The boats are built high stem and stern, with the keel rib running up into an ornament at each end, and cannot have changed in the least since the times of the sagas.

Well, the governor being gone, we had our breakfast, and then carrying big bundles of sandwiches set out for shore to amuse ourselves through the day, as we didn't expect to sail till the next morning. Magnússon took us to the store of a friend of his, a sort of place like a ship's hold, and where they sold everything a Faroese would buy, from a tin tack to a cask of brandy; we found nothing to buy there but Danish cherry-brandy, which was good and cheap. Then we went into the private house of the merchant and were kindly welcomed by his wife into a pretty wooden house very like a ship's cabin, and, to me, still unquiet: it

12

was very clean, painted white and with roses and ivy in great
pots growing all over the drawing-room wall (inside).

Thence we went out into the town, which pleased me
very much: certainly there was a smell of fish, and these
creatures, or parts of them, from guts to gutted bodies, hung
and lay about in many places; but there was no other dirt
apparent; the houses were all of wood, high-roofed, with
little white casements, the rest of the walls[1] being mostly
done over with Stockholm tar: every roof was of turf, and
fine crops of flowery grass grew on some of them: the people we met were very polite, good-tempered and contented-
looking: the women not pretty but not horrible either, and
the men often quite handsome, and always carrying themselves well in their neat dresses; which include, by the by,
skin shoes tied about the ankle with neat thongs: the men
were often quite swarthy, and had a curious cast of melancholy on their faces, natural I should think to the dwellers in
small remote islands. We were to go a walk under the guidance of a Faroe parson to a farm on the other side of the
island (Straumey), and so presently having gone through
the town we met on a road that ran through little fields of
very sweet flowery grass nearly ready for the scythe: it af-
fected me strangely to see all the familiar flowers growing
in a place so different to anything one had ever imagined,
and withal (it had grown a very bright fresh day by now)
there was real beauty about the place of a kind I can't describe. We were soon off these cultivated meadows however
and in a long deep valley of the open fells, peaty and grass-
clad, with a small stream running through it and not unlike
many Cumberland valleys I have been in: up the hillside on
the left we struck, and clomb the hill whence turning round
we could see the sound we had come up this morning, the
little "Diana" lying in the harbour with the boats clustered

[1]A good many though were white or black: the houses were pitched
down with little order enough, and in fact the town was like a toy
Dutch town of my childhood's days.

13

round her, the little toylike looking town so small, so small, and beyond it the mountains, jagged and peaked, of another island, with the added interest of knowing that there was a deep sound between us and them: sea and sky were deep blue now, but the white clouds yet clung to the mountains here and there.

We turned away and went along the ridge of the mountain-neck and looking all up the valley could see it turning off toward the right, and a higher range above its bounding hill: and again it was exciting to be told that this higher range was in another island; we saw it soon, as we turned a corner of the stony stepped grey hills, and below us lay a deep calm sound, say two miles broad, a hogbacked steep mountain-island forming the other side of it, next to which lay a steeper islet, a mere rock; and then other islands, the end of which we could not see, entangled the sound and swallowed it up; I was most deeply impressed with it all, yet can scarcely tell you why; it was like nothing I had ever seen, but strangely like my old imaginations of places for sea-wanderers to come to: the day was quite a hot summer day now, and there was no cloud in the sky and the atmosphere was very, very clear, but a little pillowy cloud kept dragging and always changing, yet always there over the top of the little rocky islet, which was by no means very high. We turned now towards the end of the sound that looked openest, and began to go down hill, and soon were off the stony ground and walking over grassy slopes full of wild thyme and ragged-robin, and a beautiful blue milk-wort: how delicious it seemed after the unrest and grubbiness of the little vessel!

We could now, when we looked behind us, see a good stretch of our hillside, which sloped steeply into the sea, and showed the home-meads of two farms within sight; and on the hillside of the opposite island we could count three farms: all the islands, whether sloping or sheer rocks, went right into the sea without a handsbreadth of beach any-where; and, little thing as that seems, I suppose it is this which gives the air of romanticism to these strange islands. We

turned another spur of the hills soon, and then the land on Kirkiuboe our side fell back, the long island aforesaid ended suddenly and precipitously, and there was a wide bay before us bounded on the other side now by the steep grey cliffs of another island:[1] the hillsides we were on flattened speedily now, under steep walls of basalt, and at the further end of them close by the sea lay the many gables (black wood with green turf roofs) of the farm of Kirkiuboe (Kirkby), a little whitewashed church being the nearest to the sea, while close under the basalt cliff was the ruin of a stone medieval church: a most beautiful and poetical place it looked to me, but more remote and melancholy than I can say, in spite of the flowers and grass and bright sun: it looked as if you might live for a hundred years before you would ever see ship sailing into the bay there; as if the old life of the saga-time had gone, and the modern life [had] never reached the place.

We hastened down, along the high mowing-grass of the homefield, full of buttercups and marsh marigolds, and so among the buildings: the long-nosed cadaverous parson who guided us took us first to the ruin, which he said had never been finished, as the Reformation had stopped the building of it: in spite of which story it is visibly not later than 1340 in date, which fact I with some qualms stoutly asserted to the parson's disgust, though 'tis quite a new fault to me to find local antiquaries post-date their antiquities: anyhow it was or had been a rich and beautiful "decorated" chapel without aisles, and for all I know had never been finished: thence we went into the more modern church (such a flower-bed as its roof was![2]) which was nevertheless interesting from its having a complete set of bench-ends richly carved (in deal) of the 15th century, but quite northern in character, the interlacing work mingling with regular 15th century heraldic

[1] Hestey (Horse Island) was the island opposite; the clouded rock N.W. of it was Koltur (the Colt); Sandey was the long island in the distance to the south. E.M.

[2] "of buttercups, ragged-robin and clover," says the note-book. Ed.

15

work and very well carved figures that yet retained in costume and style a strong tinge of the 13th century: the ornament of the bishop's throne, a chair with a trefoiled canopy, though I am pretty sure of the same date as the bench-ends, was entirely of the northern interlacing work.

From the church we went into the bonder's house which was very clean, and all of unpainted deal, walls, floor, and ceiling, with queer painted old presses and chests about it: he turned up with his two children presently, and welcomed us in that queer northern manner I got used to after a little, as if he were thinking of anything else than us, nay rather, as if he were not quite sure if we were there or not: he was a handsome well-dressed man, very black of hair and skin, and with the melancholy very strong in his face and manner. There we drank unlimited milk, and then turned back up the slopes, but lay down a little way off the house, and ate and drank, thoroughly comfortable, and enjoying the rolling about in the fresh grass prodigiously.[1]

Then we wandered back to the ship; and as we passed by the abovesaid rocky island the little pillowy cloud yet dragged over its top.

We reached the " Diana " just in time for dinner, sat down not knowing whether we were to sail that evening or not; but in the middle of it, to my great joy, for I was impatient for Iceland still, bang went the signal gun that announced our sailing in an hour's time. The evening was very fine still, the sea was quite smooth, and the tide in our favour; so the captain told us we were going to thread the islands by the sound called the Westmanna-firth instead of going round about them; so as it turned out we had the best sight of the Faroes yet to see: going down the sound we had come up in the morning, we turned round into the sound we had looked down into from Kirkby that noon, passing close by the stead itself, and so into the Westmanna-firth, that grew narrower and narrower as we went on, though here and there

---

[1] I am sorry to say though, that I spoilt it for myself somewhat by making an imbecile sketch of the stead and its surroundings.

16

between breaks of the islands we could see the open ocean.
At last we were in the narrowest of it; it was quite smooth
clear and green, and not a furlong across: the coasts were
most wonderful on either side; pierced rocks running out
from the cliffs under which a brig might have sailed: caves
that the water ran up into, how far we could not tell, smooth
walls of rock with streams running over them right into the
sea, or these would sink down into green slopes with farms
on them, or be cleft into deep valleys over which would show
crater-like or pyramidal mountains, or they would be splintered into jagged spires, one of which single and huge just at
the point of the last ness before we entered this narrow sound,
is named the Troll's finger; and all this always without one
inch of beach to be seen; and always when the cliffs sank you
could see little white clouds lying about on the hillsides. At
last we could see on ahead a narrow opening, so narrow that
you could not imagine that we could sail out of it, and then
soon the cliffs on our right gave back and showed a great
landlocked bay almost like a lake, with green slopes all round
it and a great mountain towering above them at its end, where
lay the houses of a little town, Westmanna-haven; they tell
us that the water is ten fathoms deep close up to the very
shore in here, and that it is as it looks, a most magnificent
harbour.

After that on we went toward the gates that led out into
the Atlantic; narrow enough they look even now we are
quite near; as the ship's nose was almost in them, I saw close
beside us a stead with its homefield sloping down to the sea,
the people running out to look at us and the black cattle grazing all about, then I turned to look ahead as the ship met
the first of the swell in the open sea, and when I looked astern
a very few minutes after, I could see nothing at all of the
gates we had come out by, no slopes of grass, or valleys opening out from the shore; nothing but a terrible wall of rent
and furrowed rocks, the little clouds still entangled here and
there about the tops of them: here the wall would be rent
from top to bottom and its two sides would yawn as if they

would have fallen asunder, here it was buttressed with great masses of stone that had slipped from its top; there it ran up into all manner of causeless-looking spikes: there was no beach below the wall, no foam breaking at its feet. It was midnight now and everything was grey and colourless and shadowless, yet there was light enough in the clear air to see every cranny and nook of the rocks, and in the north-east now the grey sky began to get a little lighter with dawn. I stood near the stern and looked backward a long time till the coast, which had seemed a great crescent when we came out of the sound, was now a long flat line, and so then I went to bed, with the sky brightening quickly.

Wednesday, July 12th. On board-ship "Diana" near the East firths of Iceland.

I SLEPT long and got up at nine, and found the ship making good way before a north-east wind, and no land anywhere; the morning was grey and uncheerful, and it worsened as the day wore, getting very cold, but did not rain. The only thing we saw but desolate grey sea and sky was a shoal of porpoises about 2 p.m. that came leaping after the ship, throwing themselves right out of the water; I had never seen this very common sea-sight before, and it pleased me very much.

I hung about till late that night (1 a.m.) in hopes of seeing Iceland, but was told we should not sight it till morning so I went to bed. I had better say again that we are going to stop at Berufirth, nearly 400 miles to the east of Reykjavik: shall not stay there half an hour the captain says: we have to put ashore one Captain Hammer, an old Danish whaling skipper, who goes most years to Jan Meyen for whale, but lost his ship last year, and has oily business in these East firths; and also a woe-begone East-firther, with whom I have tried to sharpen my Icelandic sometimes.

Thursday, July 13th. On board-ship " Diana " off the coast
of Rangárvalla-sýsla, Iceland.

SO I have seen Iceland at last: I awoke from a dream of
the Grange; which by the way was like some house at
Queen's Gate, to glare furiously at Magnússon who
was clutching my arm and saying something, which as my
senses gathered I found out to be an invitation to come up
on deck, as we were close off Pápey; which is an island inhabited by the Culdee monks before the Norse colonization
began, and is at the south-east corner of Iceland. It was about
3 a.m. when I went up on deck for that great excitement, the
first sight of a new land. The morning was grey still, and
cloudy out to sea, but though the sun had not yet shone over
the mountains on the east into the firth at whose mouth we
were, yet patches of it lay upon the high peaks south-west of
where we were: on our left was a dark brown ragged rocky
island, Pápey, and many small skerries about it, and beyond
that we saw the mainland, a terrible shore indeed: a great
mass of dark grey mountains worked into pyramids and
shelves, looking as if they had been built and half-ruined; they were striped with snow high up, and wreaths of
cloud dragged across them here and there, and above them
were two peaks and a jagged ridge of pure white snow: we
were far enough presently to look into Berufirth, and to see
the great pyramid of Búlandstindr which stands a little way[1]
down the west side of the firth close by the sea. The sea
was perfectly calm, and was clear of mist right up to the
shore, and then dense clouds hid the low shore, but rose no
higher than the mountains' feet: and as I looked the sun
overtopped the east hills and the great pyramid grew red
halfway down, and the lower clouds began to clear away: the
east side of the firth which was clearer of them showed the
regular Icelandic hillside: a great slip of black shale and sand,
striped with the green of the pastures, that gradually sloped
into a wide grass-grown flat between hill and sea, on which

[1] Not "a little way down," because Búlandstindr stands out at the
very extremity of the western side of Berufirth. E.M.

we could see the home-meads of several steads: we rounded
a low ragged headland presently and were in the firth and off
a narrow bight, at the end of which was the trading-station
of Djúpivogr (Deepbay): half a dozen wooden roofs, a flag-
staff and two schooners lying at anchor. There we waited
while the boat was lowered, pulled ashore with the passengers, and came back again; during which the clouds on the
west side cleared off the low shore and we could see a line of
rocks and skerries cut from the shore, low green slopes behind them, and then the mountain feet; looking up the firth,
which was all sunlighted now, the great peaks lowered till
they seemed to run into the same black, green-striped hillsides as on the east side; as we turned to leave the firth,
where we only stayed about half an hour, the clouds were
coming up from the sea, and all out that way was very
black but the sun yet shone over our heads; we were soon
out of the firth again, and going with a fair wind along the
coast, about ten miles from it at first: the sky darkened overhead, but there was a streak of blue sky over the land, and
the sun was bright on the desolate-looking heap of strangely
shaped mountains. There is really a large tract of country
between the sea and these, but being quite flat you cannot
see it, and the mountains look as if they rose straight out of
the sea: they are all dark grey, turning into indigo in the
distance under the half cloudy sky; but here and there the
top of a conical peak will be burned red with the fire, or a
snow-covered peak will rise up: at last we see the first of the
great glaciers that looks as if it were running into the sea, and
soon there is nothing but black peaks sticking up out of the
glacier-sea: this is the sides of the Vatna-Jokul, an ice-tract
as big as Yorkshire; beyond this again we come to a great
conical mass of black rock and ice which is the Oræfa Jokul,
the highest mountain in Iceland: the only way I had any idea
of its size was from the fact of our being so long off it without its seeming to change in shape at all: on the western flank
of it Magnússon pointed out to me a small river-like glacier,
and then a grey peak in front of it: the grey peak is Swine-

20

fell, under which dwelt Flosi the Burner; a little further west a jagged ridge marks the whereabouts of Hall of the Side: a most dreary region all this seems, but the pastures of course and whatever might soften it are all hidden from this distance: a most dreary place, yet it was hereabouts that the first settler came, for on ahead there lies now a low shelf of rock between Jokul and sea, and that is Ingolf's Head, where Ingolf first sat down in the autumn of 874.[1]

The wind got up and the sky got overcast as we were rounding the Oræfa, and soon it begins to rain (a little before noon) and the wind still freshening, the sea is soon running very high, the wind however is right astern and the ship making very good way and so we don't feel it much: moreover the east wind is not a cold one in Iceland, and I have felt colder on the Channel on a July night: the worst of it was what between the drift and the rain, and that we are now keeping further from shore, we almost or quite lose sight of land for a long time,[2] till near 9 p.m. when we are off Portland, which is a pierced rock a little way from the shore which a ship can sail under: this we cannot see now for the mist, but the rain leaves off now and the clouds lift, and there is a wonderful fiery and green sunset, so stormy-looking! over Eyjafell, the great ice-topped mountain which is at the eastern end of the Njala country. It is long before we can see the colour of the glacier on it because of the mist suffused with sunlight that is cast over everything, but at last about ten o'clock the sun draws behind the mountains, leaving them cold and grey against a long strip of orange that does not change any more till the dawn.

Now we see the Westman Islands a long way ahead: they lie just opposite to Njal's house at Bergthorsknoll: as they get nearer we can see them like the broken-down walls of castles in the sea: it is about one o'clock when we come up

[1] 870 was the date of Ingolf's landing. He settled down at Reykjavík 874. E.M.

[2] MS. reads "not till near 9 p.m." Ed.

21

alongside of the only inhabited one of them (four hundred
people live there); we lie-to off the trading-station where
there is a pretty good haven; the wall-like rocks run into
green slopes about here, which end in an old crater at the
south-west corner of the island. We fire a signal gun here, and
wait to see if they will send a boat for their mail (five letters &
Magnússon's Lilja), but having no answer we steam round
to a bay on the other side of the island where there is less sea,
and lie-to there, rolling prodigiously: and there after long
looking through glasses we see their signal flag run up, and
presently make out their boat coming: it was all over in a
moment when they did come; hardly a dozen words between
them, and then back they went, poor fellows! in their walnut-
shell of a boat, seven men, five letters and Lilja.[1] We had a
long look at their rocks while we were waiting: they were
not unlike the rocks as we left the Faroes, but not so high,
and were full of caves that had each a little grey strand before
them. Then we hoisted sail again, turned west, and were off
and I went to bed, thoroughly tired with the long dream-
like day: but before I left the bridge I looked north and saw
a crimson spot spreading over the orange in the sky, and that
was the dawn.

Friday, July 14th. At Reykjavík in the house of Maria
Einar's-dóttir.[2]

UP at nine and on deck to find that we were just off
Reykjaness round which we turn the corner into
Faxafirth, the bay in which Reykjavík lies: it was a
fine bright day, but rather cold. We were some time getting
up the firth as the wind was now against us; but at last we
sighted Reykjavík and were soon able to see what it was to
be like: the shores of the bay are flat and dull except that

[1] They say that the Westman-islanders watch a waterfall under
Eyja-fell, called Seljaland's foss, to know if 'tis safe to put a boat out
for the mainland: they may do this if they can see the fall reach the
sea; but if it is blown away before it reaches the sea, no boat can live.
[2] Mrs. Magnússon's eldest sister.

towards the northwest rise two great mountains, Akrafjall and Esja, of the haystack shape so common here, and black striped with green in colour; as we went on we saw another range of hills to the east, not very high but characteristic in shape, a jagged wall, with a pyramid rising amidst them; they are bare, and browner than the others, and come from the lava in fact. The town now lying ahead is a commonplace-looking little town of wood principally; but there are pretty-looking homesteads on some of the islands off it, and the bright green of their home-meads is a great relief to us after all the grey of the sea, and the ice-hills. At last we come to anchor and the boats pull off to us and the flags are run up to the flagstaffs of the stores on shore, and to the masts of the craft in the harbour, which include a French war-brig and gunboat, and several small Danish schooners and sloops: the Frenchmen are here to look after the interests of the 400 sail of French fishing vessels that do most of the deep sea fishing off Iceland: we saw several of them yesterday. We are boarded by several people now; Zoega the guide who was to buy our horses amongst others: he is a big fellow, red-headed, blue-eyed and long-chinned, like a Scotch gardener; he talks English well, and tells us he has done our bidding. Magnússon goes ashore with him, and is to come for us presently; meanwhile we go to dinner (it was about half past three when we cast anchor). A little after dinner he comes accordingly, and ashore we go and land in a street of little low wooden houses, pitched, and with white sash frames; the streets of black volcanic sand; little ragged gardens about some of the houses growing potatoes, cabbages, and huge stems of angelica: not a very attractive place, yet not very bad, better than a north-country town in England. Magnússon takes us to our lodging,[1] a very clean room in one of the little wooden houses, which stands back from the road in its potato and angelica garden, with a hay-field, where they are at work now, at the back. He tells us to come to dinner at a

[1] Lord! how that little row of wooden houses, and their gardens with the rank angelica is wedged into my memory!

23

Reykjavík certain hour, and then leaves us to our devices, so we go a little walk out into the country, hugely excited, most of all by the look of the ponies, which are much more numerous than the humans, and look delightful: here comes a string of them, about a dozen, laden with stock-fish, tied head and tail and led by a man who rides the first horse: two goodwives in Icelandic side-saddles (little chairs with gay-coloured pretty home-woven carpets thrown over them), riding with their man over stock and stone: a long-legged parson, in rusty black with a tall and stupendously bad hat, riding on a jolly round-sterned chestnut at the devil's pace; his reverend ragbagged legs going whack, whack, whack, to make you die: all these and more capped us, blessed us (veri þer sælir! be ye *seely!*), and went their ways. We went a little walk, looked at the blue bay we had just been so glad to come off,[1] and down into a marshy valley where the cotton-rush grew thick, and then back to our dinner: we had gone on a good made road so far; the country looked very barren here except just round by the sea, but there were pretty flowers and enough of them in the scant grass. To bed after dinner on the floor in our blankets, and were very comfortable.

Saturday, July 15th. In the same place.

VERY nice coffee and biscuits before we are up, and afterwards, regular breakfast, with all Icelandic matters; smoked mutton, stock-fish and the rest: I find none of it comes amiss to me at any rate. After breakfast we go first to see about our money; Mr. Fischer the agent says at first he doubts if he can get us any, as the season has been so good, more silver than usual was wanted to pay the farmers:[2] however, he says he will do his best; and then off we go to see Zoega, who is going to start this morning for the Geysirs with an English party: him we find with two ponies by our lodging, and he invites me to mount and come to his own

---

[1] Heavens! how glad I was to see it again though, six weeks afterwards.

[2] Meaning that they would be paid in kind mostly.

house where the rest are; with some trepidation I do mount, Reykjavík and all my fears and doubts vanish as the little beast[1] begins to move under me, down the street at a charming amble, that would not tire anybody. I see the other horses in Zoega's yard, sixteen of them at present, but he will bring them up to twenty before we start, and then we shall have about ten more to buy in the early part of our journey. So our saddles are shown, and have to be stuffed, the Icelandic boxes are sent down to our house, and Evans, Faulkner and I begin the serious work of packing afresh the things for the journey —that is to say, they two do, for I am principally of use as a mocking-stock, an abusing-block, how shall I call it? Magnússon meantime is away to see his friends about the place.

And now wait and consider if it isn't lucky that a good joke should not lack its sacred poet—Evans and I bought some stores the other day at the co-operative society in the Haymarket: they were to pack them in two cases and send them to us, as they did; but the day after came a message to say they had made a mistake, and put a parcel not ours in one of the cases, instead of some bologna sausage we had ordered, and which they then delivered. I asked them to unpack the case and take their property away; they said they would send the next day to do it; I agreed to that, but told them that if they didn't come that day, to Iceland their case would go with all that was in it, and that there we would eat their parcel if it was good to eat, or otherwise treat it as it deserved. Well, they never came, and here was the case, with the hidden and mysterious parcel in its bowels: many were the speculations as to what it was, on the way; and most true it is that I suggested (as the wildest possible idea) fragrant Floriline and hair-brushes—now in went the chisel, and off came the lid: there was the side of bacon; there were the tins of preserved meat; there was the Liebig, the soup-squares, the cocoa, the preserved carrots and the peas and sage and onions—and here IT was—wrapped up first in

[1] It was the pony I rode all the time, and brought to England with me.

25

Reykjavík shavings—then in brown paper, then in waterproof paper, then in more ditto, then in whitey-brown—and here IT is—four (was it) boxes of FRAGRANT FLORILINE, and two dozen bottles of Atkinson of Bond Street his scents, white violet, Frangipanni, Guard's Bouquet—what do I know? yea and moreover the scents were stowed in little boxes that had hair-brushes printed on them.

We looked at each other to see if we were drunk or dreaming, and then—to say we laughed—how does that describe the row we made; we were on the edge of the hayfield at the back of the house; the haymakers ran up and leaned on their rakes and looked at us amazed and half-frightened; man, woman and child ran out from their houses, to see what was toward; but all shame or care had left us and there we rolled about and roared, till nature refused to help us any longer—then came the inevitable regrets of the time it would take before my friends could know it, and that I should not be by to see their faces change; for how was I to keep it out of my letters?

Well, we calmed down at last and went on with our packing: afterwards I went with Magnússon to see some of his friends; the most noteworthy of them was Jón Sigurdson, the President of the Althing, a literary man whose editions of sagas I know very well: he seemed a shy, kind, scholar-like man, and I talked (Icelandic) all I might to him.

Also we went into some shops that overlook the harbour, and bought some useful things, cheese, cherry-brandy, knitted guernseys and gloves: then we went to the agent's (Fischer's) who had got our money for us, and counted and carried away 1,000 dollars in canvas bags; and now it seemed certain that we should be able to start on Monday; if those damned Icelandic locks can be got either to lock or to unlock. I needn't say I was in a fever to be off. Well, dinner and bed ended the day.

26

Sunday, July 16th. At the same place.

SPENT by me in letter-writing and fidgeting and worrying about the weather, and the iron-work: for the smith hasn't finished the necessary eyed-irons for the boxes, and the locks (made by the hatter of Reykjavík) are ingeniously useless, and drive Faulkner mad: as to the weather, it was very bright and sunny in the morning, though with a bitter north wind blowing; but in the afternoon it got warm and close, the wind shifted to the south-east (the wet wind of Iceland) and it clouded over and began to rain. As we are to camp out the first night, it would be something like madness to set out on a wet day; so I make up my desponding mind to a week's stay in Reykjavík, and express that opinion all the afternoon and evening for the gratification of my fellows, till bed-time relieves me (and them) at last.

CHAPTER II. FROM REYKJAVIK TO BERG-THORSKNOLL AND LITHEND.

Monday, July 17th. In camp at Bolavellir.

WE woke to a drizzly unpromising-looking morning, but our guides came early to us and we were to start if possible: they (the guides) are Eyvindr and Gisli: the first a queer ugly-looking fellow, long, with black eyes and straight black hair, and as swart as a gipsy; the second short, merry-looking, with light hair and blue eyes, the most good-tempered of fellows as he afterwards turned out—and also one of the laziest: we made a call of ceremony on the Governor as soon as we could: he was very civil to us and talked French: I was not glib in replying in that tongue, as the Icelandic got mixed up with it. Then we went back to the packing; during which Faulkner went and collared the smith to try to make the lock work: many a time the smith looked up cheerfully and said it was all right now: many a time Faulkner tried it, found it all wrong, and so sat down with that look of reprobation past words which I myself have winced under before now: however at eleven or so the guides brought up the pack-horses, and began to load them,

lock or no lock: they were very handy over this job and amused me vastly: we had intended starting at noon, and the weather had quite cleared up by now; but it was obviously quite
impossible, and the time went on very fast; till at last when I
had got on my breeches and boots, and was trying in vain not
to swagger in them, it was three o'clock and dinner time.
Finally the riding-horses were brought up to the door, the
pack-horses were driven out into the road, Magnússon strap-
ped on my mackintosh to my saddle-bow for me, and I tied on
my tin pannikin and mounted my little beast, & we all scrambled off somehow, following the lead of the rather irregular
pack train, the horses not yet being used to go together;
Magnússon's wife and sister-in-law, and their brother-in-
law, Helgi Helgason a schoolmaster here, and a young lady
friend mounted also to see us on our way, and there we were
off at last; I looking about the street over the queer light-
coloured mane of my little poney with great contentment.
From the high ground above the town we could see the bay
now, and the "Diana" lying there still, and her sister vessel
the "Fylla," which is still in the service, steaming up the bay
even as we look: we are up to the pack-horses here, and they
are well together now and going a good round trot, we after
them. I find my poney charming riding and am in the best of
spirits: certainly it was a time to be remembered; the clatter
of paces and box-lids, the rattle of the hoofs over the stones,
the guides crying out and cracking their whips, and we all
with our faces turned towards the mountain-wall under
which we were to sleep to-night. Always though, throughout the whole journey, the start, whenever we made it
(to-day it was a quarter to five in the evening) was a fresh
pleasure to me, yet certainly never quite as exciting as this.
Most strange and awful the country looked to me we passed
through, in spite of all my anticipations: a doleful land at
first with its great rubbish heaps of sand, striped scantily with
grass sometimes; varied though by a bank of sweet grass
here and there full of flowers,[1] and little willowy grey-leaved

[1] "The most noteworthy being a large purple cranesbill." Note
book. Ed.

28

plants I can't name: till at last we come to our first river that Bolavellir runs through a soft grassy plain into a bight of the firth; it is wonderfully clear and its flowery green lips seemed quite beautiful to me in the sunny evening, though I think at any time I should have liked the place, with the grass and sea and river all meeting, and the great black mountain (Esja) on the other side of the firth. On thence to the place where the roads branch, one going north to Thingvellir, and one (ours) east toward the Landeyjar: a little beyond this we come to a stead named Holmr; it is the first real Icelandic stead I have seen near:[1] our Icelandic friends tell us it is a poor stead, but it pleased me in my excitement, with its grey wooden gables facing south, its turf walls, and sloping bright green home-field with *its* smooth turf wall: there the bonder and his folk were haymaking, or rather standing rake in hand to stare at us, and [the] guides went up to them to buy fire-wood for our camp this evening. Meantime we got off our horses, and sat down in a pretty grassy hollow, and the Icelanders brought out champagne and glasses to drink the stirrup-cup, for they were going back here: so in half an hour's time we said good-bye for six weeks, and they mounted and turned back west, and we rode away east into a barren plain, where the road had vanished into the scantiest of tracks, and which was on the edge of the lava: soon we came on to the lava itself, grown over here with thick soft moss, grey like hoar-frost: this ended suddenly in a deep gully, on the other side of which all was changed as if by magic, for we were on a plain of short flowery grass as smooth as a lawn, a steep green bank bordering it all round, which on the south ran up into higher green slopes, and these into a great black rocky mountain:[2] we rode on over the east side of the bank, and then again a change: a waste of loose large-grained black sand without a blade of grass on it, that changed in its turn into a grass plain again but not smooth this time; all ridged and thrown up

[1] A few miles further back I had seen the wooden gables of one a goodish way off, and took them for tents as they showed among the dark grey slopes.
[2] Called Vifilsfell.

29

Bolavellir into hummocks as so much of the grass land in Iceland is, I
don't know why: this got worse and worse till at last it grew
boggy as it got near another spur of the lava-field, and then
we were off it on to the naked lava, which was here like the
cooled eddies of a molten stream: it was dreadful riding to
me unused, but still as I stumbled along, as nervous as
might be, I saw the guides galloping about over it as they
drove the train along, with hard work, at a smart trot: for
me, I didn't understand it at all, and hung behind a good
way in company of Faulkner: but we were getting near our
camping ground now, and the peaked mountain-wall lay
before us, falling back into a flat curve just above our resting place: streams of lava tumbled down the mountain-sides
here and there; notably on one to our north, Hengill by
name; on whose flank its tossed-up waves looked most
strangely like a great town in the twilight we were riding
through now. Well, Faulkner and I pushed on as well as we
could, and at last saw the lava end in the first green slopes of
the hill-spurs, where Magnússon stood by his horse waiting
for us; we rode gladly enough on to the grass, and, turning
a little, cantered along the slope and down into a plain that
lay in the bight under the hills, in the middle of which I saw
the train come to a stand: so riding through a moss at the
slope's end we came into a soft grassy meadow bordered by
a little clear stream and jumped off our horses after a ride of
six hours and a half. It was a cold night though clear and
fine, and we fell hard to work to unpack the tents and pitch
them while the guides unburden the horses, who were soon
rolling about in every direction, and then set to work dili-
gently to feed: the tents being pitched, Magnússon and
Faulkner set to work to light the fire, while Evans and I
went about looking for game, about the hill-spurs and the
borders of a little tarn between the lava and our camp: it was
light enough to see to read; wonderfully clear but not like
daylight for there were no shadows at all: I turned back
often from the slopes to look down on the little camp and
the grey smoke that now began to rise up, and felt an excite-

ment and pleasure not easy to express: till I had to get to my Bolavellir shooting which I didn't like at all; however I shot two golden plovers and came back to camp with them, where I found Faulkner rather dejected over his fire, which was sulky: but we soon got it into a blaze, boiled our kettle and made some tea, for we had brought some cold mutton from Reykjavík and did not want any other cooking: so we eat our supper, and then heated more water for grog while the guides lay about watching us, till they having a dram from us went off to a little hut of refuge near the tarn-side, and we wriggled into our blankets and so ended our first day of travel.

Tuesday, July 18th. At Mr. Thorgrímsson's house at Eyrarbakki.

UP at about nine for we were all somewhat tired: I can't say I had slept much, not that I was uncomfortable or cold, but the strangeness and excitement kept waking me up; there had been queer noises too through the night: the wild song of the plovers, the horses cropping the grass near one, the flapping of the tent-canvass, for there was a good deal of wind, and it was a cold morning though very bright; one longed for it to be warm that one might have the due enjoyment of the beautiful grass of the little meadow. Magnússon and Faulkner had *laid* the fire over night with the frying-pan on it, so we soon had it alight with bacon and my plovers in the frying-pan: I did the frying (with the help of the fire) and I confess it was with pride that I brought the pan into the tent and sat down to breakfast. That over we began to decamp, and as I wasn't wanted I wandered about up the hill-spurs and looked about me: just at the feet of the hills there was a space of bog which caught the little brooks that ran from the hills till they could gather into the streams bounding our camp; but above this the slopes were mostly covered with sweet grass, and sank into little hollows every here and there where the flowers grew very thick, notably the purple cranesbill aforesaid. Again I felt I don't know

31

what pleasure at the sight of the little camp where the guides
had gathered the horses now: it was on the chord of the arc
of a big semicircle of flat ground, some three miles at its
deepest, I should think: a grassy plain saved out of the waste
of lava, that rolling down from the mountains on either side,
spread out grey for many a mile about, the last dribble
of it reaching to the hither side of the tarn aforesaid: coming
down from the hill I went thitherward and sat on its deep
grey moss to write up my diary till I was called to saddle;
in our camping-ground that [was] all changed and unrecog-
nisable from the absence of the tents now; and so off we
went, at first straight across the plain, but turning to our
right presently came into valleys among sandy spurs of the
hills, grey or yellow or red, and then beginning to mount
are on the rocky path of the pass,[1] among the barrenest hills
I have yet seen, though here and there are stripes of scanty
green on some of the lower slopes, on one of which a sheep
was standing, and looking so much too big among the emptiness that at first we took him for a rein-deer which inhabit
these mossy parts. We rode up and down through these
wastes a long way, going higher on the whole, of course, the
path so steep that we have to get off and walk sometimes
(though I for my part felt safer on horse-back) till at last we
came to the crest of the pass, and saw the sea lying deep blue
a long way ahead, the sea we sailed over the other day before
we made Reykjaness; descending hence we soon lose the
sight of the sea; and here in the very steepest of our road we
met a parson and his man; whom, the parson, Magnússon
knew and embraced.[2]

Still down, and the hills get lower now; I note here our
riding over a huge waste of black sand all powdered over
with tufts of sea-pink and bladder-campion at regular inter-
vals, like a Persian carpet, and then over a bank of sand into

[1] Lágaskarð (Low shard) to wit.'
[2] We rarely met travellers on our way throughout the journey:
farmwork (haymaking) being at its height, and the Althing sitting
at Reykjavík, the people were little on the move.

a flat plain of smooth grass where we rested awhile, then off Olfusá this into a deep rut between two slopes, the southward-looking one grass-grown and flowery, the northward-looking one a mass of spiky cindery lava, with nothing on it but the grey moss: the gorge widening in a while we see the sea again, the Westman Isles lying far to the east. We have been descending speedily of late and are now on the verge of the hills, and nothing lies between us and the great plain that stretches right up to Eyjafell (east of Njal's country) but a short space of utterly barren shaly slopes populous with ravens: the plain before us shows to the west nothing but an awful dead grey waste of lava, but to the east are grey green pastures with the emerald green patches of home-meads lying about the shore of Olfusá, the estuary of White-water and its tributaries: of this however we can only see the lower part, low slopes hiding the rest. So we rode down the shaly hillsides, I with my heart in my mouth the while, for they were as steep as the side of a house, and so came among the lava-plain at their feet: at last we got clear of it, and rested by the wall of a prosperous-looking stead on the short grass of the pastures, and ate and drank there, getting a great pail of milk from the stead, where they were busy haymaking.

About this time began the first series of losses that I suffered, to the great joy of my fellow-travellers: for, lunch over, I missed the strap that fastened my tin pannikin (which made such a sweet tinkle) to my saddle-bow: I applied to Faulkner[1] for another, and of course he refused me with many reproaches: then afterwards, hunting about, he found the strap, but pride prevented me asking for it, so I tied my pannikin on with a piece of string, and so off we go and ride presently off the grass on to the smooth black sand about Olfusá, called the Skeið, and lo after I have ridden a furlong or so, the knot of the string has slipped and my pannikin is gone. We ride close on to the water now; a wide estuary, narrowing and deepening as we go seaward, is on our left, on our right the sand rises (above high-tide mark I suppose)

[1] C.J.F. was store-keeper and almoner to the party. Ed.

The Ferry and is grown over with tall grey-green wild oats; we are far enough off now to see a wall of mountains, dragged across by clouds, rising over the lower slopes we have just travelled over; they are black and heavy-looking, all the blacker that the day has turned gloomy and it even rains somewhat. Further east we can see the higher mountains that dominate the Njala country, Hekla first, then Three-corner and the higher ice-capped mountains that lead round at last to Eyja-fell, but the tops of them are all under clouds now.

So at last we come to the place where we are to ferry over the river; it is much narrower here, but still half a mile over I should think, and to our grief the tide has just turned long enough to be running out seaward at a great rate, the seals dropping down with it one after another with little fear of us. The river is milky-white as all the rivers it takes into it are glacier-born: Magnússon says the tide and wind are too strong for it to be safe to swim the horses over without help, as can mostly be done, so we are like to have a long job of it; we saw the boat stirring on the other side as we came down to the strand, and presently it is here, small and crank enough. The horses are all unloaded by this time and the packs lying about on the black beach, so we stow some of the luggage into the boat, and then Magnússon and the guides tie eight horses four and four together by the muzzles, Eyvindr takes one lot of strings, and Magnússon the other, and they wade into the boat while we drive the horses into the water; after a little snorting and kicking they take the water, the boat pushes off and they are soon off their legs. I watched them slowly gaining the other bank with some anxiety, but we saw them all ashore in a while and slowly going up the bank of the stream: while the boat set off for the return trip.

While it was on the way back, we saw travellers coming down along the strand to our side of the ferry, and in a while could make out one of our fellow-passengers by the "Diana" who is making for the east country, with his guide Einar Zoega: (half brother to Geir of that ilk): as they draw nearer I see something glittering at the traveller's saddle-bow, and presently riding up he jumps off his horse and greets us and

34

asks if anybody has lost this, viz: my pannikin, thank heaven:
he found it just at the beginning of the Skeið, and Einar was
for letting it lie there on the score of honesty, but our friend,
having an inkling of my ways, let us say, insisted on bringing it on.

Well, we pile the luggage up in the boat, every scrap of it,
string more of the horses together, Faulkner and I on one
side taking two each, and Magnússon and Evans other two;
we perch ourselves on the saddles, the horses are lugged and
driven in and off we go again: to me unused it is rather exciting work; we have orders to do our best to help any horse
that seems flagging, and on no account to let go; however,
they mostly swam very well with their noses up, snorting and
blowing furiously as the ice-cold water washed right over
their heads every instant; we were swept a long way down by
the tide, so far as to be quite close to the rocky bar, on which
we could see the breakers dashing, while we ourselves seemed almost level with the cold grey sea outside. Well, we
scrambled ashore presently and walked along the strand towards the place opposite to where we started: now I that
morning had forgotten to put my slippers away in my box
till it was duly on the pack-saddle, so thrust them into the
pocket of my waterproof coat, and had found them safe when
I put it on on the other side of Olfusá during a shower: but
now a misgiving coming over me, I put my hand into my
pocket, and draw out only *one* slipper—well there is no help
for it, so on I trudge, till I come up with the others, and tell
them of my loss with some hesitation on my part and much
jubilation on theirs; then we mounted, and rode about a mile
into the trading station of Eyrarbakki, our resting place that
night: a collection of a few turf-built houses, a big wooden
store and the merchant's house, all clustered about a bit of
green close to the low rock-strewn beach: a schooner also was
lying just off the bar of the Olfusá, for nothing bigger than
a row-boat (if that), can get into it[1] from the sea: the place
looks, and is, a very insecure roadstead.

We went straight to Mr. Thorgrímsson the merchant's

[1] i.e. into this harbour from the sea except at spring tide. E.M.

house[1] to ask for quarters; he was out, but Magnússon saw his wife and set the matter straight, and presently Thorgrímsson himself came in with another man, the doctor of the Westman Isles, and greeted us, of course in that queer shy way that made one doubt at first if we were welcome: however in we go and wash, and get to talk with our host, who as well as the Westman doctor, and a Danish partner Le-Folij, talks English very well: the fellow-traveller also comes in presently: he calls himself an Italian and looks like one and talks with a foreign accent; but his name is no more unenglish than just—Dapples. Thorgrímsson makes us great cheer and is very talkative and merry: his house is a pretty wooden one with big low-ceilinged rooms of the ship's cabin aspect: we have a big supper at a round table of roast mutton and all the northern delicacies, which I am quite used to now, and so to bed in various dens, I in a comfortable little room with a real clean bed, of course of the northern type, i.e. a feather bed under you and another over you: nevertheless sleep came easy.

Wednesday, July 19th. At the priest's house at Oddi.

GET up at nine and buy two horses of Thorgrímsson, a red (chestnut) pack horse which turned out very well, and a riding horse for me, which I hoped to bring over to England: he was yellowish grey with a huge hog mane; a very well made little beast, but rather young for a long journey, being only six years old: he turned out a very quick walker and ambler, and would have been an acquisition only his hoofs went wrong; he got contraction of said members and I had to bring him lame into Reykjavík, where however he sold for little less than I gave for him, his good qualities being obvious, and his defects I believe healable: his name was Fálki (Falcon) and I confess I regret him. The horses bought, we go in again pending breakfast, but presently Evans going out, comes in again shouting with laugh-

---

[1] About 6 p.m.; we had been three hours full in getting over the river.

36

ter and says I am wanted: so out I go; and lo, my missing slipper carefully laid on the gate post of the garth, and beside it a little black-bearded carle on his poney, a grey mare, who has found it on the other side of the river, and ridden across to bring it to me: I am deeply grateful and the gift of three marks (about 1s. 2d.) makes him so also, and therewith I retire, escorted by laughter, in to breakfast, which was abundant and good: after that we wander about the stead a little while the horses are being brought up; it was a most beautiful morning with those light gleaming white clouds in the blue sky that make it look so distant; I went into the little grass-garth at the back of the house and watching the fowls scratching about, felt a queer feeling something akin to disappointment of how like the world was all over after all: though indeed when I lifted my eyes the scene before me was strange enough: Ingolfsfell, a great chest-shaped mountain, rose over the lower slopes that bounded the plain many miles to the north. Thorgrimsson pointed out to us a spot on the midst of its ridge which is called the howe of Ingolf the first settler: then further east and a long way off, rose the great cone of Hekla; east of that again, and much nearer, Three-corner, looking like a huge church with a transept; then east yet the hills ran up into the glacier ranges that trended south-east till Eyjafell ended them just over the sea: the whole plain dotted over with steads was quivering with mirage, that ran together and looked like trees at the feet of the hills, or nearer to us like sheets of water: over Ingolfsfell lay, just as if it were painted, a faint rainbow (though the day was so clear and bright) but the distant mountains were astonishingly clear.

We were called to saddle in a few minutes, and so set off, riding over sand sometimes, sometimes hard turf-covered ground, and along the seaside for some time; the beach was edged seaward all the way with toothed rocks and skerries on which the long swell broke and ran up into spires of foam, as calm as it looked out to sea: we were in high spirits indeed this morning, which I think was quite the finest we had in

Iceland; we raced where the ground was good enough, and talked and laughed enough for twenty: we stopped and got milk at a queer little stead off the road at one place, and a little after that our path turned somewhat north away from the sea, and we were going over a vast marsh, mostly dry now, but not everywhere, though the road was all good at this time of the year, as the worst places are bridged by causeways: the plain changed little enough for some hours' ride, till we saw some higher ground a little way ahead, and soon came on to Thurso-water, at a place called Sandhólaferja (Sandknolls' Ferry). Here Thurso-water, running a great pace over the flat land, meets a spur of low hills, and is turned south by them at a sharpish angle: we rode over shallow streams of the river and black sand till we came to a firm sand-bank opposite the ferry, which was under a series of tower-like rocks, beneath which the stream ran swift and deep: here we unloaded the horses, while another crank ferry-boat with a rather helpless sail came leisurely across to us: there was no need to tow the horses across here, the river not being wider than the Thames at London Bridge, and there being no wind against the stream to knock up a sea, so we simply drove them in, and they swam in a compact body right across to the landing-place, making a most prodigious snorting and splashing: then we ourselves packed ourselves somehow on the top of our baggage in the boat and came across safely: the river is a white one like Olfusá, and sprawls about among black sand, as most of the white rivers do. We had victuals and a rest under the rocks on the other side, and then rode away up to a farm house on the sand knolls and down thence to a desolate little red-stranded tarn, which we skirted till the road turned off among bogs bridged over by causeways; then we hit another stream at last, and rode right up the bed of it, threading its shallow waters some dozen times in the hour: Rauðalœkr (Red-brook) was the name of it; it was deep sunk between smooth green banks, that hid away from us both the dreary bogs and the distant ice-mountains; it was

38

getting late in the afternoon by now, but the day still warm Western and cloudless, and it was soft and pleasant down in the little Rang- valley of Red-brook: the green banks gave back sometimes river into higher down-like slopes, and on two of these steads were pitched prettily enough: at last the valley took an elbow to the north, just where the banks ran up into a steep smooth-sloped hill that had a big stead with its many gables on the top of it right against the sky: against the sky, too, we saw the haymaking folk standing leaning on their rakes to watch us pass, and one man running back into the house to fetch others out to have a stare: all which was a pretty little play for me: at this place we turned sharp off east from the stream, and mounting somewhat, went over down-like grassy country whence we could again see the mountains, got much closer, the nearer ones of them, Three-corner to wit, and the neck which joins it to the Lithe, called Vatnsdals-fell. At last we go up a long hill on the topmost knoll of which a furlong to our right is the stead of Ægis-siða: Magnússon rides up to it to get us a guide across the ford, and presently we are over the brow of the hill looking down a broad clear river called Western Rang-river. Magnússon joins us with the guide on the river-bank presently, and we get ready to ford the first big river (fordable) we have met, I with some trepi-dation I must confess, as the Westman-doctor told us that Rang-river was dangerous just now: he was wrong however; the stream, as clear as glass, ran over hard smooth sand, and though it ran strong, and took us up to the girths, and the pack-boxes, to my anxiety, dipped a little into the water, yet there was really no danger at all: this ford was about as wide across as the Thames at Richmond-bridge, and the clear river running between grassy banks seemed quite beautiful to me after the wastes of Thurso and Olfus waters: we go up from the river across more of the down country, and pass a hand-some looking stead on our right,[1] cross another river and mount from that on to a bleak boggy piece of ground, where

[1] Selalœkr.

39

Magnússon tells us we are close to Oddi, so we go ahead of the train, and gallop[1] over the last bit of way up to where there lies a low green knoll on the face of the grey upland which is at the back of the houses at Oddi, then turning a corner, we ride in through the lane[2] between the garth walls and into a little yard in front of a six-gabled house of the regular Icelandic type, turf walls ever so thick, and wooden gables facing the sunny side: these are Stockholm-tarred and have little white framed windows with small panes of glass in them: both walls and roof are just as green as the field they spring from; all doors are very low: I, who am but five foot six, used to bang my head about finely when I first came to Iceland: well, we went in and were welcomed by some wo-man-kind of Dean Asmundr, who told us the dean would be in presently; the Italian Dapples was here already, and had had his bedroom assigned to him; we sat in a funny little panelled parlour, where they brought us wine and biscuits pending the priest's arrival, who turned up presently, a little hard-bitten, apple-cheeked old man, of a type very common in Iceland: he was extremely hospitable and soon summoned us to dinner, or supper rather, for it was half-past nine by now; we had smoked mutton to eat, smoked salmon, Norway anchovies, Holstein cheese (like Gruyère) and ewe-milk cheese (*islandicé* mysu ostr), queer brown stuff and quite sweet, together with some plovers we had shot which they roasted for us: the dean was very gay, and kept on calling toasts which we drank in Danish brandy, though there was Bordeaux on the table too: altogether I have a keen remembrance of the joys of that dinner. Then the dean asked us into the parlour again and we sat there and wandered out into the

[1] My word, how we split along that evening! we were at the height of our excitement, and the ponies were fresh: I ride the little chestnut at Kelmscott now; how he would be astonished at that pace in these days.

[2] These lanes with the smooth flowery turf walls are particularly delightful, and give one a sense of comfort and habitation that one needs very much as one comes in from the bleak hill or bog.

home-mead. It was a beautiful evening still, and even the eastern sky we saw behind the great mountains of the Eyja-fell range was quite red. Oddi lies on a marked knoll or slope, above a great stretch of boggy land through which Eastern Rang-river winds; the hills under Three-corner, and the long stretch of Fleetlithe gradually leading into the terrible gorges of the ice-mountains, girdle in these grey-green flats. It is a noteworthy place historically, for in fact the men who dwelt here or hereabouts still live in people's minds as the writers of most of the great stories and both the Eddas. I don't know if they actually wrote them; it was a mere guess (or tradition perhaps) of the seventeenth century that Sœmund the Learned collected the poetic Edda: but at any rate these three men, who all lived here at one time or another of their lives, Sœmund, Ari, and Snorri Sturluson, must certainly have been the great guardians of the body of Icelandic lore.

I walked round the home-field, which sloped gently down toward the marsh; the dew was falling like rain, as it always did after hot days here, and it was getting decidedly cold when I came in at last and went to a comfortable bed made up in the room where we had dined: for I needn't say that we five turned the house upside down with our requirements. That was the end of the day.

Thursday, July 20th. In camp in the home-mead at Berg-thorsknoll.

A GREY morning and raining a little: I walked about the stead after breakfast while the guides were packing, and had a good look at the knoll which rises at the back of the house, and which to my excited imagination look-ed like the fallen-in walls of the stead of the Sturlung period: it might well have been, for 'tis not likely that they would have built a house in the position of the present one with a knoll just above it, handy to burn it from: apropos, Oddi, which means a point in Icelandic, is the spit of land between the Western and Eastern Rang-rivers.

We started in very good spirits in despite of the rain under

Berg-
thorsknoll
the guidance of the dean: who takes us carefully over the boggy land down to East Rang-river, which unlike the Western stream is a white (or *muddy*) river: then over bog and black sand to Thverá (Thwart-river), a dismal white stream running through a waste of black sand; this also we cross and ride along the side of it some miles, with the long line of the Lithe (like a down, say the downs by Brighton) on our left, running along till the great mountains swallow it: these mountains, glacier-topped at the further end, form an unbroken wall at the end of the Lithe: clouds hung about them, though the day was clearing now, and spite of the rain we saw the dust over there amid the dreadful wastes whirled up into red and grey columns that looked like lower clouds themselves: the pastures we were riding over were the deadest of dead flats till they reached the down country on the north or the mountain wall on the east. To me the whole scene was most impressive and exciting: as almost always was the case in Iceland, there was nothing mean or prosaic to jar upon one in spite of the grisly desolation: not however that we were riding over desolation either but over flowery grass enough, as long as we rode by the river-side: we were in great spirits, and, the ride being a short one to Bergthors-knoll, raced and tried our ponies' paces along the turf: so passing by a poor stead, we turn away from the river over the flat marsh-land to a stead on a round knoll called Hemla; there the Oddi-dean takes his leave, and we get a boy to guide us to Bergthorsknoll; there is little variety for a long way in the flat, which is mostly peaty dried-up-marsh-looking land: at last however we see three long mounds rising up from it, in a kind of chain, one covered with the buildings of a stead, and that is Bergthorsknoll; riding nearer to it we strike the richer pastures lying along the Affall, a turbid black-sanded river, one of the branches of the great glacier-drain, that comes from the waste mentioned above. So down along the river bank we ride till soon we are at the gate of the home-mead, which is both big and rich-looking: up the lane between the smooth turf walls to the house door, where the

42

bonder comes out to welcome us: he is very kind and busy
to help; a black-haired bushy-bearded carle of about forty;
not very clean, but very contented and smiling: he makes us
welcome to pitch our tents anywhere we please in the home-
mead, and we chose a corner under the wall and soon have
them up: the hay is laying all about and there are a good many
people making hay, who somehow don't seem so curious a-
bout us as they generally were on our journey: a little horse-
play between Faulkner and me seemed quite to the goodman's taste however: the tents being pitched, I went off with
my sketch-book intending to do something, and sat down in
a place where one had the knolls and their garths against a
corner of Eyjafell; but I soon found I was too lazy and stupid for it, and so gave it up, with the firm determination not
to make myself miserable by trying it again: so I wandered
about instead, and tried to get an impression of the place into
me: the stead was a poor house built on the middle one of the
three mounds: the bonder it seems, was only a tenant, holding I believe of the Dean of Oddi; though as I said the home-
field was big and these desolate ploughed-up marshes are
good pasture (for Iceland) in spite of their looks: the longest
of the three mounds, which lay west from the house, rightly
or wrongly, gave one strongly the impression of having been
the site of Njal's house: it was about two hundred feet long
and sloped steeply away into the flatter slope of the field:
from its top one looked south across grey flats with a thin
greyer line of sea and the Westman Isles rising out of it.
Past the second mound on which the house stood, the home-
mead was divided by a lane with a turf wall on either side going right down to the home-mead wall; then came the third
mound, not many yards from the river bank, though the
bonder told us that the river was encroaching, as most of
these rivers do: I wandered about a while by myself, and
then came back to camp, where I found Magnússon and
Evans just come in with their guns, and then we all went up
to the house for coffee at the bonder's invitation: this was the
first bonder-house I had gone into, (the Dean of Oddi's be-

Berg-
thorsknoll

ing exceptionally grand even for a priest's house) and my flesh quaked for fear of—the obnoxious animal—I being moved by silly travellers' tales: the house was of turf of course, with wooden gables facing south, all doors very low, and the passages very dark: the parlour we went into was a little square room panelled with pine: there was a table in it, one chair, and several chests, more or less painted and ornamented, round the walls: no bed, as was generally the case: from the open door we could see the ladder that led up to the common sleeping and living room called the bað-stofa,[1] but (in those early days) fear extinguished curiosity, and we sat where we were, drinking our coffee, which was very good: presently Magnússon in unloading his gun managed to pull the trigger, and off it went, sending the charge some six inches from the bonder's head through the beam above the door: Magnússon turned as white as a sheet, and I daresay I did too; but nobody was killed, and the bonder laughed uproariously, and so we made the best of it: then we went down to our camp, and set about fire-making, and cooking our dinner; a wild-duck to wit, which Evans shot yesterday: him we cut up and fried with bacon in spite of the rain, which now came on very fast: Magnússon was cook on this occasion, and we dined not ill: dinner over, there was nothing for it but to stop in our tent, but it was now about ten o'clock, so we got on all right: the bonder and his wife came for a talk presently, and we passed the rest of the evening merrily enough; and so to sleep; I in some trepidation as to how the tents would behave in this their first rain.

Friday, July 21st. In camp in the home-mead of Lithend.
THE carline wakes me after a long night's sleep with coffee about half past seven. We get up presently, and find the morning fine, though the clouds hang about still, and look like rain to my inexperienced eyes. After breakfast the bonder comes and offers to show us the traditional places about the stead; so going round the knolls, he takes us

[1]There was an inner enclosure round the house, a little potato and cabbage garden: all the turf walls were smooth and green.

44

first to a hollow close by the river side, and a few yards from Lithend
the easternmost mound which they call Flosi's Hollow; the
place where he and the other Burners tethered their horses,
and lay in ambush before they set on the house: it is not big
enough to hide a dozen men now (the Burners were a hundred) but they say the river has eaten up a big piece of it even
in the memory of man: then going to the other extremity of
the home-mead, he shows us the water that Kári leaped into
to slake his burning clothes when "Life-luller was blue on
either edge."[1] There is no stream there now, but a rushy
boggy piece of land marks what has been a pond, and there
are traces of a brook that once flowed from it; a few hundred
yards further on they show us a little mossy hollow under a
grass bank which they say is the hollow Kári lay down to rest
in after the stream: a little stead close by it is called Kári's
Garth: furthermore (as noting how much the present Icelanders realise the old stories) the bonder told us that when
they were digging the foundations of a new parlour they
came deep down on a bed of ashes.

So back again to camp, which was broken up by now: we
paid for our entertainment and got to horse and away: riding
back along pastures for a while thick with a bright blue gentian
and other flowers (principally white clover) more familiar to
me: I turned back once or twice to fix the place in my memory; and here I will recapitulate and tell what Bergthorsknoll
looks like to-day, so as to have the matter off my conscience:

Three mounds something the shape of limpets rising from
a bright green home-mead with a smooth turf wall all round
it, but divided by a lane river-ward of the stead which is
pitched on the middle mound; a wide shallow "white" river
with black sands sweeping in a curve by the last of the mounds
with a strip of smooth and flowery turf running along its
banks: marshy land all round about, for the rest, all chan-
nelled with innumerable ruts, getting greyer and greyer in
the distance, till on the south side it meets the sea from which
rise the castle-like rocks of the Westman Isles, and on the

[1] "And one edge of it was blue with fire. . . ." The Story of Burnt
Njal, II, 182. Ed.

north is stopped by the long line of the Lithe, above which the mass of Three-corner shows: westward the great plain seems limitless, but eastward it is soon stopped by the great wall which is the outwork of Eyjafell, dark grey rocks rising without intermediate slopes straight out of the plain, and with the ice-mountains at last rising above them.

The morning was bright and warm by then we started for Lithend: we turned from Affall presently and struck out over the flats for Thverá, going not far from our track of yesterday: after an hour or two's ride we come into smooth green meadows on this side of Thverá, and are close under the Lithe, which is the greenest place I have seen yet, and has many steads along it: we stopped for a rest in these green flat meadows, and sat on the garth wall of a little stead called Ere-sel: they were making hay there, and man and maid ran to have a stare at us, and I assay talk with the bonder: thence we get on to the black waste of sand above Thverá: cross the river and make one or two bad shots at getting into the road to Lithend, which we can see plain enough now lying on the hill-side: at last we mount up from the river and ride along through slopes of deep grass full of clover, but with marshy streams here and there cutting through them, till at last we strike the due road leading up to Lithend which takes us in a rather rugged and swampy way up the hill-side and so to a little stead in the midst of a steep slope, but with the ground levelled in front and on both sides of it, and that is the Lith-end of to-day: unlike Bergthorsknoll, the home-mead is very small, but to make up for this the out-meadows are very rich and grassy; the hay is lying about in the home-mead as at Bergthorsknoll, but the out-meadows are not begun cutting yet: the bonder is smiling and kind and tells us we may pitch our tents where we please, so we choose a smooth mossy bit of turf to the west of the house, and about level with the tops of its roof: outside the turf wall of this the hillside slopes up steeply, and to the west of it a little stream has cut a deep ravine marshy at the bottom: looking west still one sees a long stretch of the green fertile Lithe, and

46

about a furlong from us in a biggish waterfall a stream goes
to meet Thverá: looking south is the great plain we have
been in yesterday and to-day, with the sea and Westman
Isles beyond all: Bergthorsknoll just dimly visible on the
verge of it: below our feet are flat green meadows between
the Lithe and the mountain-wall over which we can see
Gisli driving our horses to pasture, he and they looking like
mice for the distance: in the middle of this plain rises a
strange-shaped hill called Dímun, a name common to such-
like lumpy hills, and, Magnússon says, a Celtic word: these
meadows were Gunnar's great wealth in the old days, but
they are now sadly wasted and diminished by the ruin of
black sand and stones the always shifting streams of Markfleet (that splits into several branches here, Thverá, Affall,
etc.) have brought down on it: the outworks of Eyjafell
that have been running at right angles to the Lithe till just
about opposite Lithend, turn now, and run nearly parallel
with it for a space; then curving round form a huge wall at
the bottom of the valley Markfleet flows from, and are joined
there by the Tindafell range, of which this part of the Lithe
is a spur: so that turning east here, you look into a deep valley entirely closed up at the end by a wall of glacier-topped
mountains, exceedingly steep (those at the furthest end looking quite perpendicular), and nowhere broken into peaks;
except that over this western corner of the wall you can see
the summit of Eyjafell, and somewhat in advance of the east
wall is a row of jagged and toothed black hills of strange and
unaccountable shapes. The valley between these mountains
is quite flat, and as we see it from here is all grassy except for
the black stones and sand about the turbid white streams of
Markfleet.

When we are comfortable in the tents, and have got our
trench dug for cooking, the bonder comes and invites us to
coffee, so we go in, and through the usual dark passages to
the parlour, which is just such another as at Bergthorsknoll;[1]
close by the door of it I saw the loom with a half-finished web

[1] But the floor was not boarded: hard earth only.

on it: in the entrance-hall stood a great Gothic chest of carved wood, 14th century of date and North German of place: the bonder said it came from Skálholt, the bishop's seat, which is not far from here.

Coffee over, we go back to our cooking: and if I may mention such subjects at Lithend, *I* was cook, as I may say for the first time; I dealt summarily with all attempts at interference, I was patient, I was bold, and the results were surprising even to me who suspected my own hidden talents in the matter: a stew was this trial piece; a stew, four plovers or curlews, a piece of lean bacon and a tin of carrots: I must say for my companions that they were not captious: the pot was scraped, and I tasted the sweets of enthusiastic praise.

After dinner came a man named Jón, from a farm a little farther east, on the Lithe, called Lithend-cot: he was not a bonder, a working man, a saddler only who lodged there: Magnússon introduced him to us as a connection of his wife's, though he told me afterwards he was a bastard, and a man deep in old lore: he was very shy but seemed a very good fellow: he talked a little English, and offered to guide us the next day to a place called Thorsmark, a wood up in that terrible valley east of the Lithe that I have spoken of so often: we were all excitedly pleased at the idea, except Faulkner, who had suffered considerably from the riding, and found it prudent to stay and rest for a day about the camp: after this we went about the stead with the bonder, and he showed us the traditional site of Gunnar's hall, a little to the east of the present house, on a space flattened out of the hillside: below it in a hollow is a little mound called by tradition the tomb of Sámr, the dog whose dying howl warned Gunnar of the approach of his enemies. Then he leads us up the hillside into a hollow that runs at the back of the houses, which meets another little valley at an obtuse angle going up which we come at last on a big mound rising up from the hollow, and that is Gunnar's Howe: it is most dramatically situated to remind one of the beautiful passage in the Njala where

Gunnar sings in his tomb:[1] the sweet grassy flowery valley Lithend with a few big grey stones about it has a steep bank above, which hides the higher hilltop; but down the hill the slope is shallow, and about midways of it is the howe; from the top of which you can see looking to right and left all along the Lithe, and up into the valley of Thorsmark; and before you, you look down on to the roofs of Lithend, and beyond it the green pastures of the plain about Dìmun, Eyjafell and its outwork, and then the vast grey plains and the sea beyond them, Bergthorsknoll rising up between land and sea.

We lay about the howe for some time, and then toiled up the hill above the little valley till we got above the grassy slopes, and could see clearer into the Thorsmark valley, and had a sight of the spikes and glaciers of Tindafell lying north of it, which the hill's brow had hidden before: also looking north-west a little, saw over strange desolate sandy plains all raked by the wind, one of the flanks of Three-corner, which always *looks* three-cornered from every point of view. Then we came down and went slowly back home: it must have been about eleven at night as we passed the howe again: the moon was in the western sky, a little thin crescent, not shining at all as yet, though the days are visibly drawing in, and the little valley was in a sort of twilight now: so to camp and into our tents away from the heavy dew: the wind north-west and sky quite cloudless.

[1] "Skarphedin and Hogni were abroad one evening by Gunnar's howe, on the south side thereof: the moonshine was bright but whiles the clouds drew over: them seemed the howe opened and Gunnar had turned in the howe, and lay meeting the moon; and they thought they saw four lights burning in the howe, and no shadow cast from any: they saw that Gunnar was merry, and exceeding glad of countenance: and he sang a song so high that they had heard it even had they been farther off." Njála, chap. 79.

Saturday, July 22nd. In camp at same place.

ABEAUTIFUL bright morning with the wind in the east and very little of it; a good sign, as on a fine day in Iceland the wind generally goes round with the sun. A man brings us a lot of clean-run brook trout for which we pay some infinitesimal price and have them fried for breakfast. Then Jón rides in, and after many admonitions to Faulkner about dinner, Magnússon, Evans and I set off with Jón for our expedition: riding down the steep path from Lithend we come on to pleasant level dry meadows between river and hillside: the Lithe itself gets steeper as we go along,[1] and many waterfalls come down it: one (Mer-kiár-foss) a very strange one: the water (a good deal of it too) pitches over the hill some fifty feet and is then hidden by a screen of thin rocks pierced with five round holes one below another: you can see it running behind four of these holes, and then it comes spouting out of the last one, and falls a long way down to the bottom of the hill, whence it runs, a beautiful clear stream, past our path into Thverá: just past this is Lithend-cot, where Jón lives: he goes home[2] to the stead to see about an extra horse, and invites us to come in: it is a very small room he inhabits with a bed in one corner, and a bookcase in the other: there are plenty of books in the case, Icelandic, German, Danish, and English: the latter language he is very anxious to master, and has learned Danish, which as a true-born Icelander he hates of course, to help him to that knowledge: Shakespeare he has got, but says he finds him heavy: he puts two volumes of Chambers' Miscellany into his pocket, if by chance he may get a lesson out of Magnússon this day: then after a drink of milk we mount again and ride on up the valley: the hillsides still getting steeper, and crowned above the next farm (Eyvin-darmúli) by bare basaltic pillars: after this the hills fall a little back from the flat of the valley, which is grassy still where

[1] Properly speaking *ends* I suppose, the slopes are so steep.
[2] An Icelander always talks of going *home* to any stead on the road, whether he is living there or not.

50

we are riding: up in one cleft of the slopes I could see birch-
scrub growing, the first I have seen yet; it looked very dark
and rich to my eyes accustomed by now to the light green
or grey of the thin grass: about here we passed by a hand-
some-looking farm called Borkstead, on the hillside, and are
now (since Eyvindarmúli), quite in the shut-in valley, with
Markfleet no great way on our right, his white waves showing sharp every now and then above the flat. So at last we
are at Fleet-dale where the long hill called the Lithe is cut
by a valley running at right-angles to it: we have ridden
about a couple of hours from Lithend by now, and are to
change horses here before we enter the stony wastes beyond; for here the steep hills draw close together, and there
is nothing between them but the bed of Markfleet (some
one and a half miles across?). The stead here was pitched
prettily on a sort of terrace, with a cabbage-potato-angelica
garden in front of it, and below it a green meadow with one
of those little clear streams winding about almost flush with
the grass that we saw so many of: so here we leave our spare
horses and Eyvindr, who, by the way, has ridden with us,
and has a kinsman at the stead. Then on we clatter over the
loose stones till we come to the river-side and ride up it:[1]
such an ugly looking water, quite turbid and yellowish-
white, smelling strongly of sulphur, and running at a prodigious rate, all tossed up into waves by its rocky bottom:
Jón rides along looking for a ford, but we don't cross till we
come to where a sharp scarped cliff comes down to the river
and cuts our path off: here we stop; Magnússon bids me
take off my gloves so that I may have the firmer grip of the
horse's mane in case of a slip; then he takes my reins, and Jón
takes Evans', and down we go into the icy water, Jón and
Magnússon riding above us to break the stream: this crossing was soon over, the stream being narrow though deep and
strong; but we were fairly in the middle of a labyrinth of such
streams and a few rods further on had to ford again a much
wider arm: I was quite contented not to have my own reins

[1] *One* only of its many streams.

E2   51

The fords and held on to the pommel of the saddle with both hands, and I certainly could not have guided my horse a bit: then came another after a few yards of shingle which was the worst yet, because Jón had to lead us a good way down stream where the water shallowed at the meeting of two arms of the river; and this going down stream was the worst to me; the water seemed coming in a great hill down on us, running so fast by us that I quite lost any sense of where I was going, and felt no doubt that the horses were backing: so much so that I made a shift to sing out to Magnússon and ask him why: if he said anything it was lost in the uproar of the stream, and presently we were at the shallow, and heading up stream: with a curious sensation of having suddenly in one stride gone many yards, and there we were again safe on dry—stone. This was the worst of the fords by a good way: the poneys were splendidly behaved, bold and cautious, and throwing themselves sideways to the stream; Magnússon's stumbled once though,[1] and I should have been afraid but I felt that I was not responsible, and thought only of my day's sight-seeing.

From this stream we rode over the shingle, which sloped a little up to the cliffs, on to other shingle, which marked where the valley was free from water by being covered with bright yellow-green moss, thickly sprinkled with pink and red stone-crop of a very beautiful kind: the mountains on our right were both steep and high, and just before us ran up into a huge wall with inaccessible clefts in it projecting into the valley, and crowned by a glacier that came tumbling over it: but round the valley-ward tongue of this, lay fair grassy slopes, under a cliff red with burning,[2] where we rested presently gladly enough, for the day was very hot by now: this is called Goðaland, and a glacier above mentioned Goða-lands-Jokul. Then on again, and past this the cliffs were much higher especially on this side, and most unimaginably strange: they overhung in some places much more than

[1] I rode the little chestnut I brought home.
[2] Volcanic burning: he constantly mentions this. Ed.

52

seemed possible; they had caves in them just like the hell-
mouths in 13th century illuminations; or great straight
pillars were rent from them with quite flat tops of grass and a
sheep or two feeding on it, however the devil they got there:
two or three tail-ends of glacier too dribbled over them hereabout, and we turned out of our way to go up to one: it seemed to fill up a kind of cleft in the rock wall, which indeed I
suppose it had broken down; one could see its spiky white
waves against the blue sky as we came up to it: but ugh! what
a horrid sight it was when we were close, and on it; for we
dismounted and scrambled about it: its great blocks cleft into
dismal caves, half blocked up with the sand and dirt it had
ground up, and dribbling wretched white streams into the
plain below: a cold wind blew over it in the midst of the hot
day, and (apart from my having nearly broken my neck on it)
I was right glad to be in the saddle again. The great mountain-wall which closes up the valley, with its jagged outlying
teeth, was right before us now, looking quite impassable,
though the map marks a pass, leading up into one of the main
roads north and east. The mountains were about at their highest by now: I noted a bit of them like a Robinson Crusoe hut
with an over-hanging roof to it; and, on the other side of the
river, a great spherical ball stuck somehow in a steep slope of
black rock: more often the wall would be cleft, and you would
see a horrible winding street with stupendous straight rocks
for houses on either side: the bottom of the cleft quite level,
but with a white glacier stream running out of it, and the
whole blocked up at the end by the straight line of the mas-
ter-mountain: about here we crossed three streams running
from these clefts, and then turned down to Markfleet again,
for we were getting near those outlying teeth of the wall now;
also on the other side we could see the cliffs sink into grassy
slopes and valleys here and there, grown about with birch-
scrub, and that was Thorsmark. Two more streams of Markfleet we cross now, and come on a queer isolated rock or pike
sticking out of the plain; and then crossing another stream
are on the same side as the wood, for the easternmost slope

53

of which we make: nor indeed on this side can we ride any further, for Markfleet runs by the foot of the cliff, rough and unfordable, so we ride up into a little grassy valley, down into which comes the wood of low birches which clothes both slopes of the hill: this is the first Icelandic wood I have been in. Jón says that an old man told him the trees used to be much bigger than they are now, but they were pretty much all cut down in 1830 (I think). To-day they are good big bushes, rising from stocks, where sure enough the axe has been at work, the tallest of them may be about 10 feet high: they are very close set together and all tasselled with blossom and smell most deliciously in the hot day, and the grass in the little valley is deep and flowery: we unsaddled our horses here, and then struggled up the steep hill-side through the birch-boughs to look over the brow of the hill: the others outstripped me soon, so feeling tired and a little downhearted with the savagery of the place, I sat down as soon as I was clear of the wood on the bare shale of the steep slope that overlooked the valley, and turned to the mountain that rose over the bounding wall of rocks, the same scarped flat-topped mountain I have spoken of before: I could see its whole dismal length now, crowned with overhanging glaciers from which the water dripped in numberless falls that seemed to go nowhere; I suppose they were a long way off, but the air was so clear they seemed so close that one felt it strange that they should be noiseless: at right angles to this mountain was the still higher wall that closed the valley, which as aforesaid had never changed or opened out as such places generally do; below was the flat black plain space of the valley, and all about it every kind of distortion and disruption, and the labyrinth of the furious brimstone-laden Markfleet winding amidst it lay between us and anything like smoothness: surely it was what I " came out for to see," yet for the moment I felt cowed, and as if I should never get back again: yet with that came a feeling of exaltation too, and I seemed to understand how people under all disadvantages should find their imaginations kindle amid such scenes.

So when I had looked my fill I went down through the fragrant birch-boughs on to the grass and lay down there till my
fellows joined me, when I took out the glove full of biscuits
and sausage that Faulkner had given me and the whiskey
flask, and we lunched and smoked, while Jón took out his
Chamber's Miscellany and had an English lesson from
Magnússon; and so at last to saddle, and back again; Jón
talking busily, this wild place being a sort of pet enthusiasm
of his; he told us how he had gone down this valley in the
winter with the snow covering either hillside, and the moon
at its brightest: of sheep-gatherings he had been at, where
every individual sheep has to be carried on horse-back over
the fords, of expeditions he had made for the fun of the thing
up into the pathless wastes about here, & finally as we crossed
one of the streams that run into Markfleet he told us the
timely and cheerful story of how riding in the autumntide
with a party down this valley, they coming to this stream
concluded it to be fordless, but nevertheless one of the rash-
est cried out that he would not be stopped, dashed into the
water, where his horse was immediately swept off his legs
down stream, and the last they saw of the man was him
clutching with both arms round the horse's neck, in which
position the bodies of both horse and man were found driven
ashore lower down.

Past Goðalands, as we rode over the moss-covered stones,
for the first (and only) time in my journey the poney fell on
his nose, and I over it, without any sort of damage to either
however. It seemed to be rather a ticklish job crossing some
of the fords on the way back, as the river had risen with the
bright hot day; at that worst place I spoke of before, Jón
made two or three assays before he durst take us across: it
looked really like an adventure to see him sitting gravely on
his horse in the middle of the river peering about and shad-
ing his eyes against the low westering sun that was now pouring into the valley: however we all came across safely though
Evans at starting sank up to the girths in a quicksand; and
for my part, though as before I could not tell the least which

way I was going, yet I felt getting used to it all: the last stream
we were obliged to cross much lower down than we did this
morning, and a rough crossing it was; Magnússon's horse
stumbled perilously in the middle of the stream, and I certainly felt as if I had had a present of a new lease of life made
me when we were once again on the black shingle, and galloping towards the green pastures of Fleetsdale.

Biorn the boaster of the Njala lived in one of three steads
called the Mark on the south side of this grim valley, Kettle of that ilk on another: and a little way north of it is Tho-
rolfsfell where Kari lived after marrying Njal's daughter.

We changed horses again at Fleetsdale, and went into the
house for a talk with the bonder and his wife, who seemed
very pleased to see us and gave us coffee and brandy: their
house was neat and new-built, and had a prosperous air about
it: Eyvindr showed us a horse the bonder had for sale; a very
ugly one, dark dun of colour: we bought him afterwards and
he turned out the best of our pack horses.

On from thence to Borkstead afore mentioned, where a-
gain we turned in; the house was better still, better than
Fleetsdale; the bonder an old man with seven tall sons, most of
them really handsome fine men, tall, thin, with long straight
light hair and light grey eyes: of course we had more coffee
here: they were very busy bringing home hay from the out-
meads: it was the first time I had seen the poneys with their
big loads of hay, and queer enough they looked: I note by
the way that an unsavoury idiot greeted us at the porch door
asking each of us his name; he followed us into the parlour,
and took up each man's glass after he had drunk and squeezed
it, laughing approvingly at his cunning the while: the expla-
nation of him was that in Iceland where there are no work-
houses or lunatic asylums, the paupers or lunatics are dis-
tributed among the bonders to be taken care of.

It is getting late as we ride away, about half past seven I
think: the evening was lovely, quite warm still and the air
full of the scent of the hay they were getting in everywhere:
Evans rode hard away from us towards Faulkner and dinner,

while I rather loitered with Magnússon and Jón: we went Lithend into yet another stead, Eyvindarmúli, where it seems the bonder, who was very deep in old lore, was flatteringly anxious to see me. He was a grave black-bearded intelligent-looking carle of about fifty, and soon he got discussing with Magnússon and Jón minute probabilities of time and place in the Njala, pretty much as if the thing had happened twenty years ago: from that he got to lamenting the wasteful cutting of the woods in that country-side: as we departed I made a bad shot at the saddle trying to mount *more Islandico* on the wrong side, and measured my length on the turf. The bonder without the ghost of a smile on his face hoped I wasn't hurt, and only expressed his feelings by saying to Magnússon, "The skald is not quite used to riding then."

I remember thinking the little stead looked very pretty under the high slopes crested with basaltic pillars as I turned in the saddle riding through the gap in the home-mead. Conscience smote us as we left Eyvindarmúli as to how Faulkner was faring with the dinner, as we had promised seven for the hour, and it was now past eight, so we rode on our best now, and presently rode off the steep path to Lithend into our camp, where we found Faulkner standing over the frying-pan with that cold air of a man "who hasn't been," and not in a very good temper about the dinner: Evans who had been in nearly an hour took his side of course, and we had to take our scolding quietly: as Jón was dining with us I wish the dinner had been better; it principally consisted of birds the Icelanders call tjaldr[1] (they are black and white with an orange bill) and we oyster-catchers. They are waders and are very common over Iceland: Faulkner had shot them at a venture: tough they were and fishy, and—to say the truth, Faulkner has no genius for cookery. However, we were comfortable enough by then we came to the grog, and after a long talk we went to bed in a cloudless night, the wind rather cold and north as usual after a fine day; and I slept like a stone all night.

[1] The meaning of tjaldr is quite uncertain. The scientific name is hæmatopus ostralegus. Linn. E.M.

CHAPTER III. FROM LITHEND TO THE GEY-
SIRS.

Sunday, July 23rd. In camp in the home-mead at Völlr.

WE had given out that we wanted to buy horses yesterday, so this morning about breakfast time there
was quite a horse-fair in our camp: we bought about
half-a-dozen, making up our full number of thirty with one
over, a little mare Evans fancied, and speculated in privately.
Jón came in to say good-bye, bringing me a book that Magnússon had noticed at his room, an 18th century Icelandic
poet, rather rare I believe. We all thought Jón a very good
fellow and were quite sorry to part with him.

So to saddle and off, on a grey cold overcast day threatening rain; Faulkner in poor spirits and obviously not very
well. We ride west along the sides of the Lithe, and after an
hour's ride are delayed by Evans' mare finding herself near
the stead she was bred at, and running off at score accordingly: so we sit down on a little mound, and watch Eyvindr
chasing her all up the slopes, till at last he catches her and
brings her back, rather in an ill temper; so she is tied to the
tail of a stolid old pack-horse to check her exuberance, and
on we go again. We make for Breiaðbólstaðr, a church and
priest-stead[1] which we had seen on the Lithe-side from the
plain on Friday; we are to get our horses shod there, as there
was no smith at Lithend: the priest[2] was gone a preaching
at another place, but his wife, a good-looking gentle man-
nered woman, received us kindly, promised us a smith, and
gave us a splendid meal of salmon-trout and "red-grout[3]
with cream," making many apologies for the scantiness of the
meal: Faulkner ate, but was rather silent: the good wife provided a smith for us, and the horses were shod, after which,
and having presented the daughter with a bottle of our mis-
taken scents, we went on our way under the guidance of the

[1] One of the best livings in the country, worth some £140. E.M.
[2] Síra Skúli Gíslason. E.M.
[3] A sort of jelly flavoured with cherry-juice and eaten in a soup-
plate full of cream.

58

parson's son, a little lad of twelve who jumped on to his horse Völlr with much confidence. Breiðabólstaðr is near the west end of the Lithe, so we turned north now and rode over down-like country for some time till after looking up a dale through which we have our nearest view of the great mass of Three-corner we come out on the edge of the hill-country and look west over the vast plain we journeyed through last week sea-ward of this. We were very much amused by the precocity and readiness of the lad: he drove on the horses most handily, talking all the time to the guides and Magnússon, asking the latter, who was comforting Faulkner (now by no means in good estate), What did you say to him then? What did he say to you then? We could see below us the stead of Völlr which we did not intend to stop at, as we were making for Stóru-vellir, and meant a long jog the next day to Geysir, but fate otherwise willed it, thus—We rode down into the plain and soon came to the garth-wall of Völlr, and Evans and I had already passed it when Magnússon came up to us with a long face and told us that Faulkner was in great pain and could positively ride no further: a selfish pang shot through me at the news as I pictured to myself all the delay and worry that friendship might entail on me: however there was no doubt that poor Faulkner was not shamming, but had indeed been behaving with great heroism for the last few hours, so back we turned, I certainly in poor spirits (Faulkner I can *now* imagine in poorer). We all went up to the stead together: it was a handsome new-built house, and its owner was sheriff of the district,[1] and Magnússon knew something of him, so Faulkner was made as comfortable as might be, and we were soon all at coffee and cakes: the sheriff found beds for Mag-nússon and Faulkner in his house, and Evans and I were to sleep in camp which we pitched straightway, and after a talk in the stead went off and housed ourselves, and soon got cheerful enough over chocolate and supper and grog, though the rain now began to fall in torrents and it blew hard; I was quite used to tent life now and slept well enough in spite of

[1] His name was Hermannius Jónsson. E.M.

all that, and though before we got under the blankets we could hear above the roaring of the wind and flapping of canvas the steady boom of Eyvindr's nose in the other tent some twenty yards from ours.

Monday, July 24th. In the priest's (Sira Guðmundr Jónsson's) house at Stóruvellir.

THE morning breaks better than we had expected, though it is still raining fitfully: Evans and I are rather late up, and Magnússon, coming to us from the house presently, is rather lowering about Faulkner, who he says certainly can't go on to-day: so after breakfast (of chocolate, Bologna sausage and biscuit) we go into the house, and talk it over with Faulkner comfortably in bed: he is not at all low in spirits himself, says he don't feel ill, and is in no pain when he keeps quiet, so he probably will be all right after a rest: all things considered, therefore, we settle that Evans and I are to go on to Stóruvellir this evening, push on on Tuesday for the Geysirs, and wait there till Thursday, when, if Faulkner can't come, we are to have a message from him: Magnússon is to stay and dry-nurse him the while; in any case we couldn't move just yet, for the boy who was to watch our horses nodded in the night, and five of them are missing, Eyvindr and a man from the stead having gone after them.

The sheriff has gone off to a place about three miles hence, called Stórólfsvellir, to preside at a horse-fair, and Magnússon suggests we shall ride there, and so it is done: reaching a space where a knoll or two rises out of the plain under a shoulder of some low downs, we find a crowd of horses, men and women, gathered together, amongst them two Scotchmen who are buying horses: it is a simple and very dull affair as far as the buying and selling goes; the goodman or goodwife brings the horse up to the sheriff and the Scotchman names his price, and if the buyer says nay, goes off without a word: if he accepts, the money comes out of the Scotchman's bag and goes into the sheriff's (which is a glove,[1] by the way),

[1]A thumb-glove, understand.

60

the bonder's name is taken down, and the horse is driven into a pound: there is no higgling and no excitement: so naturally we soon get tired of the fun and ride off: we met our host of Bergthorsknoll here, smiling and pleased as ever; the ponies were all quite young, nice-looking little beasts, but nothing particular, the price, about £2 10s., not being high. We found Faulkner sitting up in the parlour and quite merry when we came back; Eyvindr has come back with two of the missing horses, the three others not to be found yet: however, we decamp and get ready for going, and the goodwife gets something ready for us to eat; meanwhile, who is this comes riding up the lane? a little black-haired bright-eyed woman riding astride one horse and leading two others, our runaways indeed: she has ridden thirty miles to bring them in for us, and we are proportionally grateful. Dinner of salmon-trout and potatoes and sweet soup after this, in which Faulkner plays a very respectable part, and the two halves of the expedition part, we leaving a sufficiency of horses of course, my own little red among them as the softest paced of the whole train.² It was seven o'clock and quite a fine bright evening when we started: the stead was a pleasant place if it hadn't been for the worry of wanting to get away, standing at the end of a long lane between the two halves of the home-mead at the foot of the hills which run up rather high and steep further to the north. Eastern Rang-river runs about three miles from it and a clear stream Fiská joins it: we rode down into the bed of Rang-river and crossed it, and so on through a not remarkable country to Keldur (the Springs—

¹ "They are bought principally for work in the coal mines: it seems rather too hard a fate for the spirited courageous little beasts," says the notebook. Ed.

² The fifth horse we never saw again by the way: he was an old white pack-horse and was dead lame when we started from Reykjavík: he made off it seems to the stead he came from and reached it safely: it was near the Geysirs and about fifty miles off, with some half-dozen of the biggest rivers in Iceland to be crossed between it and Vollr.

remember Ingiald of the Springs in Njala), there our guides
are at fault, and riding home to the stead, fetch out the bonder,
a very queer, stuffy old carle, who proposes to ride with us
to Stóruvellir: Keldur is just on the edge of the great lava
that has flowed from Hekla, and we are soon in the middle of
it; it is a waste of black cindery rocks, with a good deal of
sand about them, sometimes grown over with wild oats or a
sharp-leaved dwarf willow: the road is very good, and we go
along at a swinging pace, being anxious to reach Stóruvellir
bytimes: Hekla is visible on our right all the way, and the
rough ridges that lead up to it, which sink into the plain and
are cut off from the Threecorner-Tindafell ranges: and we
are nearer to it than we have been yet or shall be again: one
can see the top of the cone all reddened with burning: the
Keldur bonder names two other cones to me nearer than
Hekla, to wit, Bjólufell and Selsundsfell: it is a sufficiently
awful-looking district. As we ride on we come to two steep
conical mounds close to our road, and the bonder points them
out to me as Knafa-knolls, by which Gunnar saw the spears
of his waylayers standing up thick before the fight by Rang-
river: 'tis a goodish ride by the way, five or six miles to the
nearest point of Rang-river. Soon after this we ride off the
lava on to smooth rich meadow land, broken again presently
by wastes of black volcanic sand also as smooth as a table, and
hedged by steep grassy banks: thence again on to slopes of
grass for a goodish way: the moon near her full we saw now
luminous for the first time since we came to Iceland: the
slopes led us at last down to the bank of Outer or Western
Rang-river: deep flower grass went down right into the water
on either side, making a shallow valley; on the further slope
was a many-gabled stead: it was a beautiful night, about half-
past ten now, I suppose, the twilight deeper than we had seen
it yet, but all colours quite clear: something about the atmosphere of the place touched me very much as we rode down
into the bright smooth river: the ford was very deep, but
quite without danger, the bottom being so smooth. Hence
we rode into the lava again, which was of a different kind to

the cindery stuff on the other side Rang-river, being more Stóru-
like a curdled stream (as it was), it was much overgrown with vellir
vegetation, and was full of treacherous breakneck holes: it
was pathless, or nearly so, and we made slow way over it,
and we didn't reach Stóruvellir, after what was to me a very
pleasant ride, till nearly midnight, and I was more than half
ashamed to knock at the door of the little parsonage, with
Magnússon's letter of introduction in my hand: out came
presently Sira Guðmundr, looking very like the ideal parson
of the modern northern novelette; he held out both hands
to us and said in slow English, "You are very welcome,"
then led me by the hand through the dark passages into the
parlour: he became more genial still when lights were
brought and he had read Magnússon's letter, for he took us
at first for the Scotch horse-coupers it turned out: he roused
the house to get us supper[3] and beds, and his son, a bright,
well-mannered student of eighteen,[2] turned up and talked
German with Evans; he himself essayed Latin with me,
which I shied, preferring to stumble in Icelandic rather. The
bonder from Keldur[4] had his glass of brandy with us, and
then went back through the night some twenty-five miles,
well rewarded according to his own idea with a dollar, and
so after supper to bed.

[3] Supper, black bread, smoked mutton and salmon and ewe-milk
cheese: bed, a bed that pulled out telescope-fashion for me, and the
parlour floor by his own choice for Evans.

Also named Guðmundr, now a district physician at Stykkisholm
in the west of Iceland. E.M.

[3] On the way the old fellow hung back a good bit (we were riding
very fast) and the guides had the bad manners to laugh consumedly
at him, till at last his horse stumbled, and over his head he went to
their great amusement: afterwards the old gentleman sidled up to
me and said: "I'm seventy-seven, and can't ride as fast as I used."

Tuesday, July 25th. In camp at Geysir.

GOT up at eight very unwillingly, but we had a long day's ride before us: Sira Guðmundr was loth to part with us, and seemed to think the ride to Geysir over-long: however we were resolved: we had breakfast much the same as supper, and then Sira Guðmundr took out a little Icelandic-English reader, & got me to give him a lesson: he translated easily enough, but somewhat abroad in his pronunciation: then I got him with some difficulty to take a pretty Sallust from me, and he bade us good-bye with many thanks: he sent his son with us to show the way to the ferry over Thurso-water, the train having been despatched about an hour before to the ford which is lower down. So off we rode on a calm soft morning but threatening rain: we soon rode off the pretty green home-mead and crossing a shallow river were among the lava again, which was pretty much like the last we had ridden through last night: we were soon on the bank of Thurso-water, a terrible looking stream here, about as wide as the Thames at Richmond, white and turbid and running at a prodigious rate, in great waves; just above us it ran through a gorge formed by low cliffs, but all about the ferry and lower the banks were low; we towed our horses across after the boat, from which as we crossed we could see our train just amidst the ford lower down: we met presently and the young Guðmundr went back home: this day's ride is the one most confused in my head of all we had, our guides lost their way a quarter of an hour after we left Thiórsárholt (the ford and ferry), and they were losing their way all day long as soon as the temporary guides left us; (I paid three dollars away in small change for this help). It began to rain furiously I remember about an hour's ride from Thiósárholt as we were down in a ravine trying to get across a most hopeless looking bog: we were seldom on any visible road, and were for ever getting embogged and having to try back, passing through a country very ragged and sour with rock and swamp and otherwise with little character: but after crossing a biggish river, an affluent of Whitewater, called Big Laxá, the country altered, being all beset with ridges crested with bare

64

basalt columned rocks that made strange valleys and gorges,
beyond which we could see far away the masses of the huge
glaciers of Long- and Ball-Jokul. We came to Hruni about
one o'clock: near it by the wayside is the first hot spring I
have seen; it was confined in a little oblong artificial basin,
and the water was hot enough to bear one's hand in comfortably. Hruni is an important place, a church-stead; but we
didn't go home there not wishing to be delayed by hospitality, so we lay on the grass outside the home-mead, and
eat our sausage and biscuit with the rain beginning again:
past this we ride into a wide shallow valley through which
runs Little Laxá whence we can see a mile or two to our left
a great column of steam going up from a hot spring, (Hver,
kettle, is the Icelandic). The weather got wild and stormy
about here, and I don't remember much of the country till
we came to a stead on a knoll on the side of the high bank of
White-water: the name I didn't learn; it is marked but not
named in the map and is a little above the ferry of Brœðra-
tunga:[1] the little home-mead had just been cleared of its hay
and a crowd of sea-swallows were hovering over it, after the
worms I suppose, filling the air with their shrill cries. We
got a guide across the ford here and the guides made some
show of caution about the crossing. asking us to take fresh
horses and the like, for White-water is one of the biggest
rivers[2] in Iceland: it was quite a joke however after Markfleet, though its four or five streams running among the
black waste of stones and sand looked formidable enough:
a very bright gay red-purple flower with grey leaves and red
stems grew in great masses amidst the river-bed: I don't
know the name of it.[3] We turned north up the river from the
ford, and in a mile or two had to take another guide at a stead

[1] The name of the stead is Kópsvatn. E.M.
[2] We had crossed its estuary Olfusá on our second day's ride,
and all these rivers in fact on our way to Bergthorsknoll. You
mustn't confuse this White-water with the Burgfirth one which we
come to afterwards.
[3] The eyrarrós (shingle-rose) is a kind of willow-herb, epilobium
montanum Linn. E.M.

that lay under a steepish ridge rising from the wide boggy plain: he was a fierce-looking man, so much so that I was fain to call him Wolf the Unwashed, but he turned out to be the mildest of dirty fellows: with him our strayings were over, for he guided us right to within sight of our camping ground: he leads us up through a pass in the ridge aforesaid into a little narrow valley that touched me strangely, and through that into an open down-like country, much grown over with very low birch-scrub: presently as we ride along Gisli points out to me through an opening of the hills on our left a low hill across a flat valley, all burnt red with earth-fires, and underneath it a whitish slope with a great cloud of steam drifting about it: this (a long way off still) is our journey's end to-day, and I feel ashamed rather that so it is; for this[1] is the place which has made Iceland famous to Mangnall's Questions and the rest, who have never heard the names of Sigurd and Brynhild, of Njal or Gunnar or Grettir or Gisli or Gudrun: Geysir the Icelanders call it, which being translated signifyeth the Gusher. Well after a longish ride of these birch-clad hills we come into scanty meadows, and to a stead amidst them overlooking a river called Tungufliót, and beyond it the valley of Hawkdale in which the Geysirs lie: we rest a little on the hill side here and then go down and cross the river, one of whose three streams was deep and rough: angelica grows wild about its banks, and the guides throw themselves on it with great enthusiasm: the weather has got cold and cheerless now, and the low clouds drift all about the hills as we ride over a mile or two of rough caniculated ground: and 'tis with a grumbling feeling that I turn away from the neat-looking stead of Haukadalr with its smooth

[1] The Geysirs are not mentioned in any Icelandic writing before the 18th century: of course ordinary hot springs are often spoken of, and name many steads. [The annals of "the men of Oddi" mention hot springs coming up and older ones disappearing in the neighbourhood of Hawkdale 1294. Geysir is not specially mentioned till the 17th century. E.M.]

bright green home-mead to the red Melr[1] (as Gisli called it) Geysirs aforesaid, and the ugly seared white slope, all drifted across by the reek of the hot-springs. We can see the low crater of the big Geysir now quite clearly; some way back on the other side of Tungufliót I had taken it for a big tent, and had bewailed it for the possible Englishman whom I thought we should find there: however go we must, and presently after crossing a small bright river, come right on the beastly place, under the crater of the big Geysir, and ride off the turf on to the sulphurous accretion formed by the overflow, which is even now trickling over it, warm enough to make our horses snort and plunge in terror: so on to a piece of turf about twenty yards from the lip of the crater: a nasty, lumpy thin piece of turf, all scored with trenches cut by former tourists round their tents: here Eyvindr calls a halt, and Evans dismounts, but I am not in such a hurry: the evening is wretched and rainy now; a south wind is drifting the stinking steam of the southward-lying hot springs full in our faces: the turf is the only nasty bit of camping-ground we have had yet, all bestrewn too with feathers and wings of birds, polished mutton-bones, and above all pieces of paper: and—must I say it—the place seemed all too near to that possible column of scalding water I had heard so much of: understand I was quite ready to break my neck in my quality of pilgrim to the holy places of Iceland: to be drowned in Markfleet, or squelched in climbing up Drangey seemed to come quite in the day's work; but to wake up boiled while one was acting the part of accomplice to Mangnall's Questions was too disgusting. So there I sat on my horse, while the guides began to bestir themselves about the unloading, feeling a very unheroic disgust gaining on me: Evans seeing that a storm was brewing sang out genially to come help pitch the tents. "Let's go home to Haukadal," quoth I, "we can't camp in this beastly place."

[1] Common enough in English compounds, e.g. Melbourne, Melrose.

"What is he saying," said Eyvindr to Gisli:

"Why, I'm not going to camp here," said I:

"You must," said Eyvindr, "all Englishmen do."

"Blast all Englishmen!" said I in the Icelandic tongue.

"Well," said Evans (who behaved like a lamb on this occasion) "couldn't we pitch our tent on the end of the slope there?" For at the back of the scalded ground were nice green slopes leading up to the scarped red cliffs of the low hill aforesaid.

"Can't," said Eyvindr, "that's the Hawkdale men's mowing grass." He was rather more than half grinning at me all the time, don't you see.

"Damn the Hawkdale men," said Evans, when I told him what Eyvindr had said, "come and see whether we shall roll off it in the night or not." So off we went, but there was clearly a fair chance of our rolling off, so back I had to come, and dismount under Eyvindr's grins, still very sulky.

However I set to hard at the tent-pitching, not a cheerful operation in itself on a wet night; and by dint of our spade we made a tolerably comfortable lair; spread the blankets and crept in: nothing lothe to rest, for we had made a thirteen hours ride of it, and though I was not tired, I was hungry enough. My spirits rose considerably with the warmth and dryness of the tent, and the opening of the beef-tin, and brewing of chocolate; but we had scarcely taken three mouthfuls before there came a noise like muffled thunder, and a feeling as though some one had struck the hollow earth underneath us some half dozen times; we run out, and hear the boiling water running over the sides of the great Kettle, and see the steam rising up from the hot stream, but that was all: and these attempts at eruptions go on hourly or oftener, all day, but the big Geysir does not fairly spout out oftener in general than about once in five or six days: I confess I went back to my dinner with my heart beating rather; for indeed my imagination must have been sluggish if it couldn't suggest a new Geysir bursting out just under our

68

tent in honour of my arrival: however nothing but a sufficiency of beef, which was very good, by the way, spoiled my
appetite that night.

Dinner over, Gisli brings us a pail of cold water from the
stream above the flow from Geysir, and takes me a little way
up the scalded slope to a small pool, still and deep, with a
sort of bridge across it, and a little stream of overflow from
it; the water of it is boiling an inch or two below the surface,
and so clear that in the twilight I couldn't see that there was
any water there, as it was pretty much flush with the lip of
it; as dim as the light is, I can see, looking through the
steam, its horrible blue and green depths and the white sulphur sides of it sticking out: it is called Blesi or the Sigher.
Gisli follows Eyvindr herewith down to the stead at Hawkdale where they are to sleep, and I heat a pot of water for our
grog in Blesi, its own water being extremely foul of taste,
and go back to the tent rather glad I am not quite alone in
that strange place. So to bed at last and sound asleep enough,
bating an occasional waking from the thump, rumble and
steam of the big Gusher.

Wednesday, July 26th. In camp at the same place.

A BRIGHTISH morning at first, and after bathing in
the stream that flows from Blesi, as low down as was
pleasant, we fry our bacon and have our breakfast in
great comfort: then walk about our dismal garden, after taking our clothes to the wash in the above-mentioned stream.
The red "Melr" is really the highest point of a low ridge
running parallel to the master ridges that form this wide
valley: here it is just as if the ridge had been split in two and
half of it tumbled into the plain which indeed I suppose was
the case: north of the big Geysir is a rise of sulphury shale
that hides the crater till you are close up to it; it is divided
by a little hollow through which runs the stream from Blesi:
this ground has no big spring in it but is quite full of little
ones, most of them just big enough to put your thumb into,
if you have a mind to be scalded: then comes Blesi, and be-

69

tween it and our camp a spring of boiling mud about a yard across; a rod further south you come to the second biggest kettle, Strokkr to wit, i.e. the Churn: this is not like Geysir which has a little crater inside the big basin, but has only one

 visible crater with a ragged lip to it, the water gurgling and boiling fiercely many yards below:[1] Strokkr used to gush but not so often as the Geysir: it will not do so now spontaneously, but must be stuffed with turf first: past Strokkr again, near the mouth of a little hollow running up to the "Melr" is the little Geysir which is exactly a model in petto[2] of the big, its inner crater being about as wide as a dinner plate: it gushes three or four times a day, sending a column up about twenty feet high; there are several other springs about this, a notable one low down the slope which boils very fiercely, and where the people of the poor stead just below come to do their washing. The Melr a little past this sinks into the boggy flats about a bright little river that having run behind the ridge meets below it the stream we crossed just below our camping stead: looking south the wide valley is very flat, and you can see this stream wandering away to join Tungufliót, itself a tributary of White-water: a long way [off] a long house-roof-shaped mountain suddenly blocks the valley as with a door, and you may imagine beyond it the great flats of the Njála country and the sea to end all: to the north the Melr sinks into the plain only a little way from the stead of Hawkdale which lies under the north boundary of the valley, above which one can see on fair days the long line of Ball- and Long-Jokuls: on fair sunlit days there is something pleasant about the wide valley, especially looking south over the winding stream and green flats.

To-day the weather is very broken, and after a little we went back to our tent, for the rain began to come down heavily; and there we sit contentedly enough for some time, solaced by the snoring of Eyvindr in the other (spare) tent:

[1] The big basin of Geysir is full up to the brim except just after an eruption, when you can walk right up to the real crater.

[2] *In petto*: a verbal slip, the idea being "in little." Ed.

70

by whom sits Gisli awake but most intensely lazy, knocking
one stone against another for amusement, and smoking cig-
ars that I had provided him with: it was some hours though
before we were any less lazy; and then we bethink us that
there ought to be some fish in these streams, and I wake up
Eyvindr, who sets off to get me worms, and presently
Evans and I both set off in the rain: Eyvindr leads me to a
place at the end of the Melr near Hawkdale, where a strange
stream runs from one river into the other: strange, because
it runs mostly underground cropping up here and there in
bright clear bubbling holes. Eyvindr borrows a hook from
me, ties it to a piece of string weighted with a flat stone, lies on
his belly over one of the holes and drops in his hook, and has
a plump little trout in a minute, before I had got my line in
the water: in short we caught five trout apiece. The sun came
out while we were fishing, and showed the valley at the back
of the Melr green and pleasant looking after our horrible
camp, and it was quite a rest for me. Eyvindr and I went
back along the stream below our camp, and presently met
Evans, fishless but with a plover and a snipe he had shot,
and back we all go to camp, and begin to get ready for cooking our fish: but it soon comes on to rain again, our fuel is
smallish birch twigs not very dry, and after patient struggles
on Evans' part, and my wandering about barefoot trying to
help him, we give it up, and dine off preserved beef, entirely
to my satisfaction, but not to his, for he was ambitious, and
thought himself beaten. So grog, pipe, and sleep unbroken.

Thursday, July 27th. In camp at the same place.

THE sun was shining when we got up, but in about
half an hour it came on to rain and blow very hard:
in despite of which we, having tried the hot springs
for the cooking of our fish, and found them unsatisfactory,
turned to, to light a fire, and after we had all tried and failed
in succession two or three times, Evans at last managed it,
and we fried our fish, and carrying it into the tent, ate it in
huge triumph: to show our earnestness thereover I note
that it was a little past nine when we began the fire-lighting,

71

and in the middle of breakfast (which we were not long over once got, I can tell you), Evans said,

"I wonder what o'clock it is?"

"About half past eleven, I should think," quoth I, but looking at my watch therewith, I found it half past two. Well, we lay in our tent for a while, till at last the weather bettered, about five I think, and we set fishing, having first pinned a paper to the carefully closed tent, like a lawyer's clerk when he goes to lunch, to this effect: "Gone a-fishing in the next valley, back by eight," because you remember we expected either Faulkner, or his messenger to say he couldn't come. We went over the north shoulder of the Melr, and so down into the valley behind it, which quite charmed us under the sun of the now fine afternoon: it fell back in a great semicircle of flat grassy land bounded by the slopes of quite high hills, on the opposite side to the Melr, close under which ran the stream of the very clearest water: on the slopes of the other side was a big flourishing looking stead with its emerald green home-mead: we fished and loitered all up the stream, and I caught two fine trout, but Evans disdaining a worm came home empty: we crossed the stream again close by where I was fishing yesterday, and so home the shortest way: it made a longish trudge for us, and we didn't come into camp much before nine: there we saw three or four horses standing near the tents and I recognised my little red one that I had lent Faulkner for his ease, and presently looking about we saw him and Magnússon standing with Gisli about Strokkr, which they had been stuffing with turf: we went up to them and there was a joyful meeting, for Faulkner was gotten pretty well all right, and the expedition seemed on its legs again; though he told me afterwards that so recently as the night before he had made up his mind (at Hruni) to go back to Reykjavik and meet us as we came back from the West, and would have gone but that the man who was to have been his guide couldn't come at the last moment.

Well there was Magnússon with his nose over the depths of Strokkr, which was visibly getting very angry, the water rising and falling in a fitful way, till at last he shouted:

72

"Now he's coming up," and there was a roar in the crater as we all scuttled away at our fastest, and up shot a huge column of mud, water, and steam, amongst which we could see the intrusive turfs: then it fell and rose again several times as we turned and walked back to camp, playing for about twenty minutes in a fitful way: nay a full hour afterwards as we sat at dinner it made a last excursion into the air.

So back to camp, and the night being fine made a fire easily, fried our fish, and dined, talking prodigiously, and so to bed after a very merry evening.

Friday, July 28th. In camp at the same place.

I HAD been sleeping rather restlessly, when about 6 a.m. I was awoke by the Gusher growling in a much more obstinate way than we had heard him yet; then the noise seemed to get nearer till it swelled into a great roar in the crater, and we were all out in the open air in a moment, and presently saw the water lifted some six feet above the crater's lip, and then fall again heavily, then rise again a good bit higher and again fall, and then at last shoot up as though a spring had been touched into a huge column of water and steam some eighty feet high, as Faulkner and Evans guessed it; it fell and rose again many times, till at last it subsided much as it began with rumblings and thumpings of the earth, the whole affair lasting something less than twenty minutes: afterwards about 9.30 a.m. as we were busy washing our clothes in the Blesi-stream there was a lesser eruption: this one being over we put on our shoes and went off to the crater and walked over the hot surface of the outer one to look at the inner one where the water was sunk a long way down. People thought us lucky to have seen this, as Geysir had gushed the morning of Evans' and my arrival, and he doesn't often go off within six days of his last work: nay sometimes people will stay for a fortnight at the Geysirs without seeing it.

The weather was bright and hot at first this morning, but the rain came up about mid-day, and went circling about the hills, raining and hailing even amid sunshine, till about four

73

when it really did clear, and gave us a very fine afternoon and evening.

We lay in our tent during the rain, and Sigurðr the bonder of Hawkdale came up to keep us company, and to talk of our journey, for he was to be our guide on the morrow: the folk at Hruni had told Magnússon that the road was good this year on the east side of the great glaciers, and it would have been a desirable way of going north as we should have come out close to Skagafirth and Drangey: Sigurd however dissuaded us from it, said that White-water was very ill to cross high up, and the road very bad as you got further north and moreover that the way-marks had been destroyed: this looked as if he could not help us much at all events, and so we determined to stick to the west road through Kaldidalr as we had originally intended, and to-morrow are to make for an oasis in the wilderness called Brunnar (the springs).

We spent this afternoon in repitching Faulkner and Magnússon's tent, and in wringing and hanging out to dry our wash, stretching a line between the two tents, and hanging the things thereon, Faulkner having made some ingenious clothes-pegs out of firewood; I was quite pleased with the cosy homelike look of the camp when I came back to it after a walk and found everything in apple-pie order: you see wet weather in camp plays the deuce with order, one is so huddled up, there is nowhere to put things. We bought a lamb of Sigurd to-day, and parboiled a quarter of him in Blesi, and then fried a shoulder or so for our dinner and ate him with peas (preserved) and in fact had quite a feast. Then the moon rose big and red, the second time we had seen him so in Iceland, for last night though calm and unrainy was hazy: he scarcely cast a shadow yet though the nights were got much darker, so much so that when we sat down for our first game of whist in Iceland we had to light up to see the cards. We were all in high spirits, I in special I think, for I had fretted at the delay in this place sacred principally to Mangnall, and there had seemed a probability of the expedition being spoiled or half spoiled. So to bed and sound sleep.

74

Saturday, July 29th. In camp at Brunnar.

SET off in high spirits under Sigurd's guidance about half past ten on a bright morning, and, passing by the half-hid stream where I fished, crossed the little bright river, and went straight at the steep hill-side opposite; it is covered with a very good birch-wood, among which it is pleasant to see the thrushes (or redwings?) flitting about: we are some time mounting the hill which is very steep, and I and Evans tail off, but at last come up to the top on to a bit of rough grass full of crowberries[1] on which Magnússon, who has waited for us, is fairly browsing, face among the grass. Thence over sand, mostly, alongside a craggy ridge till we come on to a valley filled with moss-and-flower-grown lava, walled ahead of us by steep black cliffs which seem to run a long way on to the north but open to the south except for a chest-shaped mountain that partly blocks up the way: now descending a little we ride into a bight of this valley, where the black cliffs fell back into a semicircle, leaving a quite flat space, grass-grown right up to the feet of the perpendicular cliffs; it impresses itself on my memory as a peculiarly solemn place, and is the gate of the wilderness through which we shall be going now for some three days: we make for a part of the wall that is broken down into a ruin of black stones and begin to scale it in spite of its most impassable look, and somehow stumble up to the top of the pass (Hellisskarð) and there we are in the wilderness: a great plain of black and grey sand, grey rocks sticking up out of it; tufts of sea-pink, and bladder campion scattered about here and there, and a strange plant, a dwarf willow, that grows in these wastes only, a few sprays of long green leaves wreathing about as it were a tangle of bare roots, white and blanched like bones: that is the near detail of the waste, but further on, on all sides

[1] Crowberries are shiny black heath-berries growing on a resinous plant, and themselves resinous—the other heathberry, the blue berry, is the same as our bilberry, and is bloomed like a plum.

75

rise cliffs and mountains, whose local colour is dark grey or black (except now and then a red place burnt by old volcanic fires) and which show through the atmosphere of this cloudy and showery day various shades of inky purple.[1] As we ride on, we see ahead and to our left the wide spreading cone of Skialdbreið (Broad-shield) which is in fact just like a round shield with a boss; running south from its foot is a rent and jagged line of hills which shuts us out from the rest of the world on that side; on our right and closer to us than these, is an enormous wall-sided mountain with a regular roof like a house called Hlöðufell (Barn-fell). It stands quite isolated, is some four miles long I should think, and has never been scaled by any one: over its shoulder we can see now the waste of Long-Jokul, that looks as if it ended the world, green-white and gleaming in the doubtful sun; that and a faint tinge of green on the lava of Skialdbreið is the only thing in the distant landscape that isn't inky purple: it was a most memorable first sight of the wilderness to me.

After a while we come to a little meadow,[2] about half a mile across just under the side of Hlöðufell, and stop to bait there; and eat merrily enough though it begins to rain with a cold wind, and the day seems regularly closing in for wet: we can see Geitland's Jokul now over the north shoulder of Hlöðufell. So to horse again, when we are soon off the grass and on to a very rough piece of lava, over which in our excitement we ride somewhat recklessly, till the driving rain chills us, and the astounding nature of the road, heaven save the mark, makes anything but the slowest of walks impossible: for we are going now just where the edge of a lava-field tumbles over a series of slopes; imagine that we are going up and down hill, over a mass of stones from pieces as big as your fist to rocks twenty inches or so cube, quite loose, just a little sand sprinkled among them, and every one of them, large or small, with fine sharp edges, and the slopes steep enough, I can tell you. We got off and walked a good bit, but I for my

[1] On bright cloudless days the distance goes astonishingly blue.
[2] Called Hlöðuvellir (Barn meads) marked much too big in the map.

76

part had to keep steadying myself with my hand; I should
think we made about two miles an hour over this pretty
king's highway (for as I live by bread 'tis marked as a road
in the map) and there was not one of the ponies that wasn't
cut and bleeding more or less before the day was over.

Meanwhile we have put Hlöðufell behind us, but Skialdbreið is still unchanged on our left: on our right is a mass of
jagged bare mountains, all beset with clouds, that, drifting
away now and then show dreadful inaccessible ravines and
closed up valleys with no trace of grass about them among
the toothed peaks and rent walls; I think it was the most
horrible sight of mountains I had the whole journey long.
From these mountains a few long spurs ran down to join the
lava plain we are going on; and in one place the tumbling
peaks smooth themselves into a long straight wall with a
pyramid in the midst; the sun shone through the rain hereabout, and showed over this wall a boundless waste of ice all
gleaming, and looking as far away as those high close-packed
gleaming white clouds one sees sometimes on fine evenings;
just over this gap is the site of the fabulous or doubtful
Thorisdale of the Grettis-Saga; and certainly the sight of it
threw a new light on the way in which the story-teller meant
his tale to be looked on.

So on we stumble; great lumps of lava sticking up here
and there above the loose stones and sand, Skialdbreið never
changing, and the hills we are making for looking as if they
were going back from us. Certainly this is what I came out
for to see, and highly satisfactory I find it, nor indeed to-day
did it depress me at all. At last we turn the corner of a big
black sand-hill, and are off the stones on to sand thickly besprinkled with flowers, then these presently disappear, and
we ride under the sand-hills over smooth black sand, that
stretches far into the distance, getting quite purple at last,
till a low bank of sand along a stream side stops it: in which
bank is suddenly a scarped place which is deep Indian red.
Past the sand hills we get into lava again but of the solid
manageable kind: the weather has cleared by now, and we

are coming near our supper and bed, and at last can see a patch of green on a little slope side which is verily it. My pony was tired and I had been tailing for some time when I saw the sight; so now I push on at my best, and at last coming over the brow of a shaly slope see it lying before me, a little swampy river and over that a shallow valley, marshy at the bottom but with slopes of firmer grass.[1] I scuttle across the stream and the marsh, and up into the hollow on the slope side where the horses are halted, which is on the edge of a little gully of sand and loam which is handy to make our fire in; and so straightway Magnússon and I go to work with some birch-boughs we have brought from Hawkdale, which we eke out with the resinous crowberry branches, and soon have a fire, whereon we fry a joint (nondescript, Magnús-son's butchering, but partaking of the nature of a leg) of lamb parboiled yesterday in the Sigher, then we make a great pot of cocoa, and are very happy in spite of the rain which again comes peppering on our tents: the guides creep under a very primitive tent that Sigurd of Hawkdale has brought with him, and so presently to sleep after a nine hours' ride over much the roughest road I met with in Iceland: Faulkner in good condition.

Sunday, July 30th. In the bonder's house at Kalmanstunga. NO very long ride before us to-day, which is lucky as we didn't manage to leave camp till 12 o'clock. We passed by the three pools that name this place with their little patch of green, and were soon on the bare sand and stone of the waste again: after a mile or two's ride we strike the great north road from Reykjavík, a regular and tolerably wide track instead of the imaginary road of yesterday: look-ing behind us as we mounted a low gradual rise, we could see still the great barn-like mass of Hlöðufell hull down nearly now, and the spreading cone of Skialdbreið, still unchanged; right ahead are first a long line of broken down mountain-

[1]As we came up to it we couldn't see the three ponds from which the place takes its name.

wall black as ink under a dull cloudy sky, then beyond them
to the north steep cliffs that hide the ice of Geitland's Jokul
from us, then the pass of Kaldidalr (Cold-dale) through
which our road lies; hedged in on the other side by another
flat cone of a glacier-capped mountain called Ok (The Yoke):
in front of this a narrow steep tent-shaped mountain called
Fanntófell; except for this the steeps of Geitland's Jokul on
one side of the way and the flat cone of Ok reproduce very
closely Hlöðufell and Skiadbreið of yesterday: the ground
about us is no longer lava, but water-washed boulders, remi-
niscences I suppose of vanished glaciers; it is even barrener
than that of yesterday since no flowers grow amongst it, but
the road is good: despite of that we were like to have lost one
of our pack- horses, who taking fright at something set off at
score galloping furiously, the red-painted Icelandic boxes
bounding about on his sides; we all thought he would damage himself seriously, till at last one of the boxes got one
end unhooked and trailing on the ground, stopped him; of
course the lid flew open, and our candles and spare boots and
a few other things strewed the soil of Iceland: it doesn't
sound very funny to tell of but amused us very much at the
time to the extent of setting us into inextinguishable laughter; and in fact I remember still the odd incongruous look of
the thing in the face of the horrible black mountains of the
waste: well, we picked them up and jogged on, nearing the
jagged wall aforesaid for some time, till at last we headed
straight for the pass, and turning a shoulder of the near cliffs
were presently in the jaws of it: a dismal place enough is
Cold-dale, and cold enough even with a warm[1] east wind
blowing as to-day; it is a narrow valley choked a good deal
with banks of stones and boulders and stripes of unmelted
snow lying about even now: the black cliffs of Geitland's
Jokul on one side with the glaciers sometimes trickling over
the tops of them, and on the other side flatter dismal slopes
of stones and sand that quite hide the ice that caps Ok. At

[1] The east wind is warm and wet in Iceland; the coldest wind is
north-west there for obvious reasons.

Kalmans-tunga the entrance of the valley is a heap of stones standing in the middle of a small patch of grass, this is a landmark called a Carline,[1] common enough on the wilderness roads, but at this special one 'tis the custom of travellers to dismount and write a joke or a scrap of doggrel and put it under one of the stones for the benefit of the next comers, which office I fulfilled for our company now very inefficiently. Then on we go with little change for two or three hours; at last after rising somewhat we find we have turned the shoulder of Ok, and have a faraway view of more and more waste and more and more inky mountains; but may imagine if we please the inhabited dales that lie beyond these and go down to Broad-firth, and through which some weeks hence we shall be tra-velling: this is on our left; on our right the black cliffs break down and show us a huge Jokul-field, and from this run four dark spurs down into the lower land; behind the third of them we are promised Kalmanstunga. We descend now pretty sharply for about an hour[2] till at last we can see some green patches on a distant hill-side, and then after a mile or two's further ride can look into a wide deep semi-circular valley, the greater part of which indeed is a waste of black, but green slopes run down the lower part of the hills about it, and on the furthest slope is the usual emerald-green patch that shows supper and bed: We are still seven miles off how-ever, and the rain which had held up till now (say half-past 6 p.m.) through a dull sunless day, now begins to come down smartly, and I don't much look forward to the tent-pitching for the night: we turn towards the valley and a little further on crossing some little streams (the first water since the pools of Brunnar) come presently to a meadow of deep grass on the brow of a very steep descent into the valley, down into which thunders a milk-white stream through an awful look-

---

[1] They call the heaps of stones that mark the summit of the Lake-country hills "old men."

[2] I am sorry to be so vague about time: the fact is it was of almost no value to us at this stage of the journey, especially on moderate rides like this.

80

ing gorge it has cut for itself in the rock:[1] we dismount here
and have a rest in the rain for the horses' sake: then down
the slope to a swift turbid river[2] which Gisli, who is more at
home here than before, tries for a ford and does not like the
look of: so we have to mount a prodigiously steep slope again
and down on the other side into a hollow much grown over
with birch, and so pretty and pleasant looking a place in spite
of the rain that the non-Icelanders of the party were for staying and camping there: Magnússon however and the guides
say that we shall have no good pasture for the horses, which
they sorely need, last night's bite at Brunnar having been but
scanty: so we turn down to the river-side, and cross it on to
a plain of quite black stones with jagged rocks sticking up
here and there, shiny black just like coals; four more streams
run through this, and crossing the last of them we come on
to a scanty strip of out-meadow, beyond which is the wall
of the tún of Kalmanstunga: as Magnússon and I gallop
through this I can see even through the pouring rain that it
is a very sweet looking soft place with a little bright stream
running through it and grass bright green to the water's
edge: the house at whose door we are soon standing is a very
poor looking place, just a heap of green turf without the
cheerful looking wooden gables turned south one generally
has seen hitherto: however the bonder is good tempered and
invites us into the house, and offers us his parlour for our
night's lodging: it rains so hard that we make few words
about accepting the offer, though this was the first bonder's
house we shall have slept in, and I had yet to shake off my
dread of—, inspired principally by Baring-Gould's piece of
book-making about Iceland: so we are soon all housed in a
little room about twelve feet by eight: two beds in an alcove
on one side of the room and three chests on the other, and a
little table under the window: the walls are panelled and the
floor boarded; the window looks through four little panes

[1] The streams of the valley are the head waters of White-water
that flows past Gilsbank and Burg of the Gunnlaug's Saga.
[2] White-water, no less.

of glass, and a turf wall five feet thick (by measurement) on
to a wild enough landscape of the black valley, with the green
slopes we have come down, and beyond the snow-striped
black cliffs[1] and white dome of Geitland's Jokul. We sup off
the last of our lamb from Hawkdale presently, overhaul one
or two boxes (huge anxiety of Faulkner) and find the biscuits
going to powder a good deal—and so to bed after plenty of
talk.

Monday, July 31st. In camp at Búðará (by Arnarvatn).

GOT up late, and prowled about doing little or nothing for some hours waiting to see if the weather
would mend, for it was raining hard and our journey
was not to be a very long one to-day. In spite of the rain I was
in good spirits since I had slept in a bonder-house without
getting lousy, though Evans complained sorely of the fleas;
later on I should have been surprised at the presence of a
louse, but as aforesaid I had been stuffed full of travellers'
stories on this point and was troubled thereon. About 2 p.m.
the weather cleared and was bright and sunny so that we got
ready for a start; I walked about the house a bit and found
the home-mead green and fair though it lies so high up
among these dreadful wastes: the house however very poor
looking, just three heaps of turf without the usual boarded
gables facing south. Still, here as in many places, there was a
charm about the green sloping meadow and little bright
stream running through it, that one would scarcely imagine
could be attained to by such simple means. We got to horse
no earlier than three, our host going with us to guide us
through the great cave of Surtshellir[2] which lies on our

[1] The snow-filled crannies of the cliffs took queer shapes sometimes; the principal one seen from this window was just like a medieval crucifix, the body hanging on the arms I mean: we saw it just
the same as we returned weeks afterwards.

[2] Surt is the god of fire, [the demon of fire, about whom so much
is said in the Völuspá of the Elder Edda as leader of the forces of de-
struction on the day of Judgement. E.M.]

82

way: we squeezed unwilling permission from Faulkner to have a candle-end apiece with us for that expedition. So, riding over a short "neck," we come into a long valley pleasant and grass-grown, with the Norðlendingafliót (Northfolks-fleet) an affluent of White-water, running all the way on our left: looking down we can see the valley widen, and wind somewhat to the north, and our guide points out White-water-side to us and the spot where Gilsbank, Gunnlaug's stead, lies, distant only some ten miles from us, though it will be three weeks at least before we are there, as we come back from the north. The slopes of this valley sink after a while and we are riding over a plain of ancient moss-grown lava dominated by the great mass of Eirík's Jokul, a mountain round in plan and quite wallsided, deep black cliffs with a dome of ice capping them: and presently the guide leads us from the road and we let the train go its ways to await us at a certain place, while we ourselves go over the lava till we come to a steep-sided hollow which looks as if the lava had fallen in there after having been puffed up into a bubble, which indeed I suppose was the case: in one side of this hollow, all cumbered with great heaps of fallen stone, is the entrance to the cave: we tie our horses together at the entrance, and stumble over the stones and so come first into a ragged sort of porch, and then into a regular vaulted hall, with a ledge of stone running at a regular distance all round like a bench: the floor however is covered with great blocks and heaps of fallen stones, and ice lies between them very smooth but very uneven, and covered with water sometimes a couple of feet deep, all which makes it very bad going, scrambling with hand and knee in fact: and my big loose fisherman's boots are not good footclothes for such a job: this first cave is shortish and not very dark, for 'tis lighted by another defect in the lava bubble a few hundred feet further on; but getting past this it gets quite dark and we have to light up, and so go over worse floor still, the drip

Surtshellir

"The abode of the land sprites in one of the stories," says the note-book. Ed.

G2

Surtshellir from the roof sometimes putting our candles out: in spite of ice and all I dripped too—with sweat, and got quite done up, especially as the others in their enthusiasm kept well ahead of me, they all being tolerably good climbers; at last after about three-quarters of an hour I asked our guide how far we were, and he said encouragingly, "More than half way," and a little after we came to another broken bubble, and there I must confess I gave in, and Faulkner kept me company; so we hauled ourselves out on to the moss-covered lava, and sitting down fell to a most agreeable pipe, I for one quite dead beat, while Magnússon and Evans went on with the guide: after a while they came back, not having got to the end of the cave, but so far as to see the great sight of it: a pillar of ice to wit that rises from floor to roof, and a frozen waterfall, which I having missed (to my great shame and grief now) by my lachesse, can say no more about: however they said that it was hard enough to get there, and Evans had an ugly fall on his knee which he felt for many days afterwards. Nevertheless, why didn't I try it.

So back we went over the top of the long air-bubble to our horses, take leave of our guide and ride along the plain after our train, with the rain again following on the heels of us: on a rock near the cave sat a great grey gerfalcon with the plovers twittering and screaming all round him. We had spent two hours in all over these caves. After an hour's ride or so we struck the Norðlendingafliót again, an ugly stream here with wide banks of black sloppy sand: on a rock-strewn knoll on the other side of this our train was halted, so we galloped up in the middle of the now pouring rain, took our saddles off and turned them upside down, and then picked out the biggest stone to crouch behind and fell to victuals: which I mention because surely on that day Faulkner *did* distinguish himself: refusing to say a word, till cold mutton, Holstein cheese, black bread, Bologna sausage and raisins having disappeared, he lighted his pipe with a sigh and looked about him: to say the truth we were all very merry indeed, and when, in default of Falki, who refused to be

caught, I mounted a strong but rough-paced packhorse, I
followed Evans at a great pace over rough and smooth. It did
not rain so heavily now but we could look about us: the huge
Eirík's Jokul rises always on our right, but between it and
us the country has quite changed since we passed the river;
it is all little valleys and low conical sand-heap-shaped hills
overgrown with ling and scant grass, and almost every valley has its little lake in it, in one of which we saw two swans
with their brood keeping cautiously in the middle. This
waste is Ernewaterheath (Arnarvatns-heiði) of the Gretla,
where Grettir dwelt so long as an outlaw.

The day, though still raining softly, got very wonderful
as we rode on: the sun kept shining faintly through the thin
clouds and seemed always ready to break out, and the whole
sky was suffused with the light of it, as you may have seen it
in a stormy sunset in England, only this lasted for hours instead of a few minutes: two wonderful rainbows came out as
we rode; the second one of which was beyond everything of
the sort I ever saw, we were loitering past a bank of deep grass
with breaks in it through which one saw the black side of
Eirík's Jokul, and the bow came strong against the black
cliffs and white snow of it, and seemed quite close to us while
the sun, very low now, shone out athwart all the shifting
clouds from a strip of faint golden green sky in the north-
west. All faded presently and we came at last down on to Erne-
water about at half-past nine amidst a cold grey drift of rain.
It is a big sheet of water, some seven miles square with low
hills all round it, and between us and it a stretch of boggy
land that runs at last in a long spit into the lake: this is Gret-
tirs-head where he lived at the time he slew Thorir Red-beard
his would-be assassin; it is a most mournful desolate-looking
place, with no signs of life as we rode up but for a swan that
rose up trumpeting from the lake side: I had looked forward
to camping on its side, but its swamps had no pasture for the
beasts and no good camping ground, so we had to ride past
it up a small stream called Búðará that runs into it, and dark
now falling were beginning to get rather weary and impa-

tient when Gisli, who is the great man now, and knows the country well, called a halt on a patch of smooth turf by the side of the stream. There we pitched our tents in a pouring rain; I more tired than I had been yet, owing I fancy to the stumbling about Surtshellir: however, once housed it hurts us not; we sup off cold mutton and cocoa made with the etna, for we are too lazy to look for rather doubtful fuel and light a proper fire, besides it was nearly dark, being half-past ten. After supper we found the rain had stopped; the moon had shone out, and though it was obviously growing cold, we looked forward to a fine day on the morrow for our last day in the wilderness, and talked of bathing in the clear Búðará.

Tuesday, August 1st. In the bonder's house at Grimstunga. WE did, did we! I was roused from sweet sleep by Magnússon, who came to tell me that two hours before the ground had been covered with snow, and that it was sleeting, raining and blowing: I confess I felt strongly inclined to suggest lying there till the weather changed, for it was warm under the blankets: but it might not be: there was little pasture there for the horses on the oasis there, and they had had but a sorry bite for the last two nights; so it was undoubtedly necessary to hurry on to the fertile Vatnsdale, the nearest stead of which, Grimstunga,[1] was seven or eight hours off: so I groaned and got up and went out into the bitterest morning, the wind NW and plenty of it and of rain; Magnússon and I made a desperate attempt at a fire, and failed of course; the guides were standing by the horses, who stood with tails turned to the wind and heads hanging down, shaking again with the cold; well, we decamped and packed, and walked up and down eating our breakfast of cold mutton bones and cold water, and chaffing each other the while to keep up our spirits, and so, after a

[1] Grimstunga is the homestead at which the young Gunnlaug the Wormtongue gave the first proof of his prowess. See his Saga, chap. v. E.M.

86

sloppy half-hour, to horse, and away into the very teeth of
it. I don't like to confess to being a milksop: but true it is
that it beat me: may I mention that I had a stomach-ache to
begin with as some excuse: and for the rest, if it was bad in
our camp, it was much worse out of it, seeing that the camp-
ing-stead was sheltered by a low hill; as we rode now we could
not see a rod in front of us, the rain, or hail, or sleet, for it was
now one, now the other of these, did not fall, we could see no
drops, but it was driven in a level sheet into our faces, so that
one had to shut one eye altogether, and flap one's hat over
the other. Magnússon and Evans stood it out best, working
hard at driving the horses; Faulkner, worried by his short
sight, and I by my milksopishness, tailed; I was fortunately
mounted on Falki, who was very swift and surefooted, and
so got on somehow; but I did at last in the early part of the
day fairly go to sleep as I rode, and fall to dreaming of people
at home: from which I was woke up by a halt, and Magnússon coming to me and telling me that my little haversack was
missing: now in the said haversack I had the notes of this
present journal; pipe, spare spectacles, drawing materials (if
they were any use) and other things I particularly didn't want
to lose, so I hope to be forgiven if I confess that I lost my
temper, and threatened to kill Eyvindr, to whom I had given
it at Búðará: he, poor fellow, answered not, but caught an
empty horse, and set off through the storm (we had ridden
then some three hours) to look for it, and on we went. Though
of course I grew colder & colder, my stomach bettered somewhat after this excitement, but the wind scarcely lulled all day;
we went on without changing horses; rested for some five
minutes in a little cleft where we didn't feel the storm quite
as much: met two men and a woman coming from Grimstunga, and envied them for having their backs turned to the
wind: I suppose the country was something like that of yesterday, but of course we could see but little of it: the road was
not bad and quite obvious, so we made good way: I stopped
by a considerable stream to drink after we had ridden some
hours, and felt a thrill of pride as a traveller, and a strange

87

sensation, as I noted and cried out that it was running north: all other streams we had seen in Iceland having had their course south or south-west. This stream we crossed twice, and a little after we came to the brow of a steep slope over which we looked into a very deep narrow valley, cleft down from the wilderness by a biggish stream and trending nearly due north. Going down the very steep slope into this valley one of the laden horses quarrelled with his crupper, and flung up his heels so lustily that we all thought he would go head over heels down the hill, and despite our discomfort, we laughed consumedly, it looked so odd. About here, when all the others were getting to their worst, I began to revive, which I am glad of, for I got an impression of a very wonderful country. We crossed the valley and the river, and slowly wound up the other side, and so followed it towards Water-dale; the country we were riding over was high upland-looking ground with no indication of this terrible gorge till one was quite on the edge of it; it grew very narrow as we went on, and the cliffs very steep and not less than six hundred feet high, I should think; the bottom of it was filled but for a few narrow grassy slopes going down from the cliffs, with a deep green river: huge buttresses ran into it here and there nearly stopping it at times, and making a place that could seldom see the sun: this is the next dale to Forsæludalr, Shady-dale, of the Gretla, and they say is just like it, so there you have no unworthy background to Glám the Thrall and his hauntings. As we rode on we had to cross a narrow ravine going down at right angles into the main gorge, with a stream thundering down it; we rode round the very verge of it a-midst a cloud of spray from the waterfall, and a most dreadful place it looked down there where the two waters met: so on for about half an hour, till at last the narrow gorge widened into the head of Water-dale, that looked all green and fertile to us after the waste, its slopes going up on every side to the long wall of mountain that hedged it in: it was all full of mist and drifting rain, and the wind blew up from it like knives: but down below we could see the handsome stead of Grims-

tunga lying in its ample tún, and a new-built wooden church
beside it, and a sweet sight it was to us: we rode swiftly down
to the stead, and soon had three or four men about and were
bidden in; and as we sat quite out of the wind and rain in the
clean parlour, drinking coffee and brandy, and began to feel
that we had feet and hands again, I felt such happiness as I
suppose I shan't feel again till I ride from Búðará to Grimstunga under similar circumstances. I should think we sat for
about an hour thawing ourselves in our wet clothes, and talking to the bonder, a jolly-looking *fat* old man, his son Thorstein, a bright good-tempered young one, and Dr Skaptason,
who is to be our next host, and lives further down the valley
at Hnausar: then we unpacked the boxes and dried ourselves
and were, O so comfortable and were shown to two little
rooms, handy enough for our needs, and with real beds in
them: then, going out, I found Eyvindr just come back with
my bag which he had duly found at the camp: I shook hands
and thanked him with effusion and hope he will forget my
threat of this morning: then the goodman gives us supper
of Icelandic matters and we all got to bed in comfort: I wondering, I must allow, whether we should all be cripples with
rheumatism for the rest of our lives.

Wednesday, August 2nd. At the same place.

SLEPT till nine when I got up very well and light-
hearted and with a furious appetite; breakfast of smoked
mutton, salmon and curds which I think very good: I
looked up the geography of Njála and wrote my diary quite
contented with not going out into the weather, which was very
cold and raw, though not rainy: so we wore away the morning, none of us saying anything about going on till lo, it was
half past three and then we all agreed it would be too late, as
we should be knocking up Skaptason at night: so we amuse
ourselves very well; buy beautiful warm stockings of the
goodwife; clean our guns which want it sorely enough; do
our best to dry our soaked gear of yesterday: then I, seeing
a netting needle and mesh propose beginning a net for the

goodman which amuses me till it is time to get ready for cooking dinner, Faulkner meantime making a biscuit box into a sugar box for us is thoughtful over it, and Magnússon and Evans amuse themselves in a simpler way by sleeping: then I take possession of the kitchen; that is as always, a little shed with a hearth built up of dry stones, and a hole in the roof for the smoke, the rafters black and shining with soot. The fuel was good peat to-day, and as I had plenty of time I worked hard at my stew and soup: they really were both very good, or else we were very hungry: we asked the bonder to dinner (in his own parlour) and with some demur he assented, but I thought he didn't like my cookery as well as the rest. Whist after this for a couple of hours and so to bed: for I suppose we dined about nine as we generally did.

Thursday, August 3rd. In Dr Skaptason's house at Hnausar. UP rather earlier on a cold grey morning, but not rainy as yet. I must say I should not have objected to another day's idling but on we must: so got away about 10 a.m. the bonder's son going with us to show us the way and to point out the historical steads: I bought two old silver spoons at starting from the kind old goody. Young Thorstein, the son, was a bright eager fellow & very well mounted, and the whole stead looked well-doing. We were all in very good spirits as we rode off down the valley, a great flat space between two high steep mountain-ridges with no break in them, and a clear river winding down it toward the sea, with only a little surrounding of shingle, in some places none at all, for there are no glaciers in this part of the North. The valley is not clear and smooth however, for knolls rise up in it that in some places run up into spurs that join the lower slopes of the mountain wall. The hero and "landnáms-man" of the vale is Ingimund the Old[1] and most of the steads Thorstein shows us have reference to him; at the first we come to Ás [where] lived Hrolleifr, the rascal he protected, and who slew him; it lies under two little knolls with a pretty tún

[1] Vatzdæla Saga, Origines Islandicae, 275 et seq. Ed.

90

about it; under the turf wall of which grow great banks of
wild hearts-ease for as cold as the weather is; we cross the
river after this, and come upon a shut-in nook among the
knolls, the second dwelling-place of Hrolleifr[1] and the witch
Liot his mother: just before this Thorstein points out a
sandy spit running into the river which is the traditional place
of the deadly wounding of Ingimund: past the aforesaid shut-
in nook we turn round a corner and come upon Ingimund's
own stead lying on a wide slope of green. As Thorstein
leads us up the road toward the stead he shows us how
it is raised above the meadow instead of being sunk below it
as is usual, and infers from that the antiquity of the stead;
higher up than the house a low knoll rises from the slope,
and this he calls the site of Ingimund's temple which names
the whole stead (Hof). Thence we ride on along the slopes
till we come to where a great buttress of bare basalt cliff
thrusts forward from the mountain wall: on the slopes beneath this lies a handsome stead called Hvammr, where we
make a call, and have the inevitable coffee and brandy: and
then depart into the rain which has just come on again but
not heavily: the call at Hof and Hvammr has taken us up
very close to the mountains, we now ride down a little way
nearer to the river, and see many steads on the other side;
for the valley is populous and prosperous as indeed it always
has been: tradition says too that it was once so well wooded,
that standing in the middle you couldn't see the hillsides for
the trees: we saw no wood at all here though there are some
patches marked in the map on the west side. A little past
Hvammr Thorstein brings us to a place where there is a
sudden deep little dell quite round like an inverted cone
sunk in the slope-side, and tell us that hereby fairs like our
"mops" used to be held, and that the lads and lasses used
to dance in this dell at these fairs: Midsummer-night I think
being the time: the grass grows sweet and deep down it, and
it looks a pleasant place enough to get out of the wind to en-

[1]Apparently traditional, as, by the Saga, the couple only dwelt
at As and were slain there by the sons of Ingimund. E.M.

91

Hnausar joy oneself in. Now the buttresses have all sunk back into the great hills the crests of which rise higher as we get nearer the sea: down in the valley is a lake said to be made by a great slip from the hills, as I suppose it was, for little sand-knolls dot its shores: there is a traditional tale about this slip of a raven drawing the girl who used to feed him away from the danger one Sunday morning: it is told in Magnússon's book.[1] We go down into the valley a little more now, and presently come to a big fine-looking tún with a gate to it of some pretensions in Icelandic architecture, ᛞᛟ— and Thorstein tells us it is Dr Skaptason's and accordingly riding out of it we are presently in front of the house, a smart newbuilt one; he is at the door in a twinkling and seems very glad to see us and all is arranged for our stay that night. I suppose it was about half past three by now, as our ride had been but a short one. The rain cleared off somewhat now, so I went out to see to my gun and look about me: there is a little tarn in the mead at the back of the house, from the shore of which the first slopes of the hills arise: I stood looking at the hills and wondering at how much bigger they look here than I thought at first they were: our horses, now feeding on a green slope, some third of the way up seem little bits of specks: a long way above them the sheep feed on the slopes of the steps that make the mountain, and its crest is all hidden in white clouds, those very clouds we came through the other day from Búðará: below the clouds is a goodish sprinkling of snow all along the eastern hill-sides of the valley. The air was quite full of sea-swallows sweeping about: I stood and watched them some while, and thought the whole place beautiful in spite of the ungenial day: then too we were come close to the northern sea, and to our turning point: all away from this was south and home again. I had seen to my gun (my brother's) which was rather a heavy charge all through the journey, wanting as much attention as a baby with croup; and then I wandered about the front of the house and played with a month-old tame fox cub, not so

[1] Legends of Iceland. Ed.

92

very tame either; a pretty little beast he was and really Hnausar "blue." The parlour of the house was smart here, and had a stove in it (I wished it had been lighted that afternoon): our bedroom was a queer little room in the old part of the house with a six foot turf wall and four bunk-beds in it. I may mention here that a legend sprang up about this bedroom, to wit that C.J.F. was found in it when we were just come, having his boots and breeches pulled off by a female Icelander, after their ancient custom, he being resigned, owing to want of knowledge of the tongue: take said legend for what it may be worth.

After a little talk with the Doctor about the new Icelandic-Norwegian company to which he belongs, dinner is brought in to which we sit down without waiting for Evans, who is gone out shooting, and who almost *never* is in time for victuals: in this case I thought it rather bad manners, but the host didn't seem to care a bit and we had a very pleasant dinner of the best Icelandic fashion: at the end of which came in Evans empty handed to claim his share. Then we had tea, then whist, and grog, and so to bed merry enough.

CHAPTER V. FROM WATER-DALE TO BIARG AND RAMFIRTH.

Friday, August 4th. In Mr Jón Víðalin's house at Víðidalstunga.

UP rather late to a somewhat better morning, but not very bright. After a long and good breakfast the Doctor brought in his daughter dressed in gala clothes which included a really fine belt of silver-smith's work, I should think not later than 1530 in date, for there was a St Barbara engraved on the smooth side of the tag in regular Hans Burgmair style: the open-work of the belt was very beautiful, the traditional northern Byzantinesque work all mixed up with the crisp sixteenth century leafage. The doctor's surgery was a queer place: such big and dirty bottles of (I suppose) very strong physic; skins of birds, whips, and odds and ends; a small library of old books (Latin me-

93

dical) and, kicking about, a fine copy of the Guðbrandr Bible in its original binding brass-bound and very good. The train having been started some hours, we set off at last after rather more than enough drinking of stirrup-cups. We had given up all idea of trying to get further north now lest we should be too close run in the Broadfirth and Snæfell country; and so our heads were turned south again. The doctor rode with us very well mounted: he has exceedingly good horses, and has a custom that a little before they get too old for work he lets them have a few quiet years of grazing in a good pasture before the bullet ends them. Our road takes us by the head of the lake before-mentioned through a queer tumbling waste of sand knolls (with grass in the hollows however) and thence west into wide flats which are the shore of a nearly land-locked inlet of the northern sea, which takes the Víðidal waters, and is called the Hope (Hóp *islandicé*); the north wind blows fresh and strong across it, and the shore is all strewn with swan-feathers. We are come in Víðidal now, and behind us to the north-east can see the hills of Longdale, the main scene of the Bandamanna Saga: before us is a slope crowned with a stead called Borg, the place of the Saga of Finnbogi the Strong; in its present condition rather a poor characterless story; but with one touching part in it where the wife of Finnbogi dies of grief for the slaying of her favourite son by a scoundrel. They show you a grassy knoll hereby for her tomb.

We go into the stead and are kindly received by the bonder (coffee and brandy of course), who has been in Scotland and talks English, and is an intelligent man enough: not much to his benefit, I am afraid, for he seems discontented with Iceland in consequence. However he knows the sagas well, and tells me that at his stead they always read over his stock of them every winter. After a talk and wandering about his stead a bit we all go off together to the Borgar-virki, a strange piece of nature hereby: it is an old crater (I suppose) crowning a sloping hill some furlong from the stead, and has from time immemorial formed a regular

94

round tower with sheer perpendicular sides rising from steep
slopes of rocky debris; there is only one breach in the natural
wall, which is flat at the top like a rampart almost all round,
with room for about four men to stand abreast on it: we
clamber painfully up to the said breach, which is made good
by man's handiwork with huge rough stones piled up into a
fair wall, but broken down a bit now: this breach may be
about twenty feet wide: once in, the floor of the tower is
smooth sweet grass, and I guess it some fifty paces diameter;
with walls of about twenty-five feet (on the inside): on one
side is a rectangular well of bright water, and by it marks of
the turf walls of old houses, though how old I don't know.
Slaying-Bardi the hero of the Heath-Slayings Saga is the
name connected with it: the story tells how he held this
stronghold with a few men against the Westlanders, who,
finding that nothing was to be made of storming it, sat down
before it and starved the garrison down to one sausage,
which they pitched over the wall in scorn to the besiegers,
who, thinking them well victualled since they could afford
such waste, demitted in despair: a story certainly not confined to Iceland. We enjoyed ourselves very much here,
especially as the sun came out for a bit, the first time that we
had seen him since Kalmanstunga and Surtshellir last Monday. We lay about on the grass-grown rampart, and could
see the northern sea now over the bar of the Hope, and the
cold, snow-besprinkled mountains of Longdale, and at our
feet the first of Víðidal (Willowdale) boggy and melancholy
with ragged ill-arranged hillsides. There we talked and
drank to each other from our own whiskey (getting rather
bitter now from washing about in the oak-kegs), till at last
we went our ways up the dale, when the day had got grey
again, the bonder of Borg swelling our train. We rode on
the worst side of the river by a dismal way enough till we
came to a stead not marked in my map and whose name I
have forgotten, though it is named in Gretla.[1] Here also we

[1] The homestead was Lœkiamót, of old the home of Thorarinn
the Wise. E.M.

were bound to go in: at the door stood a man with whom I
held a struggling conversation in Icelandic till I found he
could talk English as well as myself: he turned out to be Bar-
ing Gould's guide, and I thought him an unpleasant, boastful,
vulgar sort of a fellow: he was travelling about the country for
the Scotch horse-dealers. After staying here rather longer
than I liked we got to saddle again, and took leave of the
hospitable doctor, but the bonder of Borg went on with us.

We had got through the worst of the valley now, both
sides of the river were smoother and grassier, and the other
side (the lower) looked pleasant enough, with grass-grown
spurs and knolls: on one of the best of such on our side
stands Asgeirsá, the house of Asgeir Madpate, father of
Hrefna and uncle of Grettir's father: As (The Ridge) where
Hrefna died[1] is waste now, I imagine, and was not pointed
out to us: Auðunnarstaðir[2] is just opposite to it on the other
side and is well placed and imposing looking. At last the
vale gets narrower and we come right on Viðidalstunga
standing on pretty green slopes thrust out into the valley.
We were bent on getting to Stáðarbakki in Midfirth to-day,
but our late leaving of Hnausar, and our stopping at Borg
and the other stead have brought twilight on us here, and
there is nothing for it but to stop. We are soon welcomed in
the stead by the bonder Víðalin, somewhat of a magnate, a
man who can trace his direct descent to a "landnámsman,"
I forget whom: he is a friend of Magnússon's too, and they
fall to talking busily about politics and scraps of antiquarian-
ism, till supper comes: said supper Evans grumbled at hor-
ribly for slenderness, and disappeared to make himself hap-
pier over our own biscuit and cheese: as for me I sat hour
after hour in the little room trying to catch a sentence here
and there, and I am afraid feeling highly bored at first, which
was very unfair considering all things, till I got into a dreamy

[1] No stead of the name of As has ever existed in Willowdale.
Hrefna went after the death of Kiartan "north," i.e. to the North-
country, and obviously to her father's house at Asgeirsá. E.M.
[2] Where Grettir wrestled with Auðunn Asgeirsson. E.M.

96

state at last which was comfortable enough. Then the host Viðidals-
showed us his antiquities; an old pewter "askr"[1] or porridge tunga
pot, which he said had belonged to bishop Gúðbrand (†1627)
and was at all events of his date; several good cups and spoons
of silver, and a fine piece of embroidery with scripture subjects worked in circles, and an inscription, which Magnússon with some trouble made out: it looked like thirteenth
century work: but, I suppose was eighteenth. So to bed, very
comfortably lodged, the whole house being turned upside
down for that end.

Saturday, August 5th. In camp by the stead of Fiarðarhorn,
Ramfirth.

GOT up pretty early and walked about the stead and
into the little turf-walled church that stands on a
grassy knoll running into the flat meads: our host
followed us in, to show us what there was to see: it was all
deal inside with a rather elaborate screen, a pretty brass chan-
delier and two old (17th century?) pictures, an altar triptych
and painted rood: there were a good many books in it; among
them a Gúðbrandr Bible; a rather valuable MS. of ecclesias-
tical annals and a handsomely written book of Sagas; Hrolf
Kraki to wit, Volsunga, and Ragnar Loðbrók, written out in
the 17th century, I suppose. Breakfast after this, and then to
horse and away on a cold grey morning with a little drizzle
on, our host going with us to guide us over the bogs between
his house and Midfirth Neck.

Just as we turn out of the valley on to the neck, we come
on a knoll, the site of Swala-stead, where Vali of the Bandamanna [Saga] was murdered: Víðalin told us of it that many
stories were current of it and of Swala's witchcraft, and repeated a rhyme that says how the day will come when the big
house of Swala-stead shall be lower than the cot of Víðidale-
tongue.

Our way is rough and boggy enough, as usual over the

[1] A porringer, made of wood originally of ash. Cleasby and Vigf.,
dict., s.v. Ed.

VIII.H   97

neck, and was a characterless tumbling waste till it smoothed
itself out into a hollow lying on the neck's top, with a high hill
sweeping up from it on our right: from the flank of this juts
out at right angles a bare cliff high over the valley, which is
called [Thoreyarnúpr = Thorey's-crag], the place where
Grettir stood to challenge Slaying-Bardi as he came back
from the Heath-slayings: and low down by the hill's foot is
a little lake, once bigger, they say, called Midfirth Water,
where the ball-play in Grettla went on. So we ride a goodish
way over bog and stones, Magnússon riding by Víðalin and
talking busily all the way, riding at a foot's pace in consequence: hence a temper, for Evans got very cross at our going so slowly, and worried me till I sung out with rage to
Magnússon to get on faster, being cross at being worried,
not with Magnússon. I hope Víðalin understood what it all
meant.

At last the ground rises up to a crest, and climbing that,
we can look down into Midfirth valley, the birth-place of
Grettir. The day is at its worst now, and the long narrow vale,
cleft by an *untidy* river and bounded by a long down-like hill,
looks empty and dead and hopeless; nor could we see the
narrow strip that runs up from the northern sea and names
the place. So we go down into it, and after a due piece of bog
come on a stead hanging on the hill-side called Torfa-stead:
Torfa was a poetess much told of in the tales of this country-
side as Skald-Torfa; Víðalin shows us a great flat grey stone
that lies in the tún as the grave of her.

Thence we are soon down into the flat of the valley, which
turns out much better than it looked from farther off, and has
a great deal of character: there are flat, well-grassed meadows
all along the river, which runs in a well-defined bed, sometimes bounded by steep dark-grey banks, that break off
sometimes and leave it bare amidst the meadows: the valley
is very narrow, and looking toward its landward end one can
see the grey banks aforesaid rising high and pinching the
river very close, and winding round beyond till they get blue
in the distance and seem to stop it.

98

Thence we are soon down into the flat of the valley which turns out much better than it looked from farther off and has a great deal of character: that are flat floral grassy meadows all along the river which runs in a well defined bed sometimes bounded by steep dark grey banks that break off sometimes and leave it bare amidst the meadows. the valley is very narrow and looking toward its landward end one can see the grey banks aforesaid rising high and to pinching the river very close, and winding round beyond till they get blue in the distance and seem to stop it.

A facsimile page of the first Journal of Travel in Iceland.

On the "ere" of the river on the other side, under one of
the grey banks, lies Stáðarbakki, a church and parsonage, not
an historical place: we cross the river to it and go in to see the
priest and his wife; they are friends of Magnússon's, and, we
heard afterwards, were sorely disappointed that we hadn't
stopped there, as indeed we meant to do. However, after
coffee the priest gets to horse to go with us to Biarg, and Víðalin takes leave of us. The priest leads us through a fine tún
of his (which, by the way is being hay-made now, so much
later they are in these north firths), down on to the river side,
which we cross presently a little below the gorge aforesaid,
and then, after a short gallop over the smooth turf on the
other side, take to the hill again, and after riding some furlong from the river, turn and go south along the hill-side:
looking back we can see the narrow grey firth now and the
hills winding about it. The day is grown better, and there are
gleams of sun, which have been rare since we came north of
Kaldidal. Presently we come on some huge flat-topped,
straight-sided masses of rock, sticking out of the hill-side,
looking like a broken castle: and turning the flank of these,
we find the hill-side scooped into three or four little valleys,
which join all together on the river-ward side into a long
slope that goes down into the main valley: on two of the
knolls that make these little hollows are sheep-houses, but
the longest and highest of them, facing the rocks, and running at right-angles to the main hill, is flat-topped & smooth,
and under it, looking seaward, lie the three heaps of turf and
boarded gables of a poor house, which is Biarg,[1] where Grettir
was born; the whole little valley is bright with newly-mown
grass, whereon there are still a few hay-cocks lying: the grey
ridges of the barren hill, strewn about with great boulders,
rise above it to the north-east, and above that again one can
see the dark slopes of the mountains over Víðidal or Vatns-
dal striped with new-fallen snow. We get off at the house-
door where come two children and a woman, looking rather
miserable and dirty: it is not such a bad farm, the priest says,

[1] Same as Burg, a castle.

but is owned by two men together: one of them comes presently, and we walk about with him; and down in the hollowest of the valleys we come on a well with a turf roof over it, and beside that is a smooth mound, bigger and taller than the ordinary tussocks of the home-mead, and this they call Grettir's "head-mound," i.e. the place where his head was buried. After this we go up the hill that looks down on all this, where is a big stone (some twenty tons C.J.F. guessed it) on another, which they call a Grettir's Heave:[1] we lie down there awhile, and look down on the place in the bright sunshine, for the day has quite cleared now, and can see between the rocks of the Burg, the firth right down to its end, and the mountains of Hrutafirth beyond them, and other mountains further away into the northern sea, and as blue as blue can be. All about us the scant grass was full of flowers, gentian and milk-wort mostly. So down to the house again, over the mound at the back of it, which shows signs of old building on it. We buy a silver spoon and a piece of queer embroidery of the bonder, and then mount and ride off slowly down the hill under his guidance, and going over a bog that lies on the slope-side, come on to the smooth river-side meadows again. They are very narrow here from hill-side to hill-side: and we can see here that what I called a gorge above, and took for the end of the valley, was only a mound cleft through by the river: for we are on flat meadows above it now, and the real narrowing of the valley is above us some quarter of a mile: so these two places are like two gates, the tumbling blue mountain-country to be seen through the upper one, the slopes of the valley and even a gleam of the firth to be seen through the lower. The sun is fairly out now, and the meadows are flowery, so we have no very savage impression left us of Midfirth as we turn toward its south-west slopes to leave it. At the hill's foot is a quite round pond, and a little way up the hill by our roadside, another round pit, but not

[1] See "Grettir the Strong," p. 32. *Grettis-tak*, " the lift of Grettir the Strong," a name for those boulders which would require Herculean strength to lift them. Icel. Dictionary. Ed.

filled with water: they are both about, say, a hundred and
fifty yards across, and the waterless one may be thirty feet
deep and is all grown with rich grass and flowers; the priest
says he has picked ripe strawberries down there; a rarity, as
you may well imagine, in Iceland.

So up on to the bare "neck" and over a bog or two, till we
come on our train halted here in a grassy patch for us: the
priest, Sveinn Skúlason leaves us here after sharing with us
what lunch we have to give him. A little higher than this and
we can see the mountains of Hrutafirth rising before us; but
still looking back can note Biarg on the hill-side by its castle-
like rocks. We still go up the neck till, crossing a ridge and
hollow we are on the tongue of land that divides the two
waters, Midfirth and Hrutafirth, and can look into both of
them, with the day gone grey again, though a few gleams of
sun yet cling about it, brightening the long lines of inky-
purple hills here and there. Still on over the heath, a few
mountains thrusting themselves up above the face of it toward the south, but not of any character; more behind us on
the north, the great ridges over Vatnsdale, dark ashen coloured, and striped low down with Tuesday's snow, are clear
enough.

Now we have clomb to the top of the neck, a very bare
stony spot, and drop down over the ridge till Midfirth and
the rest north are lost and Hrutafirth (Ramfirth of Gretla)
lies all open before us: a long narrow firth running itself into
nothing up into the land, fenced on the other side by a long
unbroken dark ridge that seems to come right down to the
water's edge: there is no keel visible on the water now, but
opposite to our steep road on the south-west side is a flat
spit of land pushing out into the firth, on which stand the
"houses" of a trading station, Bórðeyri, the chief port of
these parts in the time of Grettir: the road winding down to
the firth gets steeper now till at last we can see the lip of the
grass land by the water on our side, and washed by the water,
a great tún of bright green, a regular circle within its green
turf walls, and in the midst of it the stead-buildings neat and

new, but picturesque enough: this is Thorodd-stead the dwelling-place and death-place of Thorbiorn Oxmain, who slew Atli Grettir's brother, and was slain by Grettir in his turn. I'm sorry we didn't stop here; and Magnússon thought we were going to, and when we got on to the level ground rode straight up to the house to ask for quarters; but when he came back, he found us all meaning to go on as this made a very short day's ride, and would make our next day into Laxdale a long one, and we all thought that Fiárðarhorn had been intended for our stopping place to-day: Magnússon finding us in this frame of mind rode off back to the stead to countermand our request or order, rather huffed as was but natural; though for my own single part I was quite ready to stop so as not to hurt his feelings; but if I had known it was a historical place I would have stopped in any case. Well, off we rode again somewhat uncomfortable at first after our— discussion—but soon got easier again. It was a pleasant ride too up the firth all along its very beach of black sand and shingle bestrewn with big mussel-shells: there were steepish broken but low slopes above us, and we guessed the water at about three miles wide here: as we went on we saw big pieces of drift-wood scattered about; and now and again I saw queer-looking things something of the shape and size of the screw of a small steamer lying about; I couldn't make these out, till in a little grassy break in the steeper slopes lay a boat, and beside [it] a skeleton of a good-sized whale lacking some of its vertebræ, which were those queer things; two other such breaks grassy and pleasant we passed, and there were boats in each of them, but the steads lay a little back and we didn't see them. It was good riding here; Falki was running loose, and Mouse I found go lame at Thorodstead from having cast a shoe, so I rode one of C.J.F's usual horses, a smooth-skinned shiny piebald, that we and the guides between us had christened the Goodly Pig because of his queer looks and obstinacy.

The firth narrows as we ride on, and we could see a man on a white horse riding along the other side of the firth at a

gallop: the water in shore by us was all covered with eider
ducks, great brown birds almost as big as a goose; they had
many young broods with them, and it was pretty to see the
old ducks carrying a duckling or two on their backs as they
pitched over the low waves like heavy craft.

So we come to the very end of the firth, where the river
runs into it in many streams, and there was flat green space
between the sea-water and the encircling hills, in the midst
of which one could see the church and stead of Stad: Fiárðarhorn (Firth-corner) is visible on the other side just where
the sea water comes to an end. As we turn toward the river
to seek for a ford, the man on the white horse, who has out-
ridden us, turns to it from his side and splashes through the
shallow water, and so rides away toward Stad: so we can follow his track in the sand without troubling much to feel for
a ford: and a few minutes after are thronging the tún of
Fiárðarhorn; a pretty field sloping down to the water-side:
it is half-past nine now, and getting dusk, and all men are
asleep in the houses of the poor little stead: out they swarm
however in a minute or two, like bees out of a hive, and two
smart boys help us to pitch our tents handily enough and
laughing with joy all the time. We have the stithy handed
over to us for our kitchen, as the fire is out in the kitchen
proper: thither Magnússon and I take our tools, and smithy
soup and stew, while a grey-head big carle, not very right in
his wits, a sort of Barnaby Rudge, blows the bellows for us;
we talk to him, I taking some share in the conversation, till
apropos of something or other Magnússon says:

"This man (meaning me) can talk Icelandic, you see."

"Does he," says the carle, "I have heard him talk a great
deal, and I don't know what he has been saying."

"Don't you understand this?" say I.

"Yes," says he.

"Isn't it Icelandic then?"

"Well, I don't know," says he; "in all tongues there must
be some words like other tongues, and perhaps these are
some of those."

Now was dinner served up, and we sat down to it with a close ring of men all round the tent's mouth watching us, stooping down with their hands on their knees, and now and then dropping a sentence one to the other, such as "Now he's supping the broth:" "What flesh is that?" and so on. They were queer outlandish people, but quite good-tempered and kind, and most willing to do anything we told them.

Magnússon turned in early after dinner, and was soon snoring; but C.J.F. and I lay on our blankets and smoked: while we were at this the tent-flap was drawn aside, and a big carle, surely Wolf the Unwashed again, put in his head and said:

"I am told off to watch your horses" (which were sent down to the out-meadows to graze). I thought this was a hint for liquor, and so handed him a nip of whiskey; he shook hands with me with effusion, and then I found out that he was drunk already. However he took himself off and we thought him gone: but presently back he comes and says as if he were another person:

"I'm told off to watch the horses."

Therewith he holds out a little bottle, empty now of all but dirt, but labelled (in English) "Essential oil of Almonds." I was weak enough to put some whiskey in it, and again he shook my hand and again went away, but not so far but that C.J.F. could see him holding his little bottle up against the bright moon to see how much he had got. Then he really seemed to go, but got no further than the roof of an out-building on which he sat astride (like Glám) and presently began to howl out a dismal song; I recognised the tune as the same that Eyvindr sings when he is rather more than doubtful of the way, or when he has to do something he doesn't like: it is a "ríma" or ballad in four-line stanza with a burden at each stanza's end, and every stanza ends with a queer long note, which with our friend on the roof is a dismal bellow: it was now one o'clock and though we laughed at first, it began to be rather a wearisome addition to the due noises, of the wind piping about the hill, the flapping of the

tent, and the quacking of the eider ducks, and—Magnússon's steady snore hard by. So I began to think I should
have to wake the latter to help get rid of the singer, when all
of a sudden he left off, and I thought him gone; but lo the
tent pulled open again, and there he is, asking us, as if he
were yet a new person, if he shall sing a little song to us: this
time I was curt and peremptory, so after shaking hands again
in his new character, he does really go at last away into the
darkness, and sleep descends on us.

Sunday, August 6th, In camp in the home-mead of Herdholt.

UP about eight: two or three people look in here on
their way to church, and all the household is up and
dressed in their best, so I fry the bacon and we breakfast even more in public than we dined last evening. We ask
the people if they have anything ancient or handsome for sale
here; whereat the two bonders (for this stead is held by two
families) say that they know of nothing there older or prettier than "these two old carles." The grinning over about
this joke, after we have really bought two horn spoons, we
get the bonder to put us on our way toward Laxdale, and get
to horse, climbing the hill-side away from the firth at once.
    Our way over the neck was wearily boggy, and we made
way slowly enough: the horses were marvellously clever
among the bogs, but a pack-horse at last put his foot on what
seemed a piece of sound green turf, and down he went into
a positive hole, and hung on by his forefeet and the boxes;
so that we had to unpack him, and haul him out with ropes.
    The day was windy and cold, but the sun came out and
shone brightly while we were yet on the neck: from the highest point of it we could see on our south the heads of big
mountains dark blue and snow-streaked, looking as if they
belonged to another world than the ragged waste we were
on: through a gap in the hills we have just climbed we can
see the water of Ramfirth, and further off the Vatnsdale hills.
We struggle on till we begin to get clear of the bogs, and are

Herdholt on very stony ground and going down hill, till we see a long way off Solheimar, the first stead of Laxdale: we go down very speedily hence, and are soon in the dale: long hills stretch seaward on either side of it, but the dale between them is somewhat choked up with knolls and smaller hills, Laxá running small and shallow among them: at the very head of the dale the river running under high cliffs bounds a smooth sunny green meadow on one side, and its other three sides are nearly girded in by high green banks: but after this, which was very beautiful and characteristic, the valley loses itself in a litter of broken knolls for awhile: but getting through these we come into a quite flat plain, where we stop to bait horse and man for an hour. The wind was terribly strong and cold in spite of the bright sun; but we were merry enough, however, for an hour and a half, when we set on again: we went by a good road, crossing and recrossing the river many times. The valley between its long unbroken hill-banks is never clear of a litter of lower hills: many of these however are smooth and green, and have steads lying at their feet: it is Sunday too and at all the steads we see the horses of visitors standing. One [stead] I remember particularly lying among a nest of grassy knolls, and quite a party going on among them: we didn't go in as the day was wearing fast, but Magnússon and Faulkner and I rested just beyond the stead, and then made up for lost time as well as we could; but sooth to say, the horses don't go so well as they used; Mouse is getting thin, and they will be all the better for to-morrow's rest.

Now as we rode, we could see showing over the valley's other end, the blue peaked mountains lying about Broad-firth; it was exciting to see them, for it was visibly coming to fresh country, all the northern dales we have seen being regular trenches with great unbroken lines of hill on either side. So on till at the mouth of the dale the littery knolls grow together into a spur that narrows the valley as it draws toward Hvammfirth, and high up on the side of it we can see the houses of Herdholt: Magnússon, Faulkner and I press

106

on before the train; Magnússon has been here before and thinks he knows a short cut up to the stead; but it turns out to be nothing but a most evil bog in which C.J.F.'s horse sinks up to the girths at once and we have to dismount and lead our horses carefully from tussock to tussock before we get on to the firm ground of the tún.

The little house that stands over so many stories of the old days is rather new and trim but picturesque enough, three long gabled aisles, the turf sides of which are laid herring-bone fashion, and there are  elaborate dog-vanes on the gables. From the door of it one looks down on to the flats about the river, rising gradually into the slopes of the great bounding hill, where among long straight lines of the grey stone-banks that old ice-waves have striped the hill-sides with, parallel to the main lines of the valley, and sad dull yellow-green bogs, lie two emerald green patches, the túns of two steads; one of them Hauskuldstead, the parent-house of Herdholt. The hill above all this gradually slopes down to Hwammfirth, and above its lower end show two strange-shaped mountains like a church-roof with a turret at the end of it: the spurs of these again run down into the firth, leaving a space of low hills and boggy plain by the water-side: but beyond and bounding all to the south-west lies that sea of peaked mountains that are all about Holyfell. The actual waters of Hwammfirth are hidden from sight here because of the shoulder of the spur on which we are, the higher part of which also hides the mountains to the north. The dean (an acquaintance of Magnússon's) was out when we came to the stead; so C.J.F. and I went and sat down in the parlour while Magnússon went to fetch him from the next stead; he was some time gone, and we went out again and watched the train coming leisurely in now, Evans among them: they had taken the road on the other side the river, and had crossed the bog by a handsome causeway. While we helped in the unloading and careful stowing away of our goods, Magnússon came back with the parson and his wife,

Herdholt who welcomed us kindly and offered to kill a sheep for us: then came the necessary coffee, and then Evans and C.J.F. went off to pitch the tent, while I spent my time alone in trying to regain my spirits which had suddenly fallen very low almost ever since we came into Laxdale.

Just think, though, what a mournful place this is—Iceland I mean—setting aside the pleasure of one's animal life there: the fresh air, the riding and rough life, and feeling of adventure—how every place and name marks the death of its short-lived eagerness and glory; and withal so little is the life changed in some ways: Olaf Peacock went about summer and winter after his live-stock, and saw to his hay-making and fishing just as this little peak-nosed parson does; setting aside the coffee and brandy, his victuals under his hall, "marked with famous stories," were just the same as the little parson in his ten-foot square parlour eats: I don't doubt the house stands on the old ground. But Lord! what littleness and helplessness has taken the place of the old passion and violence that had place here once—and all is unforgotten; so that one has no power to pass it by unnoticed: yet that must be something of a reward for the old life of the land, and I don't think their life now is more unworthy than most people's elsewhere, and they are happy enough by seeming. Yet it is an awful place: set aside the hope that the unseen sea gives you here, and the strange threatening change of the blue spiky mountains beyond the firth, and the rest seems emptiness and nothing else: a piece of turf under your feet, and the sky overhead, that's all; whatever solace your life is to have here must come out of yourself or these old stories, not over hopeful themselves. Something of all this I thought; and besides our heads were now fairly turned homeward, and now and again a few times I felt homesick—I hope I may be forgiven. Also there was that ceaseless wind all day: but now towards night it was grown calmer, and was still very bright, and the day ended with a beautiful and strange sunset; not violent red in the west, but the whole sky suffused with it over light green and grey,

108

with a few bars of bright white clouds dragging over it, and
some big dusky rain-clouds low down among the Broadfirth
mountains. I stood and watched it changing, till that and
rest from the wind I suppose made me contented again, and
then we were called in to supper, and even some two hours
afterwards when we went out to our tents again to bed, the
sky had not lost all its colour—so to bed happy enough.

Monday, August 7th. In the same place.

NOTHING but rest here to-day: I did at first make a
last stand about the sketching, and sitting down on
a hummock above the house began to try to draw it
and the hill of Hauskuldstead on the other side the valley;
but I got so miserable over it that I gave it up presently;
C.J.F. on the contrary did make a *triangular* image of the
house, to which I refer you if you want to know what a modern Icelandic house is like. The rest of the day I go wandering about, or lie in the tent: the morning was fine and bright
but with a cold wind; but it clouded over about two and began raining at five, and was still raining. but warmer when
after a game at whist we went to bed.

Tuesday, August 8th. In the same place.

THIS day we were to ride (on hired horses) to Hwamm
and Sælingsdale, and the weather has changed very
happily, for it is soft and warm though not very sunny,
and there is nothing but a light wind from the east, the warm
quarter in Iceland.

So M. and C.J.F. and I rode away under the parson's guidance, but Evans, guiltless of all knowledge of Snorri or
Gudrun or the Sturlungs, stayed behind to fish in Laxá. We
go over the brow of the ridge at the back of the house, and
have Hwammfirth lying before us: a shallow inlet quite boat-
less, and to-day without a wave breaking it, scarce a ripple:
there is a flat space of sand and grass edging the water at this
end; but across the firth the hills rise up high and steep, a few
steads lying at the feet of their slopes. We cross a little stream

presently that the tide runs up: it is flowing now but the water is quite clear: a little past this is a small gorge leading down to the flat shore of the firth, which some people say is the place where the sons of Oswif hid Kiartan's sword, "the King's Gift," when they came back from the feast at Herdholt. We ride some half-hour over a broken heath till in half an hour's time we "turn a corner" and come on Liaskógar lying on a green bank overlooking the flats at the firth corner here: this was the house of Thorstein Kuggson, one of Grettir's friends and a protector of him in his outlawry: the old bonder-carle who lives here now welcomed us at the door, and being led out by the parson, was only too glad to tell us all he imagined about the ancient sites: he showed us in his tún the site of Kuggson's hall, and then of his church, and then of his bridge under which hung those "din-bells"[1] that could be heard far off out on the firth: but his faith carried him so much further as to show us a pile of smoke-blackened rafters, and suggest that perhaps they came out of the old chieftain's hall: I'm afraid Magnússon cut him up by the roots at this point.

As we stood at the door just before mounting I thought I saw surf breaking on the beach some furlong or two beyond us, and pointed it out to C.J.F. with some astonishment, as the firth had seemed so smooth hitherto; but as we rode on the surf resolved itself into swans, that glided away before us and hung about some little skerries out in the firth—such a fleet of them!

The hills on the other side of the surf show bold and full of character from here, with bare basalt rocks thrusting out here and there from the grey green slopes and shaly heaps: just opposite to us they give back into a narrow valley, guarded by three isolated knolls that are capped by basaltic pillars and stand out in the flat meads; and that valley is Sælingsdale. Skirting the firth-side we are soon under the knolls aforesaid but pass by the entrance to Sælingsdale, and, riding round the end of its westernmost boundary-hill, come into

[1] Grettir the Strong, chapter LIII. Ed.

110

the next valley, Hwamm: this is also a famous place; its first
settler is Auð the Deeply Wealthy; and it became afterwards
the home of the Sturlungs, and Snorri the historian was born
there [1173]. It is a beautiful place; a shallow valley open to
Hwammfirth on the south, and on the north bounded by a
curving wall of mountain, from which, as the valley opens
seaward, great slopes of grass go down into the bottom.

We ride along the hillside here till we come to a quaint little house with many gables (nine I think) high up the slope
and a little church below it: from here we can see the Broadfirth mountains right opposite the valley's mouth. We get
off and go into the house, and are entertained by the parson[1]
a youngish man, and the ex-parson[2] an old one who lives
on still in the same house: sixty-nine years he told us he
had lived in this valley. He seemed a very innocent kind
old man: and has written a little book identifying the
places about named in the Sagas, all which he is very
anxious to talk to us about. C.J.F. bought two old silver
spoons of him which our Herdholt host told us of; he put
such a low price on them that Charley gave him more;
but he didn't feel much interested in the whole transaction.
Then we went out and he showed us above the house Auð's
Thingstead and doom-ring, and close by the temple of those
days; though Auð herself was a Christian, and would have
herself buried on the foreshore between high and low water-
mark, that she might not lie wholly in a heathen land: they
show you a big stone on the beach that they call her grave-
stone: but 'tis covered now by the tide. Then we go into the
little church where there is an old fifteenth-century chalice,
and a paten which is obviously English; a pretty old door-
ring and some good embroidery. Then we take our leave of
all but the old priest, who gets a-horseback: he is a very tall
thin old gentleman in breeches and purple stockings and skin
shoes; he is on a capital pony which turns out to be too much
for him, so he changes with Magnússon, saying as he does so:
"All comes to an end: who would have believed I should

[1]Stein Steinsson. E.M.   [2]Thorleifr Jonsson. E.M.

Bathstead ever have to ride a dull beast like this instead of a brisk horse."

Well, we ride out of the valley again, and he shows us a dyke that marks the old wall of the tún, he says, as it was in the Sturlung time, of course a long way beyond the present one [thirteenth century]. Thence we ride over the rough tongue between the two valleys, and passing to the left of those rock-crowned knolls aforesaid, enter the dale, riding high up to avoid the bogs: a many-gabled stead on the oppo-site hill-side has the classic name of Asgarð. When we first turn into the dale we can see the stead of Sælingsdale-tongue, where Gudrun lived with Bolli, but we presently fall among a knot of little knolls (made I suppose by the slips from the hills above), which choke up the valley, and hide it from us: the hillsides here are much like [those] in Hwamm, but rockier and barer, much scarred by recent slips, and the crest of them often running up into wall-like rocks; we pass a little stead among the knolls, and presently work our way out of them, and can see on the other side of the valley Sæl-ingsdale-tongue lying rather high up the slopes: just inward of it, a strange mass of pillared rock nearly joins the hillside standing at right-angles to it, and on our side the hill pushes out a spur to meet this, narrowing the valley here into a gate through which a river runs, and through which you may see the further valley all closed up by a sweeping wall of hill-side: the valley below us is flat and marshy: on our side, halfway between where we are and the gate aforesaid lies on this slope a little stead in a green tún, for the valley bottom is yellow with the bog-grass and the hill-slopes are grey and colourless, and this stead is Bathstead ("Laugar").

They are making hay down in the marshes, and the good-man of Bathstead seeing us, comes up to meet us, and kisses the old priest, and then takes us up the hill above the house, where amidst a shaly slip is the "Bath" that names the stead: it is some three feet square now, and about knee-deep, nearly boiling of course: the priest told us that he remembered it much bigger, and deep enough to take him up to the waist;

112

but that twenty years ago, a slip from the hill covered it up Bathstead
till it burst out again as we see, a queer little boiling driblet
coming without warning from amid the bare stones, a few
yards above the aforesaid bath. A little higher up the hill we
come to another hot-spring coming out of a rock and running in an orderly bed afterwards; there are plenty of wild
heartseases about it. We sit down and eat our lunch on the
grass hard by and then go down to our horses and ride off
past the stead, a very poor one with a little potatoe-cabbage
garden round it. The day has gone grey now, though a few
gleams of sunlight are scattered about among the hills on
the other side. It is a very sad place: the sand hills we passed
through shut out from this side all view of the water of
Hwamm and the distant mountains; so sad it is that my
heart sickened somewhat as when I first came to Laxdale the
other day.

  But the old priest takes us through those gates into the
other half of the valley which we see now all closed in by high
craggy cliffs jutting out into great buttresses here and there:
he points out to us on our right the mouth of a valley coming
into this one, the only opening from it, and names it Swine-
dale where Kiartan was beset and killed; and we ride on
thence over a great waste of stones brought down by the
stream over which the poor old man has a tumble right over
his horse's head, but no harm done; thence on smooth grass
we ride quite near the head of the dale, a dreadful lonely
place, quite flat amid its bounding cliffs which are rent here
and there into those dreadful *streets*[1] I told you of first in
Thorsmark: hereabouts almost under the shadow of those
cliffs the priest brings us to a low mound showing marks of
old turf walls, and this he says is the site of the "setr"[2] or
mountain-dairy where Bolli Thorleikson was killed by Kiartan's brothers. Then we turn back again, taking the other
side of the valley, and go on the other side of that pillared
gate-post rock aforesaid: it is called Tungu-stapi (Tongue-

[1] "Flat-floored, straight-sided," the note-book calls them. Ed.
[2] The Icelandic is 'sel;' the author has used the Norwegian word. Ed.

staff-rock) and is called elf-haunted:[1] there is a tale about it translated in the first volume of that book of Magnússon's.

Up the slopes a little past this we come on a poor stead which is the Sælingsdale-tongue of to-day, where Gudrun lived with Bolli, and which she afterwards changed for Holy-fell with Snorri the Priest: here I sat down on the site of the church Snorri built, with Bathstead just opposite me, the dreadful upper valley on my right, where the clouds were beginning to roll down on the enclosing mountains, and on my left Hwammfirth, and the peaked mountains beyond, inky purple, with cold gleams of sunshine tangled among them, though all was grey above our heads—ah me, what a desolate place! Yet when I went in to coffee to a very dark little dirty parlour, there was the bonder, a good-looking fellow, and his wife, making much of the old priest, and as merry a man as might be seen.

Coffee done, it is seven o'clock, and we shall scarcely get home by nine when Evans expects us; so we mount and ride off, the old priest taking affectionate leave of us at the mouth of the dale. We rode all we might back home to Herdholt, where I, coming to our tents, find three fine salmon-trout and a headless mallard laid out as the results of Evans's sport: the mallard he got in a queer way; he saw a falcon strike it, cutting its head clean off; then the falcon pounced on it but Evans drove him off and stole the duck.

Supper and bed was all that happened else that day, which I counted one of the best and most memorable days we had.

Wednesday, August 9th. In the priest's house at Breiðabólstaðr on Skógar-strand.

DOWN in the tún below the house here is a round wall marked, which was once Olaf Peacock's temple; as I ought to have noticed before. We were on our journey again to-day, starting under the priest's guidance about eleven o'clock; we crossed the valley, and came first (over most beastly bogs) to a stead called Hornstaðir, where we

[1] "and is elf-haunted," the note-book says. Ed.

bought a silver quaigh from the bonder; then go on to Hauskuldstead, where they show us the site of the great hall in
which Hauskuld (says Laxdaela) feasted eleven hundred
men at his house-warming. Thence we turn up on the mountain-neck, and so over it into Hawkdale; a flat marshy plain
with mountains round three sides of it, and Hwammfirth on
the other side: just on the northern side of it is a slope going
down to the water, which is the site of the house of Hrut,
Hauskuld's half-brother. Then we go to a stead in the flat
lands near the water called Lœkjarskógr, for the priest is to
leave us here, and we want a guide across the sands of this
corner of Hwammfirth, which we are going to cross at low-
water. So the bonder comes with us and we are off again, and
are soon off the marshes on to the sea-beach, which is not bad
riding here: it is a windy day, and the mountains on the north
side of the firth are bright with the sun; but it is grey overhead, and the mountains on the south are hidden by low
clouds: I was in good trim and spirits, and enjoyed hugely
this clatter over the beach, with the waves breaking at our
very feet; all the more as the whole train was together, which
latterly had not been so much the case.

To the north-west now we can see under a light strip of
sky the faint outline of the mountains on the further shore
of Broadfirth, and nearer the countless islands and skerries
that stretch all across the mouth of Hwammfirth, so that you
cannot see the water between them.

After a while we turn away from the beach to a place called
Gunnar-stáðr, the house (I think) of Gunnar Hlifarson of
the Hen Thorir's Saga. It stands a little way off the beach
under a semicircle of low scarped cliffs, a sort of island on
dry land, very strange to see. We bait here and go into the
parlour, where we have some chaffer for old silver with the
goodwife, in the middle of which the bonder comes in cursing
and swearing because our horses are in his mowing-grass,
which they are not: however, it turns out that he is drunk,
and his anger soon turns into smiling friendliness, and I think
he even wanted to kiss some of us, as he led us out of his tún.

We go down to the sea again, and ride along it for a little way,
under strange gleams of a cold sun, but after a mile and a half
or so, turn inland again; a little way from the beach I picked
a horned poppy (yellow), the first flower of that kind I have
seen in Iceland. We come now into a different and odd kind
of country: barren ragged land, low ledges of rock like unfinished walls rising from scanty grass and bogs. We keep on
mounting these walls or turning them over low slopes; now
and then we dropped into gullies made by streams among
them, which are walled in on either side by steep walls of rock,
the grass growing long and sweet on the little flat banks by
the water's edge: one such I remember particularly, where
the stream fell into the gorge over a wall of rock, that having
got it in, swept round it and its bright green little meadow till
you couldn't see how it got out again; another time a sudden
ledge of rock seemed to cut the open stream we were riding
by clean off. Now and then these ragged walls broke away so
that we could see the firth on our north, or steads up the
country on our south, but the distant mountains on that side
were clouded over. Nevertheless the sun shone bright as it
grew toward setting, and we were drawing out of this strange
country, going a good pace over a wide sandy road, after
having had a great deal of trouble in driving our horses, who
had turned off for the last hour or two at every bit of green
that came in sight: they tried it twice in one place, where a
long green valley went down toward the firth.

But this broad sandy way we are on now runs at the feet of
high wave-like cliffs that sweep out of a wide sloping plain
that lies between us and the sea and is all covered with birch-
scrub, and is (I suppose) the Woodstrand (Skógarströnd) of
the Eyrbyggia Saga. Under these cliffs we rode for some hour
and a half till we began to turn round them and at last saw before us where a valley of grass cleft them, at our end of which
lay a little church and a brand-new pleasant-looking house,
the parsonage of Breiðabolstaðr, and our supper and bed; we
were there presently, and found the priest away at the Althing
(in Reykjavík), but his wife received us kindly, and we were

116

soon in bed, as we were to get up early so as to cross the sands Swanfirth of Swanfirth at the ebb to-morrow; the house was pleasant and comfortable inside, with its queer little lofts and ladders, all quite clean from being new; and I thought as I lay abed what an agreeable day's ride I had had more than on most days, though I scarcely knew why.

Thursday, August 10th. At Mr. Thorlacius' house at Stykkisholm.

WE got away about nine o'clock with Magnússon bad and bilious: we ride our best for somewhile along the cliffs of yesterday, but they fail presently, and we come into a valley where our way lies through a most awkward bog through which we straggle slowly and as best we may: this passed, we rise again, and ride along steep slopes, till we have the sea on our right, and after two hours' sharp ride from Breiðabólstaðr come to the headland at the mouth of Swanfirth (Alptafjorðr). Here we found that we had missed the ebb after all and that it would be half-flood by then we came to the proper ford, so we had to follow the firth up to its other end: a thing not to be regretted, as we were in one of the most "romantic" places I saw in Iceland: the firth is very narrow; there is no beach to it, but very steep grassy slopes rise up on both sides from the water's edge till at a great height up they are crested with bare rocks of basalt, sometimes jagged into peaks, sometimes as straight as a line, sometimes overhanging the slopes beneath them threateningly. As we lay on the grass waiting to hear about the tide we saw the water below us populous with swans: I counted a hundred and forty; but Mr. Thorlacius told me afterwards that in autumn, when the yearling cygnets are gathering to go away (south?) you may see the water all white with them.

So we go along the side of the steep slope, which must be very high, because when we were on the other side our path looked as if it were close to the sea, whereas when we were on it we seemed about half way between the sea and the bare crags above us: and how steep that hillside was! the very

117

Round the badger, who has his legs shorter on one side than the other
firth-head in consideration of such places, would have found it steep
enough. But it was a beautiful ride; when you come to the
head of the firth, the hills leave a flat green space, watered by
a winding river between them and the salt water, and then
sweep round in a beautiful curve at the same height as before,
and still crested with bare crags, and so shut in the valley from
the unseen but well-imagined wilderness beyond. We came
down on to the flat meads and crossed the river, and could see
the steads of Ulfarsfell and Karstead, two of the Eyrbyggia
places up the valley, then we rode down the other side of the
firth till we came to Vadil's-head where Arnkel the Priest,
the *good* man of Eyrbyggia, is buried: his house, now waste,
was among the slopes above us: down here also Thorolf
Lamefoot, Arnkel's father, was burned[1] and so partly got
rid of.

Then we rode away over the neck by our due road, for we
should have crossed the sands at the ebb to Vadil's-head, and
so into another valley, in a little hollow of which, sheltered
from the wind, which blows great guns to-day, we changed
horses and ate. We look on to a sea of peaked mountains
from hence, and one coming before the others (Drápuhlí-
ðarfjall) has a naked torn side of stones burnt red and yellow,
and waves of lava running through a cleft of it and down its
side, and stopping suddenly like the edge of a surf out in the
valley.

We got to horse and rode round the skirt of the torn bald
mountain-side, and so into a little valley, three parts filled
up with a tarn, from whence we can see a great flat plain, stopped again by mountains that come down to the sea: this
valley with its steep sides and sudden breach that we rode out
of, was, I suppose, a crater at one time. When we are out of
it we are on the edge of the plain and still skirting the bald
slip: on our right the grey plain ends in the sea; there are
strange indents of water, and a strange hill that we are leaving behind after a bit, and that I seem as if I ought to know,

[1] After he had been dead (and worse so than alive) for some time.

118

but Magnússon pushes on still; at last Evans who has stu-
died the map deeply, and who really has a topographical head,
calls a halt, and we talk over it whether or no we have over-
shot our mark: there is a stead quite near us, so Magnússson
rides thither, while we lie down in a little valley; he comes
back presently to tell us that Evans is right, and points out
to us a flat-topped basalt *island* in the plain which is the
very Holy Fell standing near the neck of a peninsula where
Hwammfirth widens into Broadfirth; so we ride down from
the upper ground, and after a stretch of really flat land find
our seeming plain to be pretty much the ledged country of
yesterday: it is barren and unpromising enough; but the
mountains we look back on, toothed and jagged in an indescribable but well-remembered manner, are very noble
and solemn. As we rode along the winding path here we saw
a strange sight: a huge eagle quite within gunshot of us, and
not caring at all for that, flew across and across our path, always followed by a raven that seemed teazing and buffeting
him: this was the first eagle I had ever seen free and on the
wing, and it was a glorious sight, no less; the curves of his
flight, as he swept close by us, with every pen of his wings
clear against the sky was something not to be forgotten. Out
at sea too we saw a brigantine pitching about in what I
thought must be a rough sea enough. The day has been much
like yesterday throughout, and is getting clearer now as it
wears.

While we were riding through this intricate country,
Holyfell has been hidden from us, except for a dip or breach
now and then; but all at once, turning a corner of some dyke
we come upon it: the front of that dry-land and island grey
pillars of rock with green slopes breaking away from them,
and in front of it facing east a stead and church. While Magnússon sees about shoeing a horse, and C.J.F. loafs about,
Evans and I climb up to the top of the Holy Hill, and look
thence over land and sea: as we have been going all along
the firth these two days we have not gained much way south
as yet: but Broadfirth lies all open before us now, and the

peninsula of Stykkisholm indented with little firths is as a
map before us. It blew strong and cold up there, though as on
yesterday the day is brightening towards its end; so after a
long look south down we came again and went into the bonder's parlour. He came in while we were at our coffee, and
presently asked us what time it was: we said about half-past
four, which by our time was right: said he, "You are witless;
it is half-past ten (p.m.); look at my clock then." We did and
his clock was five; still however he held by his own opinion
for a while and then suddenly agreed with us. I'm afraid he
was drunk.

A two hours' ride hence over the same kind of country by
a road winding among the little creeks of the peninsula
brought us to the edge of the sea where is a trading-station,
called Stykkisholm, from a little islet of pillared basalt that
standing in the mouth of a bight here makes a little harbour.
There are so many houses here that to our unaccustomed
eyes it looks quite a town: they are mostly neat wooden ones
with trim closes and gardens about them; we ride up to one
of the biggest of them where is a sort of a yard, and store-
houses, and Magnússon asks for Mr. Thorlacius, a kinsman
of his wife's, who lives here: he is out; but while we wait
about and unload the horses, a boat comes up to the little
pier hard by, and he gets out of it and comes towards us, a
tall thin man of some fifty-five years, nervous and gentle-
looking like so many men here, especially the better educated
ones; he welcomes us kindly and in we go and into his parlour, a pretty room enough, looking on to the yard and harbour. We talked and looked at books, sometimes with, sometimes without our host, who I found knew English though he
wouldn't talk it: for he grinned sympathetically while I was
haggling out a translation from an Eyrbyggia saga of the
Wonders at Frodá to C.J.F. Dinner, or supper, seemed a
long while coming meantime, but at last we were taken into
a much prettier room opposite the first one, in which roses
in blossom grew up with ivy over one end, and there, cages
with birds in them hanging from the joists, along with guns

120

and a net, and small gear of boats: it was all quite neat too,
and there was a view out of the window of those grand mountains, looking almost as if you could touch them in the clear
bright evening. Also a *very* good supper was there, "and I, I
was there" with my appetite of—well say eight hours' standing; a certain small delicate rock-cod quite copper-colour
caught in the harbour here I may perhaps be allowed to
mention.

So after long talk to bed, I in a little room leading out of
the first sitting-room and over-looking the harbour, Evans
and Magnússon going to another house.

Friday, August 11th. In the same place.

THE first thing I saw when I woke this morning was
the masts of a brigantine with the Danish flag flying
at the peak against the "Stick-holm;" she has come
in the night, being that same craft we saw yesterday tossing
about at sea, and there she lies looking quite important and
exciting amongst the half dozen of little fishing keels. It is a
pleasant look out over the firth here: two islands come out
clear among many, a little one close by, and some five miles
out a bigger one, Hrappsey, a monastery once, and afterwards famous as a printing place.[1] From the pier we can see
the wall of skerries that cuts off Hwammfirth from the sea,
but we are seaward of that, as you may see on the map. We
were to stay here all day, to give the horses a rest and overhaul our boxes to see if we could get rid of any of them: this
last was a business in which C.J.F. would only allow me the
share of looking on, which I did with great content and in-
dustry, especially as it was a fine bright day, warm in spite of
the chilly wind, which however did not blow strong. So there
were we three in the yard (for Magnússon had gone to see a

[1] There was never a monastery at Hrappsey, the only island in
Broadfirth where a house of regulars was established being Flatey,
where the Holy Fell monastery was founded. The author may have
confounded the two places. The Hrappsey press lasted from 1773 to
1794 when it was removed to Skalholt. E.M.

friend) roaring with laughter from time to time as various
messes turned up: for I may remark here, that no one unless
he had tried it can imagine what will happen even to very
well packed boxes (as ours were) carried on pack-horses; for
example: in one of our boxes was a wound-up ball of fine
string; now opening this box at Geysir I came across a lot of
nasty-looking fluff and couldn't make out what it was till at
last I found a little nucleus of the said twine still wound
about the stick, and all the rest was beautiful oakum; at Eyrarbakki we bought some wheat-flour and put it in a tin
box, the bottom whereof came clean out at Hnausar; at
Herdholt our tin case of mustard was found smashed, and
the mustard all over everything; here the great mess is the
medicine-chest: the chlorodyne has run into the citrate of
quinine, and made some chemical combination of it which
looks like a kind of sweet-stuff "rock;" and both these
which appear to have "gone off fizzing" have mixed with
the sulphur ointment and made a slimy jelly of it; and the
whole thing is peppered beautifully with red precipitate
(louse-powder, so please you.) One of the boxes has a mix-
ture of cocoa, grass-cut latakia and paper at the bottom of
it, which it is quite a joy to turn out on to the stones here.
As to the biscuit-boxes, why tell how the whiskey-keg has
danced a hole in one, and what a queer powder the most of
them hold now?

I must now tell to my shame, how I have had the pass of
Búlandshöfði on my mind for some days and how last night
I questioned Thorlacius upon it and his description of it
didn't comfort me. 'Tis a narrow road along the face of a
steep slip above the sea two days' journey ahead now: I
didn't really think it dangerous for capable people, but I
distrusted my head sorely, and thought how disastrous it
would be if that gave way half way across: I pray excuses for
this but from all I heard I thought of something like walking
across the third-floor joists of a half-finished house, a thing
that masons and builders do without thinking of, but which
would certainly mean a broken neck to many people. Any-

how all things considered I pretty much make up my mind
this morning to go round by another way with Magnússon
and the train while Evans and C.J.F. take the Búlandshöfði
road: the way round would be by the other side of the promontory and so over Fróðarheiði, a troublesome road, but
not at all dangerous.

I sauntered through the day, but went out a little walk
about 8 p.m. looking into the rocky creeks about the place,
and sat down at last facing those often spoken of mountains
just as the sky began to change with sunset, which turned
out a very wonderful one, the mountains going all golden-
red with it, and the distant hills on the north side of Broadfirth looking like red clouds against the green sky: then I
saw the sun sink behind the farthest ness of Broadfirth as if
it had been pulled down, and the colour faded slowly out of
the mountains, but all the western sky was covered with
rippling golden clouds, the clear green showing between
them; and hours afterwards, just as we were going to bed,
the dark clouds had a ripple of red on them and the green
sky was grown greener still. I was much impressed by my
walk and being alone, and made up my mind that it was
mean to shirk Búlandshöfði as one of the marvels of our pilgrimage, and so quite gave up the idea of going round, to
my great content in the end.

I walked about the little pier when I got back, and watched
the sun set and the bright clear water about, and a man or
two upon the little brigantine, till a boat came off from her,
and two men landed close by me, one of whom fell to talking
English with me, telling me he was the owner of the vessel,
and that it was called the "Holger;" he introduced the other
man, a young fellow quite, as indeed he himself was, as the
skipper: said skipper, who talked English too, was as like
Edmund Talboys as like could be.[1] The owner was a good-
tempered vulgar Danish Jew, I should say, very ill-man-

[1] I notice now that he is like Mr. Toft, the Yankee-Dane also;
and also like brother-in-law Gilmore: sea-faring men are apt to be
born so.

nered; he came into Mr. Thorlacius's parlour afterwards and I thought was very rude to him. However, he offered to take letters for us to England, to my great joy as you may well imagine; so I sat down and wrote in huge excitement. And a little after to bed.

Saturday, August 12th. In camp by Berserkia-hraun.

UP and to breakfast at nine on board the "Holger" where the master had asked us last night; I thought as a matter of course that he had asked Thorlacius too, but to my confusion he had not. The little ship looked clean and trim, and very small was the cabin: room for us all to sit down, and two bunks somewhere: the "Holger" was going to Liverpool with wool, and was to come back thence with an "assorted cargo;" after which she was to go to Lisbon (from Iceland) with salt-fish.

Breakfast over we loitered about a bit among our horses, which Eyvindr and Gisli had now brought in, till we found to our consternation that Thorlacius expected us to breakfast with him, not knowing at first, it seems, that we had eaten on board the "Holger:" I prayed Magnússon to apologize to him for our going away without his knowing it, and tell him that it was not our fault, if he could manage it: after which at about half past eleven in we went to one of the best breakfasts ever insulted by abstinence. The train started about one o'clock and we fondly hoped to follow it in about half an hour; but I think it was more like two hours before any break in the hospitality would let us escape. Mr. Thorlacius rode with us, and we soon came to the stark bare side of the Holyfell again, round which the road winds to the back of the stead, which lies deep sunk in a little valley at the hill's foot: the land around is waste-looking and mournful enough in these days: I suppose its nearness to the sea and consequent fishing made it good time agone. We got off here and wandered about the stead again, and Thorlacius showed us a mound in the churchyard, which they call Gudrun's grave-mound, as I don't see why it shouldn't be. Then

124

we all rode away together passing by a little creek that Thorlacius pointed out to us as Sword-firth (Vigrafiörðr) the
scene of that queer fight in Eyrbyggia where Freystein Rascal is killed, and often mentioned in that Saga: I remembered
what a much bigger place I had always thought of for that
place, where the very skerry in the middle is named after the
fight, and [called] Fight-skerry. A little afterwards we got
off to say good-bye to Thorlacius: the old man was very
warm and kind both now and before; though he had almost
quarrelled with me at dinner yesterday for saying some ill of
Snorri the Priest. He is a learned man, and comes of a learned
family, and was quite delightful company though very quiet
and shy.[1]

So we rode on our way toward the lower end of the often-
mentioned toothed mountains, whose outmost spur reaches
the sea-beach as the whole range sweeps round this lower
land. We blundered thrice about the road, but found it at
last, and after asking at two steads about our train, were
told at the second one that it had been seen three hours before: so as you may imagine it was grown late by then we
found it halted in a grassy valley within sight of the sea, but
close under the aforesaid mountain-spur, a huge mass of
black cliff, with a wild sea of lava tossing up into great spires
and ridges landward of it, and at the back of that mountains
and mountains again: the valley went up into a long green
slope from a little stead that stood at the seaward end of it;
and above the green slope showed a few dark grey peaks far
away: the sea of lava is called Berserkia-hraun (lava) memorable for the story in Eyrbyggia of the two berserks whom
Styr betrayed and boiled in the bath, after they had made a
road amidst the lava, as the tale tells.

We had ridden but a very little way (say eight miles) and
had intended to sleep at Grundarfirth a long way on: we had
still more than three hours of day-light—but, somehow, it

[1] This year (1873) C.J.F. hunting up books about the Sibyls for
our stained-glass found that the principal modern book about them
was by one Thorlacius, the uncle (or great-uncle) of our friend.

125

Berserkia-hraun was a beautiful place, and a very warm fine evening, and I looked at C.J.F. and he looked at me, and presently I had the hardihood or shamelessness to propose stopping there; so stop we did though Evans didn't half like it, and in half an hour's time I was busy over my fire. We had a very pleasant evening ending with whist; but first I climbed up to the top of the long slope, for the pleasure partly of looking at those tumbled hills again before we turned round their flanks and changed them, and partly of looking down on the green valley, and our camp with the horses feeding about it, and the grey smoke curling up from it, as I had done at that first camp on Bolavellir; O how long ago it seemed! It was a fine sunset again, but not like yesterday, for there were no clouds except a long bank all along the sea: and afterwards when I came out of the tent after our whist, and it had grown darkish, this cloud bank was grown so inky-black and the sea beneath it was yet so bright, that it was long before I was fairly sure that it was not a strip of brightest sky beneath the cloud.

Sunday, August 13th. In camp at the stead of Skerðings-staðr.

UP fairly early, and away before ten. We found out the meaning of that bank of cloud, for this morning it was blowing hard, and there were fleecy clouds hanging about the mountains, and half hiding them: happily the wind however strong was warm. We rode straight out of our camping valley into the lava through which however there was a good road, whether the berserks made it or not: it was the strangest place this lava, all tossed up into hills and fantastically twisted ridges, greyer than grey, for it is altogether covered with that grey moss I have spoken of before; it was indeed "clinkers" of the monstrous furnace, no less. Thorlacius told us of it that unseen rivers run beneath it, and break up into fountains through the sea-beach below even ordinary low-water-mark: their sources are known higher up among the mountains, and trout come up there, having passed all underneath the lava from the sea. We went on through

126

the windings of our path till in about two miles we came to a
very steep descent, which brought us to a chasm in the lava:
neither better nor worse was our road here than a broken
flight of stone steps over which we and our horses had to
stumble separately as well as we could; and the horses did it
much the best. The bottom of this stair was the end of the
lava, and we came into a long narrow valley of grass shut in
on the other side by a green slope, and on our side by the
heaped-up mass of grey mossy lava, quite strait and regular
like a wall, but jagged and broken at its summit. They say
that this lava flowed from no mountain-crater, but burst out
of the earth just where it is.

It blew harder and harder now, from the south-west; just
over-head it was quite bright and sunny, but a drizzle reached us from the mountains where the shifting clouds lay. Out
of this little valley we turned into a wide plain with high and
steep mountains all round it, except for a narrow firth[1] that
ran up from the sea and let daylight in; this was near us and
on our right hand as we rode on; and on the other side of the
water the hills ran up so high in one long green-striped black
slope that where a little stead stood by the water and above
it were sheep feeding on steep slopes, yet when you got to
the top of them you were only at the mountains' foot: these
mountains seemed to run on from this firth a long way and
then, turning, shut up a long valley's end against us, rising
higher still there into an awful crowd of wild shapes, cones
and peaks, and inaccessible ledges, whence long strings of
water fell, and hollows unsunlighted and snowfilled, or with
the clouds dragging into them which now and then sent a
sharp drizzle into our faces. From these highest mountains
again came lower ones towards us which gave back some two
miles from where we were now to make the wide plain aforesaid; over the shoulders of them we saw a strange-shaped
peak far away. There were two or three steads at the feet of
these lower slopes, from one of which Magnússon got us information of where our way was: so we rode off from the lit-

[1] The Hraunfiörðr (Lavafirth) of Eyrbyggia. E.M.

127

Tröllahals   tle firth's end up the long valley aforesaid right in the teeth of
a most tremendous wind: the light shaly stones of the river-
bed we were riding along were driven before it as our horses
kicked them up; every bit of water we passed had a sheet of
spray driven from it: and as to us, the horses stopped nearly
dead sometimes, and I really thought I should have been
unhorsed; all the while the clouds never got away from the
mountain-tops, and the sun shone bright above us. So we
went on till we had got to the head of the valley when we bent
across to the seaward side of it, and mounting a steep hillside
came into a pass, a path winding about over the steep preci-
pices with great cliffs of basalt on either side of it: up this we
straggled as we best might under the mingled rain and sunshine; once or twice I looked back at the valley we had left,
and saw it swept across with mingled rain and sun too; it
looked a great hollow far below us soon; a wonderful sight
with those terrible mountains at its head. All the while as we
went, the noise of the wind about us, entangled in the ridges
and peaks of the cliffs, was not less than of loud and continu-
ous thunder; it was a wonder of a day, and most exciting: I
stuffed my whip and my hat one into one boot, one into the
other, and held on by the poney's mane, till at last we got to
the brow of the pass;[1] and looked down into the other valley,
and could see the crowd of peaks and cliffs at its head: we
went, down a descent so steep into it, that we had to get off
and lead the horses, the wind lulling no whit till we got into a
little hollow at the foot of the pass, where we rested a few
minutes. The clouds had looked black and threatening round
the mountains at our back, but now as we rode on they seemed
to melt away before us, and the sun shone gloriously: though
when we were fairly in the flat of the valley again the wind was
as strong as ever but it was at our backs, where also was the
black mass of clouds whence a light rain reached us still. The
hills on each side of this valley were much lower than in the
last (Hraunfirth): those on our right, the wrong side I sup-

[1] The pass is called Tröllaháls (Troll's Neck) and is noted for its
fierce winds. E.M.

128

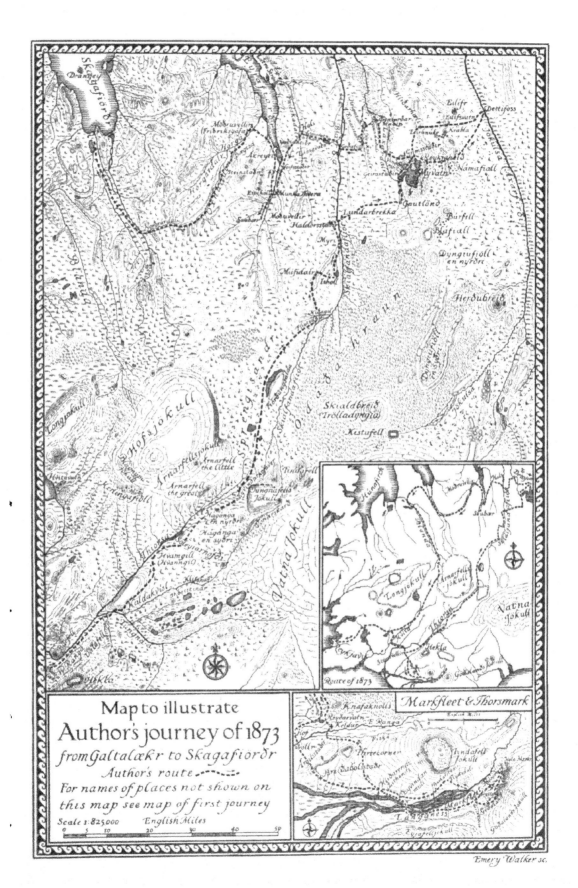

Map to illustrate
Author's journey of 1873
from Galtalœkr to Skagafiorðr
Author's route ------
For names of places not shown on
this map see map of first journey
Scale 1:825,000   English Miles

Markfleet & Thorsmark

Route of 1873

Emery Walker sc.

pose of the steep slopes above told of, were of the rubbish-
heap kind and buff of colour; before us lay the end of a long
firth that led out to sea[1] (Kolgrafa-firth) where it ended in a
ness of the buff shaly hills:[2] its waters were intense dark-blue
flecked with "white-horses" from whose tops the spray
drove in white showers like salt thrown on the wind. As we
rode we saw a rainbow begin, lying over the firth and the
shaly hill; it brightened, and then grew very bright till it had
two more behind it; it was not a great soaring arc, but quite a
flat segment: it lay on the lower slopes of the hills now, and so
seemed to move with us as we rode along the strand of the
firth, till it was clinging round that outer headland, and half
lay over the sea. This was not the last time we saw the segmental rainbows in Iceland where we also saw the usual kind;
and I don't know why they came like that.

The rain left off and the rainbow faded, and the wind fell
by then we were come to the lower end of the firth, and we
turned away to our left over a neck of flat land that was shorn
out of the hillsides there; after a three miles' ride or so we came
out on to the strand of a wide bay called Grundarfirth, that
seemed a noble kind of place, where the mountains lay in a
semicircle round a green flat plain, some five miles deep from
the chord of the mountain arc to the sea-beach; but the
mountains we could scarcely see now the clouds hung so low
about them, though the day grew finer and finer. We made a
regular halt of it here, and unloaded our horses, standing
awhile close to the sea to watch the great seas coming thundering on the shingle: amidmost of the bay a long slender
craft which Magnússon knew for the "Fylla," the sister-ship
of the "Diana," and still in the war-service: after a while we
were asked into the house hard by, whose master was a silver-
smith, & who gave us coffee, which we accompanied with our
own lunch, and there we sat for an hour I suppose, smoking
and talking, and looking at snuff-mulls in course of manu-

[1] Kolgrafafiörðr (Coalpitsfirth) of Eyrbyggia. E.M.
[2] The Ere (Eyr), originally Öndverð Eyr (Onward Ere), once
the family property of the Eredwellers. E.M.

Kirkjufell facture. Then we came out again to such a lovely surprise, for though the great waves still fell on the strand, there was scarce a breath of wind; there was no cloud in the sky, and those mountains unseen just now, you seemed as if you might touch them, so clear and bright they were: the plain went right up to them without a knoll or ridge; and they seemed utterly impassable, unless anyone might crawl through a black gully in their very midst that let a stream through to wander about the green plain. A little way south-west of this a great ledge of dark grey rock thrust forward from the mountain-sides, but running parallel with them for about a quarter of a mile, and rising some four hundred feet, was capped with a quite level space of bright green grass, from amidst of which fell a thin stream into the plain below: other ledges rose above this like a great stair, but not clear like the one below, and these were capped by a jagged line of peaks torn into all manner of strange shapes and with snow lying in their higher hollows, which swept round seaward till they ended in a cliff of regularly-ledged rock that looked as if it had been built; this runs on parallel, or nearly so, with the general line of the strand, and there is a flat tongue of land going out toward the other horn of the bay, from which rises suddenly the steepest mountain I ever saw, standing quite alone and in shape exactly like a French château roof, and called Kirkjufell (Church-fell).

Just as we were getting to horse here, a man came up, who offered us five beautiful pink-fleshed sea-trout, which we, mindful of supper, bought. Then on we rode through the freshest and brightest of afternoons, skirting the strand; just as we passed the furthest bight of the bay I noticed many eider-ducks again, also eider-drakes, which for some reason or other I had not seen before; they were handsome birds, with gleaming white breasts, whereas the ducks are dull-brown and dowdy; they were splashing about in high glee.

Out of Grundarfirth we rode into a flat marshy valley, with that cliff always on the left, and on the right Kirkjufell,

till we turned the flank of it, and found a long shallow reach
of sea running into the flats on our left, with another isolated
mountain on the tongue of it that looks at first just the shape
of Castle St. Angelo at Rome, but turned out, when we saw
the flank of it next day, to be long like Kirkjufell: its sides
are mere scarped cliffs. Hereabout the bogs got so very bad
that we were fain to turn to a poor little stead lying on a knoll
under the cliffs aforesaid, to ask for guidance; there was quite
a crowd of girls and children there, with an older woman or
two, some twelve or thirteen in all, I should think, with three
ponies to ride: they were just mounting as we came up, from
three to five on a horse: they had been blue-berrying and had
"askar"[1] full of the berries, with which their teeth were blue
also; exceedingly happy they seemed. We got a little lad of
some eleven winters here to guide us on a bit and in half an
hour come to a little stead[2] by the waterside aforesaid, the last
house before my dreaded Bulandshöfði; the cliffs are quite
near the house on the one side, as the water is on the other,
and there is a pretty hillocky tún in which we pitch our tents
to the accompaniment of a rattling wind, for it is blowing
again: "we" means Evans and C.J.F., for I went at once
gravely to the stead's kitchen, where I cooked in a queer little
den just big enough to hold me, my pots, the smoke, and a
little girl of five, whose name was Augustina: the rest of the
community stood in the doorway of the kitchen, I should
mention, and I—I streamed with sweat till my soup was
made and my trout were fried, when I must say I found the
coolness and *elegance* of the tent quite delightful.

Whist after dinner, and then Evans and Magnússon to
bed; but C.J.F. and I sat up (I writing up this journal), till
it was past one, and dawn was in the sky again; and then we
went out and walked about a bit, listening to the sea breaking outside the mouth of the firth, and most unaccountable
noises of the sea-birds, with which this place is populous beyond everything I ever saw. There was a little haze about,
but no cloud, and the night is grown warm again and still,

[1] See p. 97. Ed. [2] Skerðingstaðir. E.M.

and I felt very happy with our warm ride and the pleasant time, though true it is that I really thought it an even chance that I should tumble over Búlandshöfði to-morrow. So to bed.

Monday, August 14. In the church at Ingialdshóll.

WE got up to a most lovely morning, still, sunny, and warm, so that I can shake off the last remains of the depression that fell upon me in the North. We rode over the sands first from Skerðingstaðir, having with us a new horse that we bought last night; he looked so fat and sleek after our journey-worn nags that we called him Butter-tubs, which the guides took up at once and translated into "Stampa." We jogged on in high excitement (for Búlands-höfði was just before us, you will remember), and soon mounted from the sands on to a sort of low under-cliff, which kept rising till it too was high above the sea, but still with a high cliff landward off it, leaving some furlongs' space of smooth sward betwixt; these cliffs are quite full of gulls, especially in one place where they ran up into a peaked ridge: there are heaps of broken land at the cliff's foot, and huge boulders lie scattered about the gentle slope we ride on, some all grass-grown, some with their edges sharp and black as though last winter had brought them down.

Our path holds ever nearer to the edge of the sea cliffs, & the other cliffs draw ever closer in on us till at last we are at the end of the soft green slope, and there is nothing for our road but to pass over a rugged, steep mass of broken cliff that goes down sharp to the sheer rocks above the sea: this is Búlands-höfði, a headland that is thrust out by the tumbling mountains that fill all the inside of this peninsula; the steep slopes of this slip are all in grooves, as it were, in and out of which the path must wind, and above them rises a steep crest of this shape so common in Icelandic hills. We rode before the train as it was necessary to drive the horses, the laden ones at least, with some care, & we had gotten a man from the

132

last stead to help us in it; they are to drive the horses over in
divisions of about five, tying them together nose and tail.[1] As
for me, there I was presently on the dreaded pass, about which
I confess I had been feeling serious these two days, and if you
must know the truth, had pretty much made up my mind for
the worst. After all I had discounted my fear, and was quit
for a beating of the heart, not unpleasant, and a little trem-
bling about the knees. Indeed, the path was narrow enough,
but quite sound for some way; below us the hillside was not
sheer, but so steep as not to be much short of it. It was broken
rock, turf, ling, and here and there a little brush of birch-
scrub, till you came to the brow of the unseen cliff, and there
lay the sea below, bright green and dark blue at first, with a
little white fringe here and there round a skerry, but soften-
ing off to light grey-blue farther out till it met the sunny
haze of the horizon; the sky was cloudless except for some
faint white lines high up, and there was no sail to be seen on
the sea, and no wave breaking. I couldn't help feeling rather
light on my horse every now and then, especially when, as I
neared one of the *grooves* in the hillside, Magnússon, who
rode before me, looked for all the world as if he were riding
straight off into the sea, nor do I quite remember how I got
round the corners myself. So we rode on a while, till turning
round one of these places, we had before us a much steeper
slope where the slip is recent and bare, a great heap of loose
shale and stones; and certainly when one first came on it, it
seemed hard to think how we were to get across. Magnússon
bade me dismount here, which I did rather anxiously, tying
the reins loosely on Mouse's neck, and then leaving him to
come over as he liked best; Magnússon and C.J.F. also dismounted, but Evans rode across; I had, as was before arranged, Magnússon before me and C.J.F. after me; but
after all I did not want any help, for when I got on the path,
I found the foothold good on the loose stones though the

[1] There was talk of doing this, but I prevented it; an accident
happening to one of the ponies so tied together might drag the whole
train over the precipice. E.M.

133

path was only about a foot broad; also the very steepness of
the hillside above was a help, as I could steady myself against
it with my left hand; so that altogether I didn't find this part,
which is reckoned the dangerous part, so frightful as the
smooth road. C.J.F. didn't improve my nerves though by
kicking a loose stone or two over the path for the pleasure of
seeing it shoot down the steep and over the cliff; about three
parts over, Magnússon called out to us to look down below,
where was a seal eating a salmon; and sure enough we saw
the black head down in the green sea, dubbing away at a big
fish.

The way got broader after about a hundred yards of this,
and we were round the furthermost head of the ness, and
soon the slopes spread out and got flatter towards a wide
shallow valley that the hills sweep round as at Grundarfirth,
the furthermost horn of them dropping down toward the sea,
and ending in a kind of breakwater of low black rocks in the
very sea; this valley seems only a bight in a bigger bay, the
further side of which we can see beyond, its outermost horn
ending in a huge pile of rocks; just below us on our right the
land fell quickly toward the sea, and it too was broken at last
into a row of sea-washed skerries.

A little further, and we lay down on the grassy slopes in
great comfort, I for my part well contented that the danger
was little or nothing, if a little ashamed that my imagination
had made much of it, C.J.F. rather disappointed, I think,
and Evans scornful of the whole affair: by which you may
see, I suppose, that I ought not to have spoken of it as a peril-
ous pass at all. It was pretty to look up and see from where
we lay, the horses coming one by one over the steep brow of
the headland, the loose ones grazing about anywhere where
the hill became a little less steep, in the most unconcerned
way.

So we rode down into the valley, which is quite flat for the
most part, a mere sea-beach really, with scanty grass over it,
and shallow pools one-third covering it, with plenteous sea-
birds on them; but just underneath the mountains is a long

hog-backed ridge on which are two steads, the northern of Fróðá
which is Máfahlíð (Mewlithe) which plays a great part in the
earlier half of Eyrbyggia; over a lower piece of the mountains one can just see the top of the double snowy peak of
Snæfell. So, splashing through the pools of the flat, we came
into a little valley over a neck, whence more of Snæfell shows
far away and sharp, but looking small and near from the very
clear air to-day, and from its own bright snow.

Then over another neck we came into another valley something like the last, but with its surrounding hills cleft by a
great gully from which runs a small river, that scatters over
the plain and loses itself in a shallow backwater, divided from
the sea, with which it is parallel, by a bank of stones and sand:
the head of the valley, instead of the long ridge in the last one,
has many small mounds scarped on the seaward side, and
looking [like] pieces of some ridges that once ran at right-
angles to the big hills: many of these have some sort of a stead
upon them: we ride up to one of the innermost of these (while
the train goes steadily along the bank of the backwater, the
chord of the arc) and find a church standing in its churchyard
hanging on the seaward side of the mound, but the stead,
which is turned sideways of the mountains, is half ruined and
deserted. This is the stead of Fróðá haunted once by those
awful ghosts of the pest-slain and the drowned in Eyrbyggia:
a little past the house we come on the river aforesaid, Fróðá
(Frodi's-river): it runs between two ledges of rock like walls
built to hold it in, but breached here and there; it is strange
and awful to look up this channel filled with the rattling
stream, and see the black rent in the mountains that it runs
from. We cross the river and ride along at our best under
the bounding cliffs to meet the train, and so come into a quite
flat reach of land overgrown with rather scanty grass that lies
between the cliffs and their broken pieces and the backwater.
We halt when we come up to the train halted near the sea,
the packs are taken off, and we settle down for a long rest,
for we have heard that we shall not be able to cross the sands
of Olafsvík Enni (the next bay) till eight o'clock, when the

135

tide will have been ebbing some while, and it is now only three; so Magnússon went to shoe a horse while the rest of us loitered about well pleased. We were on the banks of a little brook that ran down to the sea, and C.J.F. and I bathed in a little clear pool of it, and were in no great hurry to get our clothes on; whereby you may see that it must have been warm that day. Then we fell to meat hungrily enough: after which Magnússon proposed whist to which I agreed though I didn't want it. As we were playing a man galloped up who addressed himself to Magnússon, and said he hoped we were going to stay at Olafsvík; Magnússon returned his salutation in the shortest possible way and said no in that sort of tone that implies the addition of damn your eyes, and the man rode away again presently. I, who thought he had been very civil and very ill-used, asked Magnússon what he meant by it; who said that it was what the man was just worthy of: he was Jón Englendingr, the clerk of the Olafsvík merchant. After talk about his misdeeds,[1] we found our time running short: I wandered down to the beach just where the backwater joined the sea, and finding the fish rising there went back and told Evans, having a mind for sea-trout: he got two pretty good ones in a few minutes, and then we had to get to horse, and rode over the rough ground of the necks always somewhat near the sea into Olafsvík; in the last scoop before we came into that valley we crossed a strange stream, running between regular walls of rock over a bottom of flat slabs as if it had been paved, and falling after a straight course of a furlong below us right into the sea, its mouth some two feet above high-water-mark.

So we came into Olafsvík—just a narrow strip of land below high cliffs which run up into a peak at the further horn, and the strand of a wide deep bay, amidst which lay a small schooner, which no doubt was dealing with the merchant station. To this latter, a wooden house on the beach, we rode, and to my dismay were received there, and very politely too, by the very man whom Magnússon had snubbed

[1]He was only a bore, but one of a very marked type. E.M.

136

just now, for the merchant[1] was ill abed with rheumatic fever:
moreover we found we should have to wait there a bit for we
were still an hour too early for the tide. As we went into the
house a very drunken man tried to push in with us, but Jón
shouldered him out, and he avenged himself afterwards by
taking up handfuls of small stones and throwing them up
against the windows: but he waited till we were all sitting
quietly in the parlour.

Outside too was a funny little white-haired boy with his
little breeches buttoned down behind like in Richter's cuts;
he was hugging the most ridiculous of cur-puppies, so Magnússon chaffed him and said we would eat his puppy and the
like, whereon he ran away and shut himself up in an out-
house: but when his Mama came in with coffee and cakes he
came in with her, but beholding our ferocious faces, shot underneath the table with a yell, and sat there nursing his be-
loved puppy till our visit was over.

Coffee done, we went into the store, whereby it seemed
that the ship in the bay had taken and not brought, for the
lack of all things was plenteous: candles we asked for, gloves,
socks, plates, cups; to all of which askings a most cheerful
and happy man said "no." Finally we bought some few
horse-shoes and I a sixpenny knife (for I had lost three);
there seemed to be nothing else there except two barrels of
brandy, a cask of sugar-candy, a cask of biscuits, and various
boxes of "Damp-Chocolate," whatever chocolate that may
be.

And now for the sands to the gallop over which I had
been looking forward to this hour: we rode through the little
green tún of the stead, and there we were on them—ugh! the
smallest grain of these sands was as big as the bowl of a wine-
glass and the biggest was a huge boulder as big as a big four-
post bed: as big as an arm-chair was a favourite size. Over
these precious sands we toiled most painfully, principally on
foot, I for my part not finding it easy even to lead my horse
after me. Magnússon and I were ahead of the train, but C.J.F.

[1] Torfi Thorgrimsen. E.M.

who was with it, told me afterwards that Eyvindr got quite
a bad fall, his horse and all tumbling head over heels into a
crevice among the rocks, and all their legs being up in the
air together. There were steep high cliffs above us made of
earth and boulders mixed together; they were undermined
with strange-looking cliffs, and at a regular height all along
them water gushed out, running so plenteously sometimes
as to make little waterfalls on to the beach. Magnússon was
kind enough to tell me (halfway) that this beach was looked
upon as a dangerous place because of the stones falling con-
tinually from these cliffs. At last however we found the cliffs
drawing away from the sea and us, and after about an hour's
ride or walk came on to smooth black sand over which we
really had a gallop for a few rods, and then turned away from
the sea on to a sandy plain that the cliff wall still bounds, going nearly at right-angles to its former course. It is getting
quite dusk now, the west before us is orange still with a
cloudless sunset, but the sky behind us at the back of the rock-
wall is dark with night and haze, and the cliffs themselves are
almost like a darker shadow upon it: I noticed this as we rode
away along the plain, and then, turning presently, saw it all
darker still from the wearing of the evening and my having
been staring at the bright west, but above the shadowy cliffs
showed now two sharp white peaks, so much brighter than the
sky, so much nearer-looking than anything else, that I started
almost with terror as if the world was changed suddenly; but
it [was] nothing else [than] the top of Snæfell again. As we
rise higher, from the plain on to the slopes of a broken land,
we see Snæfell clearer yet, but with the magic of it somewhat
gone. Ahead now we can see a round hill with buildings on
it, which are of the stead of Ingialdshóll, our lodging to-night,
and we make towards it with good will enough. A waterfall
tumbling over a rocky ledge was what I remember best seeing through the dusk a good way off, as I rode by myself
driving a knot of horses while Eyvindr and Gisli were kept
behind tying up our refractory bundle-burden to the one-
pegged pack-saddle our old enemy, and the other three rode

138

on ahead: at last I saw their three outlines clear against the
sky; Gisli and Eyvindr ran in on me with the rest of the
train, and we all drove together up a steepish hillside on the
top of which lay a comfortable-looking stead and a church
bigger than usual, which was Ingialdshóll, the scene of the
(fictitious) Víglundar Saga. The folk were abed when we
came, but they all tumbled out in the greatest good temper
when we knocked them up: then as the night was now well
on, and gotten windy too, we asked leave to sleep in the
church, in which all things were soon arranged while I sat by
the kitchen fire to make cocoa and milk hot, all the household assisting: lo and behold in the middle of all this comes
in the much maligned Jón Englendingr from Olafsvík, who
has ridden after us to bring Evans a pair of gloves (as a present) to whom Magnússon was still obdurate.

So to bed on the tombstones of Icelanders dead a hundred
and fifty years, within the screen much and prettily carved:
the stones were hard, and there was a goodish draught
through the church floor, but all that made little difference
to me five minutes after I had settled my blankets.

Tuesday, August 15th. In camp by Stapi.

UP rather early to a cold bright morning, and had a fine
breakfast of fish in the stead, which is a very good one,
the room we breakfasted in being larger than usual
and quite pretty. We didn't get to horse very early, as the
goodman was loth to let us go: a lodger in the house, an ex-
parson I understood, brought us a couple of MSS. to see
if we would buy them: one was well written in a hand of the
17th century: it was a copy of Jónsbók, one of the old law-
books, but was in such an evil plight that I wouldn't buy it.
At last we got away with the bonder to help us through the
lava, and rode down the knoll on which the stead stands
turning somewhat seaward: the knoll was quite round and
rather steep on this side; bold slopes led away from it towards
the lower spurs of Snæfell which is plain enough to see from
here. It is some four thousand feet high but doesn't look a

very big mountain; I don't think any peaked mountains do:
its double crown of dazzling white snow all crumpled like
curd showed much the same from whatever side we saw it.
We soon rode off the grassy slopes into the lava that has flowed from the big mountain; it was a very old lava all grown
over with heath and grass and flowers and dwarf shrubs, and
was pleasant riding enough especially as the day began to get
hot among it. At first when we left the slopes of Ingialdshóll
a cliff hid Snæfell from us, but as we went on it ran into spurs
of the mountain itself on the very lowest parts of which we
rode and now could see the sea before us as well as on our
right. It was as blue as blue can be: between it and us was a
plain not high above the sea level, except that westward
on the very land's end of this promontory was a cluster of
strange-looking crater-like hills turned all sorts of red and
yellow colours with burning: the land's end; for we had now
fairly turned the corner; at least when after the goodman had
left us we rode over the plain to a poor stead called Beruvík
close down on to the sea: here we got the goodman to guide
us, for almost all the rest of our day's journey lay through a
very troublesome lava. It was characteristic of Iceland that
when we asked him he wanted at first two dollars for his
pains, but when a maid of his found his horse he agreed to
come for one dollar; you see he would otherwise have had to
walk back. We rode into the lava at once from here; there
was a good deal of change in it; now it would be all in little
hillocks flower- and herb-grown, now a flattish plain roughly
paved with lava and now over wide slopes of stones leading
right up to Snæfell, with little streams, grey sometimes and
red sometimes but always muddy, running through it: the
stones themselves being queerly mingled of grey, red and
black; the red ones being the ruin of the red sides of a broken-
down crater thrusting up from halfway (as it seems) up Snæfell. Three or four hills rise from the flat ground betwixt us
and the sea; they are all conical in shape, and craters no
doubt: to one of these we rode off our way; it was quite
round with smooth grass-grown sides about the breach by

140

which we entered it: the floor of it was all covered smoothly
with round black and red stones: the tradition runs that this
is the burial place of Bera, the " Landnáms-woman " of these
parts, who would be buried in such a garth as that the sun
should not shine on more than half of it at once. The sun is
bright enough on half of it as we turn away and ride into the
hillocky lava again, and look over the hazy blue sea clearer
now than before, though we have never lost it since Ingialdshóll. We are turning the flank of Snæfell now, whose side is
a mass of frightful ridges of inky grey lava running down
into the plain from the snowy cap. Another mountain lies
before us now, joined by lower necks to Snæfell: it is called
Stapafell and is of the hipped house-roof shape and prodigiously steep, and crested with most fantastic pinnacles; it is
right over our resting-place of to-night.

Just above here we see a little schooner out in the offing
which is the second craft we have seen to-day, the other was
a fishing smack before we came to Beruvík. Then presently
from the sea-side, just beyond the grass slopes of the stead,
rises a rock that looks at first like two straight pillars, but as
we draw round it turns into a church with a steeple beside it;
Tröllakirkja (Troll's Church) is its name therefore.

Then we rode along the edge of a wave of new lava, whose
heaped up ragged stones hide the mountains from us for a
while, and so presently come off the lava on to a wide grassy
valley that slopes up to the feet of Stapafell, on whose sides
for as steep as they are we can see the sheep grazing: between
Stapafell and Snowfell are great spurs of slip and rock running up to the latter close in the valley. Our road, going
over a low neck out of this valley, brings us again into a lava
whose stones, when one sees them bare and broken, are black
and smooth like bottle glass. We are now at the end of Stapafell, and can look down a valley running toward the sea. The
lava ends some way on seaward and leaves a smooth grass-
grown ness between it and the sea, the hither horn of a wide
shallow bay, which bay is backed by a sweeping range of
peaked mountains, that drawing very near the sea, leave a

flattish plain along it, with a low spit of land to make the further horn. On the end of the hither horn aforementioned is a group of little cottages, which is Stapi our resting place. We ride swiftly down the hill and on to the grassy ness, and soon come upon the houses where we soon make all arrangements for things needful, and buy some fish for supper (for the people here are fishermen), and presently have our tents pitched in the tún. It is quite a beautiful little camping place this: a small hollow lying under the mound on which the houses stand, the grass soft, fine, and smooth; the tents are pitched just outside the grass-grown remains of an old stead (for there was once a grand house—for Iceland—here). A swift clear little stream runs round about this meadow on its way to the creak on the side toward the bay, and just beyond the stream is a green turf bank all along it, over whose smooth top we can see the huge steeps of Stapafell, and round the shoulders of them the last white fragment of Snæfell Jokul. The sun set in a sea of crimson clouds, and the night was calm and clear and warm. We lighted up to eat our dinner, and a lot of girls and women sat meanwhile to watch us on the bank on the other side of the stream, just as if it were a show they had taken places for. So to bed well pleased.

Wednesday, August 16th. In camp in the home-stead of Staðastaðr.

I DREAMED very distinctly this morning that I had come home again, and that Webb was asking me what sort of climate we had in Iceland; I cried out "atrocious!" and waking therewith heard the rain pattering on the tent, and found C.J.F. busy drawing the things from the edges of the tent; I helped him therein, and fell to sleep again almost before I had got under the blankets. Waking again later on and hearing the talk of Eyvindr with some of the countryfolk, I lay for some time puzzled to think where I was, and with an unhappy feeling of being a long way from where I wanted to be, and there and then began an access of homesickness for me.

142

Eyvindr brought us coffee at six instead of seven by mistake; but our early rising didn't avail us much, as one of our
horses had run away in the night, and Gisli had to mount
and go after him. Meantime we had to breakfast, and C.J.F.
and Evans busied themselves with rearranging the boxes,
while I sauntered toward the sea, and going down a sort of
rough stairs, came to a little bit of strand, smooth and dip-
ping into a smooth sea, between two walls of rock one of
which is continued out to sea by masses of pillared rocks
which give the place its name (Stapi, Staff). Close down by
the sea, and not all troubling themselves about my presence,
are five ravens stuffing themselves with fish-guts, and all the
near sea is alive with eider-duck, sanderlings, gulls and cor-
morants: there is no ripple on the water, and the sun shines
bright on the mountains that fence in the wide bay: the said
bay is Broadwick (Breiðavík) which names Biorn, the Broadwick champion of Eyrbyggia, him who was found in America in the last chapter of the saga. Just opposite me is a long
range of cliff down the face of which tumbles fifty feet of grey
glacier stream right into the sea. So back to the camp where
I notice that the little stream running round our meadow
which was quite clear last night has gone all turbid now, I
can't think why. Gisli had just come back with the missing
horse when I got back to the tents, and we were off in a few
minutes, and riding out from our ness-meadows, came on to
a high plateau under the mountains that ends in the cliffs
(the same I saw from the beach), close to whose edge we had
to ride presently. Many streams running down from the
mountains fell from the cliffs' edge besides the big grey one
above mentioned: some of them had cut a passage through
the rock, but the more part fell right over the bare edge; it is
strange riding through these to see the sea below over their
waters. As we rode over these cliffs an eagle flew to meet us,
and sailing quite close to our heads, pitched down on the
cliff's edge not twenty yards from where I rode. Off these
cliffs we rode, down into a shaly hollow and then on to a
rushy plain: to the left of this lay the stead of Kambr, the

house of Biorn above mentioned. This plain was quite on a level with the sea: we noticed several great drift-logs on it; and one part for several acres was all strewn with little sponges: I am too ignorant to know if they grew there or had been washed ashore. After a mile or two of very good riding over this we had to come into lava again: a lava not hilly like yesterday's but all honeycombed with holes, burst bubbles I suppose; the flowers and grass grow very thick and rich at the bottoms of these holes, meadow-sweet, cranes-bill and buttercups mostly. Amidst this lava, which a little way off would look like a quite smooth plain, rises a steep conical hill of black stones called Búða-klettr (cliff); round the landward side of this we wind and getting clear of its flank see the trading-station of Búðir (the booths) up a creek, and between it and the sea a schooner lying to, waiting with hoisted flag for the tide to bring her in: there are masts visible by the houses also and it all looks very near in the bright day, but proves over two hours of very troublesome riding; for the road (?) was all beset with false paths ending in ragged holes, in slippery ridges and pitfalls: one of the horses fell clean into a hole, and we had to pull him out with ropes; I wonder he didn't break his neck, but Icelandic ponies fall soft, and he was only a little bit scratched about the nose and legs. After a while the lava gets sprinkled with sand, which soon partly covers the rocks and then is grown over with wild oats, and then we come out on to sand and grass alone and are at the station of Buðir where are several neat houses and a church, on the top of whose cross sits a raven gravely watching our arrival. Here we had to swim our horses over the creek and have our luggage flitted over in a boat, so having seen this done and the horses all happy in the fields beyond, we went into the merchant's house, who would fain have had us stay the night with him, which was impossible; so we had to put up with chocolate and biscuits for entertainment, and afterwards went into his store to see what we could buy, for he boasted he had every thing up to live falcons. We bought some blue-fox skins there, and presently afterward crossed the river and went our ways over flats near the sea, with a wall of mountains always on our left: Stadastadr it was bright still at about three in the afternoon, and I thought it pretty, as we rode along apace, to see all the hoofs glittering in the sun.

We rode on what seemed a longish way at last till Magnússon, beginning to have doubts about the road, turned off to a little stead, and finding an old woman there, asked the way and thus reported to me the dialogue that followed.

She: What men are you?

He: Four travellers and two followers.

She: Where do you come from?

He: London.

She: What is your name?

He: I am called Eiríkr, and am Magnússon.

She: Where are you going to?

He: Staðastaðr: is it a long way hence?

She: Yes, long.

He: How far?

She: I don't know.

He: Do you know the road?

She: No.

Nevertheless about twenty minutes afterwards we turned round by some big pools, and saw the church and stead of Staðastaðr lying on a low mound a furlong off, and were soon in the tún of it, the day now, at about seven o'clock, getting spoilt, grey clouds covering the hills and spreading downwards as it seemed. The priest seemed glad to see us and offered to kill us a lamb which we accepted, and then I went off with Faulkner and Evans to help pitch the tents, and coming back presently saw a sorry sight, for the lamb was killed, and the poor old ewe was bleating and rubbing her nose against the skin in a way to make you forswear flesh-meat for ever; happily however the ending relieved one somewhat, for one of the sheep-dogs sniffing about, came rather too near the ewe, who suddenly charged him, hit him in the ribs and bowled him over howling.

To dinner in the stove, and soon after to bed in our tents, the rain coming down a little.

VIII.L

145

Thursday, August 17th. In the bonder's house at Miklaholt.

WHAT a night that was for wind! I woke up in the middle of the night with a start, thinking that tent and all must be carried away, such a flapping and tearing as there was; all held well however, and I didn't dislike it, though I kept on being woke up every hour or so; at last at seven I awoke for good, but lay there some time pretending to to think that C.J.F. was still asleep: for you see it had been settled over-night that we were to get up at seven and ride to Hítardale; but soon came coffee, and then C.J.F. confessed he had been playing the same game as I had, to my great pleasure. The wind was blowing furiously still, the rain peppering on the mountainward side of the tent, the sun shining bright on the seaward side: but cold it was, when one stirred a little.

We had scarcely finished our coffee when Evans came and wanted us to get up at once, but I am ashamed to say we received him with jeers, for we were most beautifully comfortable where we were; moreover we had broken the handle off our frying pan the day before, and here we were at a good stead where we could mend it, and we would stop a bit. So we didn't get up till it was just breakfast-time (ten o'clock), after which I spent my time in watching the heroic efforts of C.J.F. and Magnússon in smithying on anew the handle of the frying pan, which, having been accomplished somehow, did really seem to us all an admirable work. But all this had taken us some time, and we had no chance of getting to Hítardal, and so we had to aim at Miklaholt, starting at four o'clock on a raw, uncomfortable afternoon. Though the sun had been shining out at sea and sometimes over our heads, the mountains were all covered with clouds, and the furious wind had driven the rain down upon us all day; by then we started, the clouds were higher and it was not raining, but it was bitter cold, as aforewrit. It is only a ride of four hours before we see Miklaholt lying away amid marshes near the sea; the mountains had come nearer to our left on the way, and were now very wild-looking and striking in shape, jagged and peaked

146

mostly, but with a pyramid lying amidst a gap of them. It is a wild sunset, fiery and cloudy behind these high peaks whose shadows seem cast right and left by it over the eastern clouds.

So we turn away toward the bogs of Miklaholt, getting a boy from a little stead to guide us: an imp of a lad who, riding one of our horses barebacked, never ceases to wag his legs and twist about on the saddle; it was a three miles ride over the very worst bogs, over which however there was something of a road made, before we came on to a little rise on which was the tún of Miklaholt with its house & church: the folk of the house were all standing in a row to welcome us as we came to the house-door,[1] but were rather puzzled as to where to lodge us, saying, when Magnússon spoke of the guides among other difficulties, "Ah, an Icelander can be thrust into an Icelander's dog-hole—but these foreign gentlemen!" However we got very good quarters in the parlour, and all of us were well satisfied, saving Evans, who was very angry at having had to come out of his way over the bogs. In fact there was some plain speech passed between him and Magnússon, in which he was quite in the wrong; but in fact he was somewhat sick, it turned out, so had a right to be sulky. So to bed on the floor.

Friday, August 18th. In the priest's house at Hítardal.

WE got away at about half-past eleven, our day's ride not having to be a long one to-day, and were led away through the bog by our host, over another road than that we came by yesterday, to say the truth a very much worse one: C.J.F., who by the way was always the unlucky one in bogs, had his horse go through, and after he had floundered out and was riding on, he suddenly disappeared under the horse's belly by reason of a broken girth.

Once out of the bogs we ride under the face of huge cliffs looking as if they had been built in regular lines above, but with slips from them all grass-grown now: the sea, breaking

[1] "Overflowing with good-nature and laughing at everything," says the note-book. Ed.

on a flat strand, very sandy, was close to our right at first, and
a wreck lay amongst the sand (a French vessel cast away some
two years ago), making the sea view dismal. The great cliffs
leave our road after a while, and turning at right angles to it
get lower, and form one side of a wide valley half full of lava,
which is stopped by a river (Haf-fiarðará) which runs through
the midst of it: high up the valley are two little conical hills
burnt red, and further east near by the sea is a crater-like rock
amid the lava called Eld-borg (Fire-burg). The hills on the
further side of the valley run up into great scarped mountains
capped with many strange shapes, the hipped house-roof
one predominating. Our hosts (father and son) take leave of
us just as we drop down from the mountain-spurs into this
valley, and we presently cross the river above-named into a
wood growing amid the lava, where Evans shoots four ptarmigan; after this we make a pleasant halt by a flowery bank
among the lava, where the blueberries grow very abundantly,
and then turn up towards the mountains again. There is the
mouth of another valley showing beyond the last-named
mountain boundary, and the furthest wall of it is the range
called Fairwood-fell (Fagra-skogar-fjall), the haunt of
Grettir once. Riding over steepish slopes we cross the mouth
of this valley, a narrow place where the mountains show like
gate posts of a great pass, though the valley is closed up
at the end; most desolate it is to look into: the mountains
are very steep, and high up the valley a spur from the east-
ward mountains, running half way across, has been ruined
once by who knows what, and lies there now a mass of black
sand and ragged grey spikes and rocks, and the waste of it has
been driven down the valley and over the slopes that lead to
the plain, and torn up grass and bush and all, and left great
rocks scattered all about. We pass this, and ride up the slopes
of Fairwood-fell, and looking back thence can see our journey of the last two days all along the sea under the mountain-
wall, Stapafell being the last headland, with Snæfell showing
over the shoulder of it. Then on we ride, turning as the hills
turn over slopes steep but green, except where they are

148

wasted by some slips from the mountains above, that are Hítardal
crested by rock built up in regular terraces and ending in
teeth-like pinnacles. We turn round the end of these mountains at last where they fall back from the sea by a long valley that lies down below us with a river (Hítá) running close
under the mountains; this valley opens into the great plains
of Burgfirth, and you can see the mountains on the other side
of White-water (Hvítá) in the distance; the lava goes along
the river for some way, looking dark grey and dreadful
among the grey green pastures and yellow green marshes.
We ride along the slopes still heading up the valley, and presently we see ahead of us a spur rushing at right angles out
from the mountains, a great ruin spoiling the fair green
slopes; it is a huge slip of black shale, very steep, and crested
by thin jagged rocks, like palings set awry, in one of which
is a distinct round hole through which the sky shows: under
these palings on the top of the grey ruin was Grettir's-lair,
and it was down this slip he rattled after the braggart Gisli.
It was such a savage dreadful place,[1] that it gave quite a new
turn in my mind to the whole story, and transfigured Grettir
into an awful and monstrous being, like one of the early
giants of the world.

When we got to the foot of the slip we turned down to
the river which ran below us; it ran clear and shallow through
a deep gorge with a wall of lava on the other side, and winded
so that above us it seemed to be running through an impassable wall. Good store of birch-scrub grew in the crevices of
the lava, and at the top of the wall we came into a regular wood
of gnarled birch-bushes; they grew thinner after a while as we
wound through the lava which was very old, so that we rode
through a labyrinth of grey mossy rocks with soft flowery
turf all between them, and birch-bushes here and there. So we
rode awhile near the river, but presently had to turn across
the river to the stead Hítardal, whose many gables and emerald green tún we could see lying on a mound under a spur
of the opposite hill-sides: so turning away from the river we

[1] The Fairwood-fell (Fagraskógarfiall) of Grettis saga. E.M.

149

Hítardal were soon amidst sand between the lava-rocks instead of grass; the wind blew strong and cold, and drove the sand fiercely into our faces, so that we were glad enough to come to our journey's end at the stead, a pretty row of sheds and standing prettily on its grassy mound looking as if it would be sheltered by the spur aforesaid—which it was not that afternoon at all events, for the wind howled about it in all imaginable eddies. In a bight below the mound and a few hundred yards from the house was an assemblage of fantastic rocks, which I fairly thought were ruins of some minster as I rode dreamily, half forgetting where I was, into the tún.

It was somewhat late by now, and the wind was so strong and cold, and Evans withal was still sick, so we gave up the plan of pitching our tents and asked for lodging in the house, which the priest,[1] a little shy kind-looking old man, very gladly gave us, two beds to wit and the parlour floor. Magnússon after a talk with the priest came to us with a long face, saying that there was bad news: to wit there was a fever at Reykjavík, and several people (eight I think) had died of it already, whom he knew. I confess I was coward enough to feel dashed by this, and as if I should never get away home again: please to allow something to a woeful grey day and this terrible though beautiful valley. However whatever forebodings and sentimental desires I may have, I have to indulge them over the kitchen fire and under its shiny black rafters, for the others are hungry, and Evans' ptarmigan are waiting a stroke of my art. So we dined and I got back some part at least of my spirits; but when I went outside afterwards in the dead of night, and looking up at the black mountains opposite, thought the moon lay on them brightly high up, and found presently that it was snow that had fallen since we came in, halfway up them, a sort of pang shot through me of how far away I was and shut in, which was not altogether a pain either, the adventure seemed so worthy. So to bed, I in a box-bed in a pleasant little room with books in a shelf of the bed over my head.

[1] He died last year. [His name was Thorstein E. Hjalmarsen. E.M.]

150

Saturday, August 19th. In camp in the tún of Borg.

THIS morning I saw for the first time the ancient Icelandic fiddle called Langspil: it was a long box with the strings stretched along it, and lay on the table to be played with a fiddle bow; a little maiden played "Eigi má ek á ægi" (out of the Viglund Saga) on it, but it was sadly out of tune.

It was an evil morning of wind and sleet, with the snow above mentioned visible enough on the mountains. So I suggested staying where we were, especially as we had heard very dismal reports of the bogs of the Mýrar (Mires).

Evans was sick and didn't care: C.J.F. suggested going half way to Borg, saying, as was reasonable, that the weather might be just as bad to-morrow, and then we should have to go on in any case: so I agreed, whereat C.J.F. seemed downcast, for he had hoped I should be obstinate. However he brightened up presently, and said why shouldn't we ride all the way then: I wouldn't say no, and we got ready as speedily as might be, and were off not much before noon. The day brightened up somewhat for our reward, and when we got alongside of these ruined-minster-looking rocks, a gleam of sun made a mist-rainbow of that flat-segment shape on the mountain-spur above the house.

We rode along the feet of the hills on this side the valley till it opened, and the great plain of the Mýrar lay before us with the sea beyond, and the Snæfelsness promontory came in sight again on our right hand. We were now come to the point whence we needed a guide so we rode to a poor stead down the slope, and got the goodman of it to go with us, and so start again after sitting awhile with him and his wife (who is an acquaintance of Magnússon's).

He led us by a way that seemed to turn away from Borg again right under the mountains that fell away to the east, though the crow had not a very long way to fly straight over the bogs to Borg. The hills above us were broken cliffs, and their spurs that we rode over were much begrown with birch-scrub, twisted more than usual by the wind, a tree with a stem

151

as thick as my leg often creeping quite along the ground. At last we came on where Langá (Long-water) split these cliffs and ran right away for White-water:[1] there we turned toward the plain going on the seaward or west side of the river. The plain is a very wide one; it rises into broken ridges as it gets toward the east, but these for a long way are not high enough to take away its character of a plain: seaward it looks from where we are a quite unbroken plain, though it really is not so. Southward where the mouth of White-water would be, and on the other side of it, is a group of grand mountains that seem set in a circle as if they had once been the sides of some enormous crater. They end abruptly on the seaward, but landward drop gradually till they become mere hillsides along White-water: over the tops or between the gaps of them we should see, but for the clouds of this sullen day, the jokuls we passed by earlier in our journey (Long, and Ball Jokul). As we get clear of the mountain-spurs behind us we can see the north-east boundary of this great plain, which is a range of hills not very high or characteristic except for a pyramid which thrusts out from them called Baula (the Bawler).

We ride some little way along this west side of Langá, a shallow clear river, and then cross to the other side, and turn straight toward Borg. There turns out to be nothing dreadful about the bogs, for there is a good road through them; the marshland too is varied by sudden shelves of rock and grassy islands rising from its surface, and between these the birch-scrub grows thick mostly, and is higher than I have yet seen it in Iceland: the day though sulky was not very windy now, and was gotten much warmer. The day was far spent by then we came in sight of the water of the firth lying under

[1] Really for Western Burgfirth, the estuary of White-water. Taking his position high up on the west bank of Langá, the author has swept the country with his eye, east-ward to Long Jokul and Ball Jokul, west away to the Snæfell promontory, up north to the pyramid of Baula. He has embraced the main features of the country with general accuracy and breadth of vision, and one or two discrepancies in detail need not be noted. Ed.

the great mountains aforesaid, and we were hungry, and I Borg
for my part, when we came first to one stead and then to another, lying each on its own knoll, thought that it must be
Borg: at last rounding a corner of one of those rock-ledges
we come upon a creek that runs up from the firth, and standing back from the water-side across the space of gentle green
slope is a five-gabled stead under a sheer cliff, the highest of
any of those ledges of rock, and that is the house of Borg,
with a little church standing beside it.

It was quite dusk as we rode up to the door, and we got
leave to sleep in the house that night, on the condition that
we should turn out early enough in the morning to give them
time to get the parlour ready for the dean of Stafholt who is
coming to preach. So came supper and bed.

Sunday, August 20th. In camp in the home-mead of Borg.
WE turned out of the parlour as soon as we had had
our breakfast according to agreement, and pitched
our tents in the tún which is separated from the
house by a sort of yard as often here. It was a fine sunny
morning though the wind thus early was still rather cold. It
is a church-Sunday to-day and the people soon begin to drop
in and wander about, or sit happily on the green turf walls,
and there is a good deal of kissing all round: the men look
like great big school-boys in their wide trousers, short jackets
and low-crowned rough beaver hats.

While the bell was ringing the people in to "confession"
(the ante-mass service, to which, by the way, nobody but
women seemed to go), I turned away, and mounted the
"Burg" under which the house stands, a straight grey cliff
grass-clad at top, sloping gradually down toward the lower
land on one side. There are plenty of flowers in the grass at
the top, clover and gentian chiefly, and I sat there in excited
mood for some time; of all the great historical steads I had
seen this seemed to me the most striking after Lithend; yet
for some reason or other I find it hard to describe: southward
lay the firth, quite calm and bright, those great mountains

reflected in it with all detail, and over their shoulders the bright white jokuls are to be seen from here: the great circle of mountains is very awful and mysterious under a beautiful peaceful sky: they come nearly to the firth-side at the mouth of it, but from their outmost buttress a long low spit of land runs out into the sea, and beyond this is a line of skerries, beyond which one can see the surf breaking at the deep sea's end; a creek runs up from the firth toward Borg and a little stream falling through the rock ledge, of which this cliff is the highest end, goes into it. Eastward the country, ending with the low hills broken by Baula, looks little different hence to what it did from horseback, the plain somewhat flatter and the hills somewhat higher, that is all. Burgfirth, I may mention in case you forget it, or are hazy about your saga geography, is one of the great centres of story in Iceland: Egil lived at Borg, and his son Thorstein, father of Helga the Fair; some way up the river [1] is Gilsbank (Gilsbakki) Gunnlaug the Worm-tongue's house: and between that and this is Deildar Tongue, where Odd of the Tongue lived; a little north of that is Thverar Lithe, the dwelling of most of the folk in Hen-Thorir's Saga, and finally, Reykholt is hard by (to the south-east) where Snorri the historian lived and died.

When I came down from the Burg I find that mass proper has begun, and most of the men are gone into church, Magnússon among others; I looked in at the door and saw him sitting in state by the altar, and so retired not wanting to be caught and set down there: there were candles burning on the altar, and the priest was dressed in chasuble and was intoning the service in Icelandic in doleful key enough: altogether it seemed a dry reminiscence of the Catholic mass and rather depressed me, though I am glad they have kept so much ceremony for their amusement too; I am told they really do like sermons if they are flowery enough in style.

So then I lay in the tent till church was over, the end of which brought most of the worshippers in front of our tents for a stare; there was about a hundred of them, and if they

[1] Whitewater. Ed.

"came out for to see men clothed in fine raiment," they must Borg have been sadly disappointed, for dirty and worn we were by that time.

After that came dinner and then for me a wandering about on the creek sides and up on to the Burg again: the rest or something made me homesick again, and I turned over scraps of verse that came to nothing, and felt low till I met Magnússon wandering about shooting, and we came in together, and it was supper and bed presently, a calm warm night, rather cloudy.

Monday, August 21st. In camp in the home-mead at Stafholt.

UP pretty early and away at about eleven on a bright warm morning that put us all in good spirits. About the country there is not much to say, because we partly retraced our road of Saturday, and for the rest it was the same sort of country, ledges of rock making shallow valleys grown about with birch-bushes; the same mountains were in the distance also, and too far off for our short day's journey to change them much. We stopped for coffee at a bonder's house, which I have got put down as Giallar-loekjar,[1] but can't find in the map, and after a short ride thence came into a wide plain across which we could see Stafholt lying on a slope under a grey ledge of rock on the other side of a wide shallow clear river, North-water (Norðrá). The river is rockless and sandy, and has an evil reputation for quicksands, the only experience of which that we had was C.J.F. floundering in the black sand up to his saddle-girths as soon as he took the water. Over the river we passed through pleasant pastures to the dean's stead, where his wife in his absence gave us good welcome in a pleasant house though now growing somewhat old. We were to have two beds in the house, for Magnússon and Evans, which latter was somewhat sick still, and C.J.F. and I pitched our tent in the tún for the

[1] Probably Galtarhorn, which is the only place-name that suits. E.M.

155

rest. We dined luxuriously off roast mutton at 8 p.m.; but the dean came home at nine and was very cheerful and glad to see us: he swore a good deal in his talk, but swearing in a foreign tongue does not sound very dreadful. He showed us two very handsome seventeenth century brass candlesticks out of his church, by the way.

So to bed in our tent, where in the dead of night C.J.F. and I quarrelled—in this wise; I who upon my honour was lying awake, heard him snoring violently, but bore it well for a time, till it rose to a roaring snuffling climax, and I thought I should go mad, and shouted out "damn!" This woke C.J.F. who said, as if he had never been asleep in his life, and in a most disagreeable tone of voice, just as if he were seeking a quarrel,

"What's the matter now?"

Justly indignant at this speech and the tone of it, I said rather hotly,

"You were snoring like the devil."

He (and in a most unpleasant tone, as if I *must* always be in the wrong),

"I have been awake for half an hour."

I (still indignant, but willing in my good nature to give him a loop-hole for honourable escape),

"You must have been snoring awake then, and I wish the Devil you wouldn't."

He (sourly and obstinately), "It so happens that I particularly noticed that I was awake, for I was thinking that the wind was getting up and that it might rain in the night, and that I had better move the things from the tent-walls."

I (rather curtly, for I was getting roused), "Why did you snore then?"

He, "I didn't."

I, "You did."

He, "It was you who were snoring, and dreamed it was I."

Indignation should have kept me silent after this, but I thought it disrespectful not to answer an old friend, so I exerted myself to say: "It so happens that I particularly noticed

that I was awake, for I was just thinking of getting up to Stafhol
move the gun-case away from the tent-walls."

He (most disagreeably) "Rubbish!"

Speechless indignation now indeed: and so to sleep.

Tuesday, August 22nd. In the priest's house at Gilsbank
(Gilsbakki).

BUT waking this morning it occurred to me that
something amusing had happened, without remembering what it was at first, till at last it smote upon me
and I fell a-roaring with laughter, as did C.J.F. no less and
no later; so small a joke moving our little minds in those
waste places—owing to the fresh air, I suppose.

Evans elected to stay here and nurse his cold this day, and
meet us to-morrow at Reykholt, so we left him in very comfortable quarters with two or three Icelandic phrases for his
help. Eyvindr and the greater part of the train stayed with
him, and we went our ways with Gisli and the rest: the dean
and his son led us on our way.

Just past the house they offered to show me a seam of coal
that lay, they said, in the cliff-side above Northwater; but I
in my hatred of coal was incurious and refused; I was rather
sorry afterwards, for I heard that it was not coal but Surtr-
brandar,[1] a sort of fossil wood that lies in certain places in Iceland (mostly in these same parts) quite unchanged in form
amid layers of leaves, poplar, birch and alder.

The mountains over against Borg look from here, as we
have turned round them somewhat, more still like a half-
ruined crater of monstrous size.

We rode up the course of White-water, though not very
near it, through that same ledged country, till after crossing
Thwart-water (Thverá) the ledges grow bigger and run into
long low hills, and on our left make Thverá-lithe, the chief
scene of Hen Thorir's saga, which is a narrow [valley] shut
in between the low hills: another range, bigger and higher

[1] Surtr is the God of fire (soot, *cocknice*, sutt). [Surt means Swart;
he was a demon, not the god of fire. E.M.]

Gilsbank and going right up to the Jokuls, is the north-west bank of White-water, whose south-east is the continuation of the mountains opposite Borg fallen into downs by now: a long way up the north-west bank (which is called White-water-side) is Gilsbank whither we are bound: some ten miles east of it at the very head of the valley lies Kalmanstunga, where we stayed some three weeks before though it now seems such a long time ago. We turn up into the valley presently and then the Stafholt folk leave us, and we jog on soberly by ourselves: the valley soon narrows so much as to bring our road within sight of White-water, and we are fairly riding along White-water-side. A monotonous and dreary valley it seemed to me that day, with its endless slopes of thin grass, dotted about however with steads here and there, and the lower part of all filled with banks of stones brought down by the rage of the river, and with the great white dome of Geitland's Jokul filling the valley at the further end. The wind blows strong and cold from the ice to-day too, and no winding of the valley seems to stop it: but the sun shines, and we were not unmerry when we stopped to eat our bait under a bank as much out of the wind as might be, which was not much. The valley bettered as we drew toward its closed end: the rubbish of stones ended, and we rode through green flat ground for a while near the river side, till before us rise the spikes and cliffs of an old lava all grown about with birch and deep rich grass, which birch turns out presently, as we ride along a clear stream that skirts the lava, to be the best wood we have seen yet. The hill side on our left is near us too, a great bold down here, which presently we see cleft by a deep ravine, through which runs the stream aforesaid; this ravine is the "Gil" from which the stead of Gilsbank once the house of Illugi the Black, father of Gunnlaug the Worm-tongue is named. We turn aside to it, and ride up a bare bleak hill to a poorish house built high up the hillside, with the evening clear, but cold and even frosty. So cold that we found it hard work keeping warm even in the priest's little parlour.

158

It was not a very cheerful evening, for Magnússon had Gilsbank heard bad news again about the fever at Reykjavík and was naturally anxious, and I am afraid his long face infected me also. The old priest was at all events most kind and hospitable to us, and so at last to bed we went, Magnússon in the bed, C.J.F. and I on the floor in our blankets.

Wednesday, August 23rd. In the priest's house at Reykholt.

UP on a windy cold morning with drizzle and gleams of sun succeeding one another, and as we are getting ready for going, one of those flat segmental rainbows comes out over the Jokuls on the north. The priest takes us to the edge of the ragged gill and shows us the traditional place of burial of Hermund the brother of Gunnlaug, in which he himself doesn't believe, because Hermund was a Christian and would have been buried in a church.

The whole side and part of the gable and roof of the house here was covered with ox-eye daisies in full blossom.

The view down into the valley is but gloomy: the birch-grown lava indeed looks grey-green, and not unhopeful, but it only lasts a little way toward the Jokuls, and then comes a second wave of lava upon it, new comparatively, and naked, a great leaden sea that stretches up through the narrowing valley between its low boundary hills till the higher land at the end with the Jokuls above it ends all.

We sent Gisli on with our lessened train, and then the priest and his son (a Reykjavík student this latter) led us away down the hill, and into the lava at its feet: it was that newer lava we went on, just at its edge where a clear stream ran at the bottom of the last cliff of it, and beyond the stream the birches grew thick on the earlier wave: indeed now we were on it we found the naked lava not wholly bare, there being a good deal of the heather and other herbaceous plants growing in its crannies, especially one beautiful plant with olive-shaped leaves and bright red berries. We followed up the course of the stream toward White-water, and about the highest of the lava-cliff above it the priest said:

"Come see where I take my trout in autumn."

So we got off our horses and leaning over, saw a bubbling spring that came out of the lava and made a big pool before it fairly joined the swift-running stream aforesaid; it was very deep, some thirty feet the priest said, but you could see every point of rock at the bottom all bright blue on this sunny day (for so it was gotten to be now). The priest said it never freezes, this hole: the trout gather in it before they go up the underground streams of the lava.

Now we saw where the clear stream fell into White-water, splitting round a little islet at its mouth; this islet, and all the flat banks along the stream under the cliffs were very bright and green, and tall birch-bushes, quite the biggest I had seen in Iceland, were scattered over them; they grew fair and ungnarled too in bunches of straight staves: the whole place seemed very beautiful to me. We were now close on the bank of White-water itself, which runs deep and swift between steep ledges of basalt rock, on the top of which the lava lies on our side; the river is not so turbid as other white waters we have seen, being rather greenish white: it looks most terrible here. A little further on and a turn of the river shows us a most strange sight: White-water gathered up between narrow rocks some ten feet wide at its narrowest is a mass of foam there, and below this where it widens into a still furious torrent the bank on our side is basalt rock cut into steps like the steps of a bath, over which pours into White-water a small river that runs from out of the hidden caves of the lava, and is quite clear.

We left our horses just by the mouth of the afore-mentioned stream, and now stumble on, on foot, round a swell of the lava just by the gates of the gorge that hides the river from us for a few minutes, and so come right on the Barnafóss (Bairns' Force) which is what the priest has been taking us to see. It is a wild place enough; a mile below Gilsbank White-water is about as wide as the Thames at Reading, two

160

small rivers come into it between this and that, and here is
all the rest of it shut in between straight walls of black rock
nowhere more than twenty feet across; far up the gorge we
can see the mountains towering up, and the white dome of
the great Jokul beyond everything: about the narrowest of
it, where it is certainly not ten feet across, the rocks stretch
out to meet each other, overhanging the stream like the
springings of some natural arch; which indeed the story of
the place says was once complete, but that a certain witch
once lured two children of her enemy to cross the place, and
then raised a wild storm which swept away them and the
keystone of the bridge: wherefore is the fall called the
Bairns' Force. We lay a little while on a grassy, berry-grown
bank near the water watching this marvel, and then turned
back to where we had left our horses. I came up panting, and
threw myself down on the grass, and when the priest made
an astonished face at me, explained that I was heavily clad
and booted: he nodded his head, and then tapped me on the
belly, and said very gravely: "Besides you know you are so
fat."

He led us away back up the first clear stream, which we
crossed just above the deep hole afore-mentioned into the
older birch-grown lava, and so into a most beautiful little
nook of it; a grass-grown space quite smooth and flat, with
a clear streamlet running level with the grass at the end of it
we came in by, and all round it otherwhere a steep green bank
crested with thick-growing birches smelling most sweet in
the sun: he got off his horse here, and said he had brought
us to this place because it was good to take leave in a pretty
place: so we said good-bye to him and he went back home
leaving his son to bring us further on the way: a bright-look-
ing youth whom I had overheard this morning telling C.J.F.
the story of the Froðá-wonders in dog-latin.

So we wound on through the wood, and found many
pretty places of a like kind to the first in it; and the whole
place had a softness about it that saddened one amidst all the
grisliness surrounding it, more than the grimmest desert I

had seen. We came out of the wood into wide flat meadows bounded on our left by the stony side of White-water, and on our right by the grey bush-grown cliff of the lava washed by a clear stream, all of which was still sweet and soft, so that it was with a shudder that we gained our road of yesterday leading us down the grim valley of White-water. We rode on till we came to a stead on the slopes called Hawkgil where dwelt an acquaintance of Magnússon's who had his name and calling (saddle-making) written on a board over his house, which looked queer in such a lonely place: we went in here and were treated to coffee and most excellent cakes of rye sweetened; and when we rode out again the priest's son turned back home, and the bonder rode on with us to the next stead, Sámstaðir, and got us a guide for the fording of White-water, and down the slope we went, and into the deepest ford we had come across, though not the most dangerous. Magnússon had to lead me again, for though my head didn't swim, and I was not at all nervous, I could not tell as we went through the swift-running water whether we were going up stream or down. We turned round on the other bank and watched our guide recrossing, and I was surprised to see that he went very nearly in a straight line, for as we were in the water I seemed to be making quite a long bow upward. I thought White-water-side looked grand and solemn from here with its long unbroken hillside running toward the Jokuls. We turned from it to Reykholts-dale over a waste sandy neck, topping one of whose knolls we came among most evil bogs, and the road dying out among them, as commonly happens, we fairly lost our way and wandered about till we met a carle on the queerest of queer horses: white, so please you, but had dipped his head into a tub of red ochre, and had his tail nailed on by a patch of the same colour: that's what he seemed like.

Horse and rider led us a little way over a bad road into a valley shorter than White-water-side, its hills more crested with bare rock, and over the shut-in end of it the top of Jokul Ok showing. There were many steads on either side of it, and at this western end of the dale jets of steam going up from the hot-springs scattered all about: just below us was a stead and church well placed on the hillside, and a little behind the stead went up a column of steam wavering about, that showed the whereabouts of a great kettle (Hver). This stead is a famous place indeed and worthy to be remembered, for Snorri the historian lived and was slain here, and has left marks of himself here, of which more presently. We rode down to the stead and found Gisli and Eyvindr and Evans at the door; there was another fellow-passenger of ours here too, Dapples to wit, "the Italian man," as they call him here. The day has got to be cold and rainy now, and we were glad enough of shelter in the priest's parlour, where we soon had a fine dinner of roast mutton, and so presently bed: one bed for Magnússon and floor for the rest.

Thursday, August 24th. In the same place.

A COLD raw morning when I went out to bathe in Snorri's Bath, so that I felt grateful for the hot water up to my middle. The said bath is a round one sunk in the earth some twelve feet diameter, lined & paved with smooth cut stones cemented with bitumen; there is a groove cut from it to the hot-spring [Skrifla] which is some hundred yards off, and can be turned off by a single dam into another channel, so that you can have the water as hot or as cool as you will: all the water for the house comes from this hot-spring, by the way, and smells evilly of sulphuretted hydrogen, but smell and taste go off when it has been boiled again; and we made very good tea with it last night. The bath is a few yards from the stead, and close by it rises a steep artificial grassy mound, which is Snorri's castle. I wandered about the mound a bit and then in to breakfast; after which befell a counsel as to whether we should go on or not; we had intended to go to Brunnar where we had camped before, this day, and Thingvellir the next; but the day was so cold and raw and we in good quarters, so we felt disinclined to move, and the end of it was we agreed to go on next day all the way

M2   163

to Thingvellir, and so coolly sat down to whist now; at which
we played, with an interval for dinner, till about five in the
afternoon, when C.J.F. and I wandered out, and down to the
river where we talked about when we should be home again,
and then, after an interval of making ducks and drakes in the
water, back to the stead again, taking the hot-spring on our
way; a sloppy and untidy piece of boggy land lay all about it,
but the spring was a queer one, always playing about two feet
high. Evans, by the way, as he came from Stafholt, had seen a
strange hot-spring in this valley, one rising out of the midst
of a cold river with an accretion of flinty deposit all about it.

So back to supper in the stead, more whist (if one must
tell the truth) and to bed as before.

Friday, August 25th. In camp in the home-mead at Thingvellir.

SET off quite early (about 8 a.m.) under the priest's
guidance, the day being little, if any, better than before.
The priest led us right up the dale, and we passed by a
pretty stead, whose home-mead had been levelled altogether
of the usual hummocks: this lay on a spur of the bounding
hills, and when we rode away from it we were presently on
waste ground of the roughest, and mounted speedily the
south hill boundary of the dale, riding alongside a stream that
had cut for itself a gorge that got deeper and deeper as we
went on: from this also we soon turned, and were fairly on the
open "heath," and had mounted so high that we could look
into both White-water-side and Reykholts-dale, and could
even see the scar on the hill-side of the former that showed
where Gilsbank lay. Thence away over a bad and doubtful
road until we run into a real and trodden way called the "Way
under Ok," which is one of the north roads and goes just on
the west side of that mountain Ok on the east side whereof is
the Kaldidal road that we took in going north. Ok has been
on our left for some time now, but when we are once in the
road we soon begin to leave it behind, and the outline of the
mountains gets familiar to us, in especial the great boss of
Skialdbreið that rises up straight before us.

164

Whether it was accident or not I don't know, but certainly as soon as we had passed Kaldidal going north the weather got much colder, and now as soon as we were past Ok it grew warmer again: for the wind dropped and a long strip of blue-green opened in the south-west and widened and turned bluer and let the sun out.

It is exciting to us to see the indigo coloured peaks whose shapes we know rising up one after another over the dull heath: and soon we note the ragged screen of rocks before Ball-Jokul, and that other range that runs south from Skiald-breið, and the whole tumbled sea of peaks that rise between us and the plain of Thingvellir.

The heath bettered as we rode on, and we got to riding into little valleys now, boggy or sandy at bottom (oftenest the latter) but with the banks about them grown over with heath berries, sweet grass and flowers, much as it was with our old encampment at Brunnar; at last these open out before us into a wider plain, and we can see Skialdbreið clear to his feet and the grey lava we journeyed over the other day,[1] and the aforesaid toothed screen of mountains ending in a gap through which show mountains a long way off, bright and intense blue under the now bright sunny sky; on the other side of this gap rises a lumpier range gradually drawing toward us, which is Armansfell: and through this gap lies our way to Thingvellir. We are now come to our old camp-ing-stead of Brunnar, and there we bait, not at our encamp-ment on the hillside but on the grass meadow about the pools: we rest about an hour and then set forward, I greatly excited by the warm day and the thought of the Thingmeads before us.

Then passing by our old camp we follow up a willowy stream that runs under bents edging a sandy plain somewhat willow-grown also, with Skialdbreið ever on our left, look-ing no otherwise than when we saw it weeks ago from the east side of it, for in short it is quite round. Then over a neck of shale and rock called Tröllahals (Trolls' Neck) into a great wide sandy valley, going utterly waste up to the feet of

[1] See pages 76, 77. Ed.

Skialdbreið, and with a small stream running through it. We
are now turning round Skialdbreið,[1] and can see on his south-
west flank two small hills lying that are perfect pyramids to
look at from here. We are drawing near to the spurs of Armansfell now, and the wide plain narrows as a hill on our left
shuts out the view of Skialdbreið, and then we are in a great
round valley of dark brown sand as flat as a table and almost
without a pebble on it: the shoulder of Armansfell, the haunt
of the land-spirits, rises on the south-west of the valley, and
in that corner is a small tarn, for in fact in the wetter times
of the year the whole valley is a lake except these slopes on
which we are riding now: the valley, open at the side we rode
into it, is quite shut in everywhere else, but at the east corner the hills sink into a low neck, which we make for, and
scaling it, are in a pass with shaly sides scantily grass-grown
here and there. My heart beats, so please you, as we near the
brow of the pass, and all the infinite wonder, which came upon me when I came up on the deck of the "Diana" to see
Iceland for the first time, comes on me again now, for this is
the heart of Iceland that we are going to see: nor was the
reality of the sight unworthy; the pass showed long and
winding from the brow, with jagged dark hills showing over
the nearer banks of it as you went on, and betwixt them was
an open space with a great unseen but imagined plain between
you and the great lake that you saw glittering far away under
huge peaked hills of bright blue with grey-green sky above
them,[2] Hengill the highest of them, from the hot-spring on
whose flank rose into the air a wavering column of snow-
white steam.

Down through the pass now, which gets so steep that we
have to dismount, and so narrow that its sides hide the distant view as we get lower, till where the pass, still narrow,
widens into Jóruskörð, so called after a witch-wife of ancient times, we can see the great grey plain before us, though

[1] The note-book says they had now been round three sides of
Skialdbreið, "and he is just the same on every side." Ed.
[2] On the other side of which was our first encampment.

166

the nearer mountains now hide Hengill and those others
beyond the lake: now as we get toward the mouth of the
pass there rises on our left a little peaked hill, called the
Maidens' Seat, because the other side of it looks into the
meadows of Hofmannaflöt (Chieftains' Flat), where the men
returning from the Althing used to hold games, the women
looking on from the hill aforesaid. The pass comes out presently on to grass and bush-grown banks above the meadow
which lies perfectly flat and green under grey cliffs on the
other side which fall away as they sweep round to us into
grass-grown slopes. Westward it opens into the great plain,
which is hidden from us again by the slopes on our right: it
was a beautiful and historical-looking place.

So on we rode till we were fairly in the plain: I had hung
back a little to pick up one of the horses, who had gone wandering after the sweet grass on the banks of the Chieftains'
Flat, and when I galloped down after the others I found them
all halted in the first of the plain laughing preposterously, on
these grounds: you must know that the Icelandic ponies
don't jump much, rather running down and up a ditch or
up and down a wall: well, as they galloped down into the
plain there lay before C.J.F.'s horse a deepish rift, unseen by
C.J.F., whose little dun ambler saved him from losing all
chance of laughing again by suddenly making up his mind to
a good jump, so that there they were safe on the other side,
and we all looking at it as the best of good jokes.

We were now fairly in the plain of the Thingmeads; the
great round masses of Armansfell scooped here and there into
shallow dales (dal-verpi, dale-warps), with a bunch of snow
lying on them in places, is the north boundary of it, and opposite to that on the other side of the now unseen lake is the noble Hengill, and its flanking mountains: these two change no
more for us, but on the south-east we have at first a ragged
toothed wall of clinker running down from the flank of
Skialdbreið, which fails after a while, into a gap through which
pours the great sea of lava down the slowly sloping side of
Skialdbreið. As we ride along (over the lava now) we come

167

opposite to a flat-topped hill some way down the lava-stream, and just below it opens a huge black chasm, that runs straight away south toward the lake, a great double-walled dyke, but with its walls tumbled and ruined a good deal in places: the hill is the Raven-burg, and the chasm the Raven-rift.[1] But as we turn west we can see, a long way off across the grey plain, a straight black line running from the foot of Armansfell right into the lake, which we can again see hence, and some way up from the lake a white line cuts the black one across. The black and the white line are the Great Rift (Almanna-Gjá) and Axewater (Öxará) tumbling over it. Once again that thin thread of insight and imagination, which comes so seldom to us, and is such a joy when it comes, did not fail me at this first sight of the greatest marvel and most storied place of Iceland.

When we first came into the plain, it was on the edge of the lava, sandy but grown over with willow and grass; we are on pure lava now which is also far from barren, being much grown about with grass and willow, but chiefly birch; every-

 where, however, the bare molten rock shows in places, never tossed up in waves but always curdled like the cooling fire-stream it once was, and often the strands or curdles are twisted regularly like a rope.

 Over this lava-plain we rode to a little stead called Hrauntún, that lay on a low mound of soft grass, with a few great boulders scattered about it, rising like an island from the much riven lava-sea; there we struck the regular road from the south-east to Thing-vellir, and hastened along it at about eight o'clock on the loveliest and clearest of evenings. On our way we crossed by a narrow bridge-like rock over a terrible chasm, deep, straight-sided, and with water at the bottom, into a little sunken plain nearly round, all grass-grown and smooth and flat, round which the lava has run without breaking into it: a small stream follows the inside of the lava wave

[1] Hrafna-björg, Hrafna-gjá.

168

nearly all round this strange place, and through its opening we ride into the lava again; over a wave-top and into the trough of it, as it seems, and then on to another wave—and lo, there we are on the lower side of the Great Rift, a grass-grown, shrub-grown slope, with a huge wall of grey rock rising on the other side of the chasm, as perpendicularly as though a plummet had ruled it. It was getting dusk when we got there, and we had hit the Rift rather high up, so we rode straight down toward the lake along the Rift-side, the great wall with a fantastic coping of clinker ever on our right till we saw at the end of a bight of the lake, an undulating bright green tún with a church and stead on their little mounds, and between us and them a flat green plain with Axewater wind-ing about it most sweetly, till, straightening itself on the Rift-ward side of the stead, it ran straight for the lake widening as it went. So we rode down into the flat and galloped over turf and stream till we were in the lane of the stead, and pre-sently came to a halt before the door of the priest's house, having made a thirteen hours' ride of it from Reykholt. We found here two set of travellers who had come over with us: one a hair-brained queer chap named Watts, who had a great turn for climbing everything, and who had possession of the church with his photographic gear; the others who were housed in the stead were two Cambridge men who had had a queer journey from Reykjavík to Stykkisholm by smack first, and afterwards to Skagafiörðr & Drangey, and so back, nearly without a guide. As for us, we got leave to encamp in the tún down by the side of Axewater, and soon had our tents up on a beautiful piece of mossy turf close to the water's edge, almost under the shadow of the Great Rift, whose wonderful cliff rose into the moonlit sky a few rods on the other side the river, and was all populous with ravens that kept crying out and croaking long after we were settled there. There, Evans compelling me, I lighted a fire and did my cook's office, sore against my will; for partly I was somewhat tired, and partly I was lazy and dreamy: bed came shortly after that, and then sleep with happy dreams enough, as almost always in Iceland.

Saturday, August 26th. In the same place.

WE got up to a most beautiful morning, warm and
soft like a fine day of latter May in England. We
were most delighted with our camp and all about
us: the flat of the meadow ends a few yards lakeward of us
in grassy mounds that come close up to the water's edge:
the little Axewater is spread out before us shallow and slow-
running as it nears its end in the lake: between us and the
stead-garth lies a queer little washing-tub of a boat to ferry
one across; on the other side is a smooth space of grass gradually sloping up to the lower or broken-down wall of the
rift, which is pretty steep too at this end, except where a gap
nearly opposite the house leads one into the rift itself.

Breakfast over, I go with Magnússon to call on the priest,
who leads us presently on to the Lögberg (Hill of Laws),
the heart and centre of the old Icelandic Commonwealth.
One passes by the church and through the church-yard which
is on a higher part of the mound than the house: in the
church-yard stands a stone called the Yardstone which is as
old as the thirteenth century, and has the Bremen ell marked
out on one side, and the English yard on the other. Thence
we go down a little and come on to the side of a deep rift in
the lava which splits into two arms, leaving a little island in
the midst bridged by a narrow space on which two men could
barely stand abreast: when you are in the island it widens
and slopes upward higher and higher till at last where the
two arms of the rift meet there is a considerable cliff above
the dark dreadful-looking rift and its cold waters: a dozen
yards from this is a little mound rising from the surface of
the island, which, if the HILL of LAWS is the heart of Iceland, is the heart of the Hill of Laws, for here stood the
Speaker at Law, and every year gave forth the law: the whole
island is not a large church for the ceremony: it might hold
some five hundred men close packed, but surely 'tis one of
the most dramatic spots in Iceland, and Grim Goatshoe,
who picked it out for the seat of the Althing, must have been
a man of poetic insight. It is a good deal raised above the

'* He had a penny for his pains from every householder of Iceland.

170

level of the valley of Axewater; the rift all round it is deep
and wide; I should say sixteen feet wide at the narrowest,
where you can see many many feet below the rocks all blue
and purple through the clearest water in the world; this is
the place that they call Flosi's Leap, for tradition (not the
Njáls Saga) says that Flosi the Burner leapt across it to join
his men who were drawn up outside the Berg: and they say
he was in all his arms when he leapt.

The Hill of Laws is all covered with sweet deep grass and
the heath berries grow all down the sides of its rift. As you
stand here you look, as I said, across the grassy valley through
which Axewater having tumbled over the sheer height of
the upper wall of the Great Rift, and cleft the lower wall
through, wanders serpentine, making little sandy or grassy
islets as it goes, the most obvious of which, a mere patch of
turf nearly level with the river, but in the very midst of the
plain, is called the Battle-Holm, because there the judicial
combats were held.

You must suppose that only the Lawman and some of the
chiefs with the jurors of the courts had their place on the
Hill of Laws, the main body of the people were on the other
side of the water-filled rift, which in fact made the Hill of
Laws a fortress easily defensible in those days so lacking in
good shot-weapons.

Across the plain of Axewater, on the first
slopes of the lower wall of the Great Rift were
set up the booths of the different districts[1]
going all down the Rift-side right to the lake:
just opposite where the stead now stands is a breach in this
lower wall through which runs the Reykjavík road; and the
slope on the lakeward side of this is known as the site of
the booth of Snorri the Priest, whereby he stood with his
men in this very gap in the Rift-wall at the Battle of the Althing, prepared to help the winners moderately, and make
peace if he could do so to his own advantage.[2]

Just in the very midst of the Hill of Laws rises a low mound

[1] Consult the plan of the Althing in Dasent's Burnt Njal.
[2] See Njála: The Battle at the Althing.

regular in shape, and still having on it signs of the concen-
tric rows of seats on which the jurors of the courts sat.

You must not forget when thinking of all this, that the
huge wall of the Great Rift does verily bar the whole plain
from the slopes of Armansfell to the lake, so that no ordinary man could scale it except in that one place by Snorri's
Booth aforesaid; and the long line of it cuts clean against the
sky with never a mountain rising over it till Armansfell
thrusts up a broad shoulder at the further end.

So back to the stead, for we have a mind to catch fish for
our dinner: the priest tells of the whereabouts of his boat,
and we have a half-hour's stumble over intricate lava till we
come to the side of a little creek of the lake where the boat
lies: we launched it and got in and rowed out into the middle
of the lake, a great sheet of water some twelve miles by eight
with an island lying in the middle looking like a broken-
down crater, but all grass-grown now. The day was most
beautiful and sunny, but if all lakes are as I fancy melancholy,
just think of an Icelandic one! the great spiky hills on two
sides of it, the black rift and heavy grey Armansfell behind
us, and on the other side the grey lava going up in one long
slope to the boss of Skialdbreið, bounded by that rocky
screen aforesaid, and three separate hills thrusting up out of
the lava-sea: the spiky hills were very dark in spite of the
sunny day and the deep water (how deep it must be) green
like a cold sea.

We had to sit (five of us) pretty close in our boat, Evans
and I holding the rods, while Gisli and C.J.F. rowed, and
Magnússon baled with a used-up tobacco tin, for the boat
was both crank and leaky. We pulled across a wideish bay,
toward some scarped rocks where in one corner was a beautiful little grassy slope: near by there where the water shallowed to some fourteen feet, and was so clear that one could
see every smallest cranny in the rocks below, we caught two
trouts and a char, and then landed on the grass slope aforesaid, and ate and lay about a while till the afternoon was worn
somewhat, and then pulled back quietly, skirting the shores

172

of the bay: we saw as we pulled along a company riding along Thing-
among the lava toward Thingvellir by the Geysir road. So vellir
back to the creek from which we started, where by the priest's
desire we drew his set nets for him, taking out of them seven
great char and a trout. The Icelandic char by the way is a
strange looking fish, purple-black on the back of him, getting lighter and greener down the sides, and speckled with
grey spots, and then his belly orange-chrome as if laid on
with a house-painter's brush: and the fins are dark grey bordered with white. Back we stumbled to camp, and as we came
into the home-mead met the company aforesaid, dismounted
now & wandering about: they are a parson, Frank Holland,
son of the old carle Sir Henry, and two other quiet-looking
people: but the parson looked a queer phenomenon out
there. We asked news of England where nothing had happened, and so went off to our own place to cook and eat dinner. After dinner the Cambridge men invited us into the
house, to have a glass of grog: we pricked up our ears at this,
as our own grog had by this got so bitter from kicking about
in imperfectly seasoned oak kegs, that it was better physic
than grog: so we sat down in the little parlour, and hot water
and sugar came out, and then a tin bottle of whiskey, which
coming out of the tin bottle proved to be as black as a shoe;
and the end of it was that I had to go back to our camp to
fetch up a keg of our own bitter whiskey to treat ourselves
and the rest of the company withal. So to bed somewhat late.

Sunday, August 27th. In the same place.
I LAY abed while a light rain was falling on a warm morning, and listened to the ravens croaking and sweeping
round our tent, wondering sleepily whether they would
get our fish, that hung up on our tent-pole, as they brushed
quite close to where we were lying, and croaked the while in
an excited manner; however, when I got up presently I found
the fish untouched, and the morning clearing and so we made
our breakfast in great content. I had heard a report that the
Anglican parson meditated church after the manner in Eng-

land, so, wandering about presently, I met him and Magnússon just come in from the Lögberg. I told the latter I was
thinking of going across into the Great Rift: whereon the
parson offered to ferry me across the Axewater by the washing-tub of a boat aforesaid; thereto I agreed, and C.J.F. went
with me, and the parson went his ways back when he had
seen us safely on the grass on the other side, and as I heard
afterwards, straightway led the whiter sheep of his flock off
to the little church where the ceremony ran its course.

All that had nothing more to do with us than that I thought
it civil of him. C.J.F. and I went along this side of the Rift
till we came on the mound that still marks Snorri's booth
beside the steep road that leads into the Rift: between the
two walls of which here the space is clear of rubbish and is
smooth and grass-grown, and two or three of our own
ponies are grazing hard by. When you are fairly withinside,
the broken-down wall, though of course both lower and
more irregular than the other side, does still nevertheless
look like a wall; but on the other side the courses of rock lie
square and regular as if a mason had built them, and their
face is generally, not smooth exactly, but smoothly facetted;
dark grey of colour they are, save that where anything sticks
out, the flat top of it gets covered with heathy plants. The
top of this wall is a crest of most fantastic shapes; a pillar here
with a skull on the top, a slim pinnacle here carrying a huge
stone, a row of stakes eaten into and crumbling: all manner
of strange things. Looking down the Rift you can follow up
its two walls till the sky is blocked up at last by Armansfell
grey and heavy. The sun was shining brightly now, and as
we walked on away from the lake we agreed that it was the
hottest day we had had.

Some furlong's space from where we entered the Rift the
way was blocked by Axewater, which, falling over the upper
wall about three hundred yards higher up, brings down a
wall of rubbish here, and at last cleaves a way for itself through
the lower wall into the plain, though once I imagine it must
have run all along the Rift till it reached the lake: however it

174

has now made for itself a clean breach of about six feet wide
in the lower wall, through which it runs after having collected
its waters together in a deep clear pool; so that standing on
its splashed stones one can see, looking over the edge of the
water between the gap, the plain below with its winding
stream and the cows and horses feeding about, and the long
line of the slope where the booths once stood.

The deep pool above mentioned was the place where they
used to drown warlocks and witches in the later or mediaeval
times, casting them down from the top of the Rift above it.
Past this we came again on to a most soft and beautiful space
of sward, and then we came to the falls of Axewater, the
middle fall, that is, where after its first sheer tumble, it has to
scramble out of the ruin of stones it has washed into the Rift.
We both set about climbing over this but I found it rather
too much for me and gave it up. C.J.F. went on without me
right away to the foot of Armansfell, and told me afterwards
that at first the Rift was yet clearer than before and very beautiful, but that as you got to Armansfell it got more blocked
and kept on getting less and less open and defined. As for me,
turning back, I climbed the lower wall near the breach aforesaid, and walked along its steep side till I came to the gap by
Snorri's Booth, and so into the Rift again, with my face turned
toward the lake now. This is the highest and most wonderful part of the Rift; it makes a slight turn toward the east a
little way nearer the lake than opposite the gap by Snorri's
Booth, and just there it sends out a huge bastion as regular
as though it were really nothing else: this bastion the Reykjavík road climbs by a sort of broken stair, up which I went
now, and came out on the great lava-plain which lies level
with the lips of the Rift, ten paces from which you could have
no guessing of the stupendous chasm, or of anything but
some gentle wave in the once molten sea of rock. There were
strange deep clefts in the lava up there that I looked into, low
down, in which the ferns and meadow-sweet grew richly,
though the snow lay yet at the bottoms of them. So I went a
little further on the road and then sat down on a flat stone and

looked about: I was a little higher now, so I could see all
across the great valley, and all the lake was spread before me
with its winding bank of huge dark-blue mountains; and
over the shoulder of the lower wall I could just see the stead
and its bright green tún, and our own little camp beside the
clear shallow water: it was a most lovely day like the finest of
May days in England (when we get them fine) windless and
warm but neither hot nor close. I sat there a long time and
then slowly wandered back to the ferry, where I found the
boat on my side, but mooning managed to drop first one, and
then the other scull over-board, and there floated helpless
till first a little girl tried to shove me over one of the sculls;
second a boy came down to help her; third the priest tried to
reach me with a salmon spear; and fourth Geir Zoega (whom
I had'nt seen for six weeks) stepped gravely into the shallow
water, and pulled the little cockle-shell ashore. Then I went
to the camp which I find, rather to my joy, deserted, and lay
down and tried to write my journal, but could not, for a
strange lazy sort of excitement that was on me, made up of
half a dozen things. At last I saw the others coming, all save
C.J.F., who was still in the Rift, so I set off again to the Hill
of Laws and lay there a long while in the mossy grass, while
the day grew fairer yet if it might be as it drew towards evening, and over the slopes of Armansfell lay one of those (to
me) unaccountable flat rainbows or mist bows.

So at last I turned to go home [1] remembering that I had to
cook the dinner, and just by the garth wall I found the Anglican parson, Evans, and one of the Cambridge men: the two
latter were handling their guns and fidgetting about, so I asked them if they had taken them out to clean. Whereon they
nodded and winked at me most mysteriously, and presently
the parson turned his back and walked away, whereon my
two fools ran like skirmishers down by the wall, trying to
hide themselves and guns, pursued I must say by my indignant scorn, which was not voiceless. So they crossed the river
and presently rose up a noise like the bombardment of a

[1] He sat about the rocks and ate blueberries till he could find no
more, and then remembered about the dinner. Ed.

town,[1] for of course a very pop-gun fired off among these huge cliffs sounds tremendous: still however they seemed to think that the parson would not be the wiser if they came back quietly, which they did in about an hour, hiding their guns under their coat-flaps, and pulled out from their pockets three or four brace of ptarmigan. Excuse this stupid story but the undying respectability that these gentlemen had carried out to Iceland really did strike me at the time.

So we fell to dinner, and it was growing dark when we had done; the evening had clouded over; strange heavy clouds hung above Hengil, mingling with the steam of the hot springs there; a soft wind blew from the south across the lake, and we went to bed expecting a wet day on the morrow.

Monday, August 28th. In a house at Reykjavík.

NOR were we disappointed: I gathered the wreck of my last cooking together under a thick drizzle, and by then we had breakfasted it had begun to pour; in the midst of which by nine o'clock we rode away from our last camp in Iceland, going into the Great Rift, and up that broken stair of the bastion aforesaid. The rain increased rather than not, but the wind was warm, and we minded it little. The two Cambridge men and their guide went with us, so that we were quite a big body of horse; the road was good steadily, and we went a fine pace; we could see little because of the driving rain; but if we had seen more I could tell you little about it, for excitement about my letters quite swallowed up everything else in me; and I was only glad that we went so fast. We stopped to bait in a fine valley surrounded by great cliffs called Seliadal, & there we ate in the downpour and rode on again in about half an hour. I remember I noticed after that a troop of men driving home sheep, who seemed to cross our path without our meeting them in some queer way. At last we stopped again, with the rain nearly done, in a little plain near Helga-vatn, and a mile or two further on we came (with a great jump in my heart) to the sea, and riding past a creek or two, we could see, a long way off, the beacon

[1] "of Paris" the note-book says. Ed.

on the hill above Reykjavík, and very dimly the harbour and ships lying there. Then we turned from the sea a little, and presently our road ran into the one that led to Bolavellir, our first camp in Iceland: thence away the road was almost like a road in England, and we swung along a great pace, keeping quite close together, the horses knowing well that they were coming near their journey's end. Nothing happened except that once Gisli, charging over a stony piece of ground after a straying horse, fell horse and man such a fall that I thought he must have broken his neck this time, but he was none the worse for it, and only laughed as he picked himself up. There we were, past the beacon, and into the little town, and I, heeding not other people, galloped my best to Mistress Maria's house, jumping off my horse (Mouse to wit) just six weeks to the minute since I had mounted him before by the paling of the queer little weedy-looking garden before the black, white-windowed cottage that I have seen in night dreams and day dreams so often since. Well, Miss Sæmundson, who met me, presently told me that there were no letters for me there, so off I galloped for the post office. Why doesn't one drop down, or faint, or do something of that sort, when it comes to the uttermost in such matters? I walked in quite coolly in appearance, and gave Mr Finsen my name scribbled big on a piece of paper; he shuffled the letters and gave me eleven; I opened one from Ellis there and then, thinking that from him I should hear any bad news in the simplest form; though indeed the eleven letters at first glance did somewhat cure my terror, for there was no one dead at least.

So home I went soberly to another lodging than last time, and thence, after reading my letters with not more than the usual amount of disappointment and wondering at people's calmness, I suppose, to Mrs Maria's house again, where was dinner, and the courtly old carle, Sir Henry Holland, whose age (eighty-four) I thought was the most interesting thing about him. I was rather low, after all, and cowed by the company, and a sense of stiffness after our joyous rough life just ended. So to bed.

178

Tuesday, August 29th. In a house (Geir Zoega's I think) in
Reykjavík.

A WILD broken morning: the "Diana," which was away
at Hafnafiorð yesterday, came in again in the night,
and lies there now, a sweet sight to my eyes. It was a
day of nothings, inexpressibly dull after our old life: trouble
about selling our horses, a business full of shilly-shally—
early bed was the only comfort.

Wednesday, August 30th. In the same place.

A WET day and stormy: the only thing that happened
was our going to see the museum which has a great
deal of interesting things in it, ancient, mediaeval, and
modern art even the latter differing little from the thirteenth-
century forms. All else was shilly-shally about the horses,
and people saying that we could never start on Friday the
day appointed. In spite of all that my spirits rose towards
evening; for I felt somehow that nothing could keep me from
starting now. This day also we overhauled our stores, and
gave the greater part of the surplus to Eyvindr and Gisli to
their great joy and handshaking. Also we sold the horses this
evening to Geir Zoega.

Thursday, August 31st. In the same place.

WEATHER worse than ever, raining fearfully, and
blowing great guns right in our teeth for Berufirth.
Also this morning, as I lay in a very clean bed in a
very clean room, I saw a Louse crawl just below my chin
across the bed-clothes: the place was so clean that the infer-
ence was that I myself was lousy, which probability was plentifully rubbed in by my fellows, I assure you.

There seemed little chance indeed of our sailing next day,
but my assurance that we should did not abate at all. We
turned to at packing up which took us till about four in the
afternoon, at which time we went to dinner at Dr Hjaltalin's,
a great feast honoured also by the Governor. We are merry
enough there drinking all kinds of toasts, and at last, when

we had gotten to coffee, comes a message from the skipper of
the "Diana" that the mails are on board and that we shall
sail at 6 a.m. to-morrow.

So going out I find sure enough that the rain has left off
and the wind fallen, and home we go to our lodgings to see
about getting our luggage on board, Eyvindr and Gisli
working with us in great joy at their gifts. So to bed very
tired, for a few hours.

Friday, September 1st. On board the "Diana" off the south
coast of Iceland.

UP at half-past four, and after finishing packing, down
to the strand whence Eyvindr and Gisli rowed us
aboard at about a quarter to six. The ponies were
taken aboard last night, and there they are now looking prepared for everything. The wind changed to a fair wind in the
night; but the weather does not look promising, and the
captain is inclined to chaff us about our probable fate.

There lay a large English schooner yacht just ahead of the
"Diana" which had come into the harbour yesterday afternoon; a boat put off from her presently and discharged a man
on our deck, a friend of Evans, who after having been three
weeks in coming here from Glasgow and walking about
Reykjavík in the wet for an hour or two yesterday afternoon,
is going back this morning with us to England.

Well, we shook hands with Eyvindr and Gisli, and they
got into their boat and went back home: they had been very
hard-working friendly trusty fellows to us, and contented
and good-humoured to a marvel.

Then came the Magnússons on board, late and hurried,
the anchor came up and the ship's head turns south again,
and in a minute or two we are steaming down Faxafirth. We
got sail on the ship when we were round the corner, and went
on steadily enough: poor C.J.F. collapsed at once into his
berth; I was a little sick at first, but soon got better again.
About nine o'clock p.m. we made the Westman Islands, and
lay-to under the huge cliffs in the dusk to deliver our *one*

180

letter: a light came up on the sea and faded, then came up South
again, and presently a boat was by the ship's side, a man coast of
clambered on deck, and three minutes afterward we had left Iceland
that melancholy place behind. So to bed.

Saturday, September 2nd. On board the "Diana" off Berufirth.

UP and on deck, whence there is nothing to be seen
but rainy grey sky and sulky grey sea not very rough.
We get on well enough till about 3 p.m. when the
weather gets somewhat thick, and we sound again and again,
the captain being nervous of getting too near this iron coast
with its toothed hidden rocks. At last we see a fishing smack
lying-to ahead, and the captain hails her for information and
finds we are about seven miles from shore, which is too close
as things go. I was touched at the sight of the round-bowed
craft washing about on the grey seas, and her men hanging
over the bulwark with their fishing-lines, all looking so familiar to that unresting hard life. So on again, but before night-
fall the skipper gave up all hope of getting into Berufirth that
night, and we lay-to at last for the night, rolling quite as
much as was pleasant; yet I slept.

Sunday, September 3rd. On board the "Diana," somewhere
between Iceland and the Faroes.

THE first turn of the screw woke me about three this
morning, and we were soon in the head of Berufirth
but had to wait for a pilot to take us in to Djúpivogr
(the trading-station) as it was still rather thick. A sad dripping
misty day it was when we cast anchor in the harbour; after
the first quarter of an hour the mountains were not to be
seen, nothing but the dripping shore, and the black houses
of the merchant-stead. We went ashore for an hour or two,
had coffee in the merchant's house, looked over his store for
fox-skins and found none: then C.J.F. and I wandered away
among the rocks inshore, happy enough if not exactly extremely well. At noon the signal-gun was fired, and we went

aboard, and were off presently, and the last I saw of Iceland was but the shadows of the rocks dimly looming through the mist. The pilot's boat towed alongside of us; I watched it going through the water cold green under the shadow of our sides: the pilot's son sat in the stern, a tall handsome looking youth about eighteen: "wide-faced, grey-eyed and open-eyed," the very type of a northern youth, as he sat looking dreamily out to sea. His father went over the side into the boat presently and they cast off, and soon even the shadows of the rocks faded into the mist, and I had seen the last of Iceland: the last for ever I thought, though it seems now (June, 1873) that I am to see it again.

We made good way toward the south-east all day and toward the evening the rain ceased, the wind blew fair, and we were running ten knots an hour. I had been sick in the morning but was better now; well enough to stand well pleased in the waist of the ship, which is very low and near the water, and watch the moon come out over the shifting horizon made by the great Atlantic rollers, that came on thence till they towered over us and sank under our keel, and were away again to leeward. So to bed.

Monday, September 4th. On board the "Diana" in the harbour of Thorshaven.

UP at eight on a beautiful soft morning, the wind fair for the Faroes. Later on it clouded over and the wind got somewhat ahead, so that we didn't make the north-west Isle—Mykeness the headland of it is called—till about six in the evening: and it was about four hours' run thence to Thorshaven, for we couldn't go through the Westmannafirth this time, but round about by the sea way all along the outside of the islands.

It was a wild evening as we ran past them; a bright but watery sunset out to sea with great masses of clouds piled up on the horizon: over the islands brooded a heavy horizontal cloud, hiding them from the first hundred feet above the sea and upwards, except where here and there a sharp peak or

182

pyramid came up above the cloud. The sea was dull grey,
and then would strike the cliffs so that a great sheet of white
foam would run up them, to their top as it seemed: I still
thought it a solemn and wonderful place, though we were
not seeing much of it now. As we sailed on we passed by a
strange place I had heard of, where a stream running out of
a little lake falls right into the sea over the cliff's edge: every
now and then as we looked at it, the waves running in shore
would break at the rock's foot and run right up the cliff, and
"put out" the waterfall as it were.

So we sailed on through the gathering night, till we had
passed between the big island and a little skerry and so round
the last ness into the Thorshaven Firth. The sky had got
quite clear by now; the stars were very bright, and the moon
was rising from among some low fleecy clouds when I went
into the cabin for a while: thence Magnússon called me out
to look at some faint show of the northern lights: there was
a broad double belt of luminous white cloud all over the
middle of the sky, which as we looked at it was combed all
out into long streamers that at first kept their arched shape
over the sky, but gradually broke away into pieces, till the
moon growing high and bright seemed to scatter them, and
there was left only one long stripe like the tail of a great
comet going from the horizon to the zenith: that faded too
in a while, leaving nothing but moon and stars in a cloudless
sky. The anchor was down by now and we were lying close
off the little town, whose lights shone bright before us; and
so to bed I went in a quiet bed at last.

Tuesday, September 5th. On board the "Diana" between
the Faroes and the Orkneys.

ABRIGHT morning to begin with, but as the day wore
the sky clouded over and the wind rose; amidst which
we set off again at about 11 a.m. I watched the islands,
which were clear enough now, and noted all the openings to
their labyrinths till the day began to get very gloomy, when

I went into the cabin not wishing to have an ugly last impression of so beautiful a place as I had thought it, for I never thought to see it again.

The wind rose still and the sea with it, and we made but slow way, for we were going very near the wind, and at last I went to a very uneasy bed in which my feet were often much higher than my head; nor did I sleep much, though having my sea-legs now I was not sick.

Wednesday, September 6th. On board the " Diana" off the North coast of Scotland.

A VERY rough night it had been, and was rough all the early part of the day, and the wind was foul so that we made way slowly. We sighted Foul Isle about noon and Fair Isle a little after, and made the Orkneys about half-past three: after which wind and sea fell, and by then we had passed the Southernmost Orkneys about seven we were sailing on a quite even keel; we could just see the low bank of the islands against a beautiful golden sunset, as we sailed along in great rest and peace, and so went to bed joyously after last night's tumbles.

Thursday, September 7th. In England again.

U P at eight and on deck: a soft warm grey morning, the sea calm and grey; on our right is a long grey line, which is the Scotch coast, and a fleet of small undecked luggers we are running through is the Aberdeen fishing fleet. It turned out a beautiful day, but I thought the Scotch coast wondrous dull after all the marvels we had seen; even the Firth of Forth and its islands.

So there we were at last about seven in the evening laid along the pier at Granton, glared at stolidly by a line of Scotch men and boys, whom somehow it occurred to most of us Englishmen to fall to and chaff, which amused them and us till the gangway was thrust ashore, when I for my part departed without tuck of drum for Edinburgh as I had come.

I went into a tavern there with some of the Icelanders and
184

there was a drinking of healths, and farewells, and then Magnússon and Jón Sigurðsson went with me to the railway station, and I stood before the ticket-door quite bewildered,
and not knowing what to ask for. Lord, how strange it seemed
at first! So into the train, thinking what a little way it was
from Edinburgh to London.

I was curious to see what effect the trees would have upon
me when day dawned; but they did not have much; I thought
the houses and horses looked so disproportionately big for
the landscape that it all looked like a scene at a theatre.

So there I was in London at last, well washed, and finding
nobody I cared for dead: a piece of luck that does not always
happen to people when they are fools enough to go away beyond call for more than two months.

This is not meant in disrespect to Iceland, which is a marvellous, beautiful and solemn place, and where I had been in
fact very happy.

WILLIAM MORRIS finished writing this journal (from
notes made in Iceland at the above dates) on the 30th June
1873, intending to sail from Granton for Iceland the second
time on July 10th of the aforesaid year 1873.

> Æ man lifa
> Nema öld fariz
> Bragna lof
> Eða bili heimar

A DIARY OF TRAVEL IN ICELAND
1873

Thursday, July 24th. Resting at Breiða[bólsstaðr], on F[leet] L[ithe].

I BEGIN to make a few notes of our journey.

We sighted Iceland in the early morning of Tuesday [July 15th] about 1 a.m.; a bitter cold morning and the sea rather high, but bright enough: the first sight of land was just a few peaks thrusting up above a bank of cold grey clouds. After I had looked a bit at it I went to bed on a sofa in the cabin, and only woke again when I heard the bell go for half-speed: then I got up about five and found the morning nearly as cold as ever but brighter: the captain was about, we were just off Papey again, and unimaginably strange it seemed to me to be seeing all this over again on just such a morning as last time: I think I was no less impressed by it than before, and even the captain, a soft sailor sort of chap, told me that though this was the seventh time he had seen it so, he never failed to be moved by it—no wonder indeed. So we wore away an hour or two in the bay and then were off again with a very smooth sea, but cold enough it was with much more snow on the mountains than last time.

The Westman Isles were in sight next morning, the ship still going smoothly but a sharp and very cold wind blowing: the Westman Isles looked very green and inviting to us as we lay close under the great sheer cliffs of the off island where high up on terribly steep pieces of grass the sheep were feeding: the sea birds were a wonder to see here, as thick as bees about a hive, and lying on the lower grass slopes like great masses of white flowers. The wind blew harder and harder as we got from under the lee of the isles, so that we made up our minds that we should not get to Reykjavik till quite late to-day,[1] but we were not even so lucky as that: we went on pretty well till we had to turn the corner at Reykjaness and then

[1] Hecla white.

186

as I was sitting in the cabin expecting something to happen,
all of a sudden up went her bows, and a huge lurch sent us
all in a heap together, and presently a man came in and said
we had turned tail to the wind and were to lie-to till the gale
lulled.

Happily the wind blew off shore so we could lie-to comfortably quite close to land, under which conditions I went
to bed thinking we might be kept there twenty-four hours
unless there was a lull about sunrise. I slept, however, and
even dreamed a very pleasant dream of pretty farewells
from home and so forth, from which I only woke to hear the
screw going full speed and fell asleep again, well pleased to
think we were going on. When I woke again we were knocking about furiously but were really getting round the Skagi:
so I dressed and came aboard very sick, on a wild bright
morning, the wind blowing a gale, and rising still again. In
this wise we stumbled up the bay to Reykjavík and cast anchor about eleven on the Friday morning, and after a little
time Jón the saddle-smith came aboard and accosted me. I
confess I only half knew him at first; he is a regular type in
Iceland, broad-faced, stout-made, and blue-eyed: he gave us
good news of our horses and presently we got into a boat
and went ashore, and in an hour or two had settled everything, even our journey, and made up our minds to be off
the next day if we could, having only to wait for horse shoes
and the bringing up of the horses. Jón introduced the other
guide presently—Haldor, from Eyvindarmúli, on Fleet
Lithe, a little fellow with the most good-tempered of faces,
and not ill-looking either—I suppose him a crony of Jón's.

Dinner after this, packing of boxes and bed.

Saturday, 19th. In camp on the Battle Holm, Thingvellir.

WE really did get off this day about two, a fellow passenger[1] known to C.J.F. at Oxford who is bound for Geysir going with us to Thingvellir, and the usual troup of acquaintance riding out with us. My spirits, which had been rather low these two days with thoughts of distance in time and space and obstacles boded and unboded, rose again when I was once in the saddle and on the path made more familiar to me by the one intense sight of it than many years might have made another place: it was a bright day too, and not at all cold, though we hear on all sides that the early summer here has been the coldest that men remember. So when at last we took leave of our Icelandic friends in a thymy valley and rode away I felt happy and light-hearted and quite at home, to wit, as if there had been no break between the old journey and this.

This first day's journey was our last day last time; but then we rode it in furious rain and now it was fine but for a shower or two. Seliadal looked no otherwise than before, but when late in the evening the near hillsides failed, and showed us the great ridges and peaks of the Armansfell range with broken lights striking among the wildest and most awful of gorges among them, it was something new to me, for the rain had hidden all that before—and then at last I remembered all I had come to see and the land conquered my misgivings once for all, I hope. We sat down just here and let the train go on while we eat our bit of lunch (9 p.m.) and then rode on swiftly over a great upland plain—Lord, how waste and wild these lava deserts were, the great mountains on our left with the clouds drifting among them, and the stretch of grey (like hoar frost, remember) on our right, a few black peaks showing over them.

There was little change for a long time as we rode, till at last we began to see the great plain of the Thing-meads over the nearer brents: and still we rode on—it said something for my feeling at home, by the way, that when a horse ran

[1] John Henry Middleton. Ed.

188

over stock and stone about here and the two boxes came down with a crash my heart never rose to my mouth. So on and we grew all agog for the Great Rift after we had seen the Lake—it was a long [way] first though, down by brents running parallel to the rift mostly and so at last on to a plain of bare lava, and then without warning the horses stopped, Jón turned round and began to quote poetry to me, and indeed my own heart came into my mouth as we began to wind down that broken stair into the rift unseen as yet, till turning a corner of the stair there lay the great black wall before us in the midnight twilight, for that was the hour now.

We wound out of the rift to south-east and I settled on a smooth holm amidst the Axará[1] for our camp, which I afterwards remembered was the veritable battle holm. So we fell to work, and were some time housing ourselves and getting our dinner—for four make easier work than two. We went to bed about two and just before, I heard voices and saw a train of horses coming out of the rift carrying boards for the more part. So strange they looked and the whole scene was such a drama to me—but to bed I went and slept without dreaming.

Sunday 20th. In camp at Snorra Staðir—in Laugardal.

UP at 8 on a beautiful bright morning and C.J.F. and I on to the Logberg after breakfast, the sun quite hot and summery. The Logberg I find would hold quite twice as many people as I said before; it was unmown now and the grass was high in it and quite full of flowers, Loki's purse (money-rattle), buttercups, milkwort, white clover, cranesbill, one or two alpine flowers I can't name, and a most lovely little dark blue gentian: it was a very happy morning. Then to cooking dinner at which we feasted on the best of char, orange-coloured inside, and then the horses came up and we were off about two. We rode up by the rift awhile and then still on our old path to Hrauntun where we turned along the shores of the lake; and so up a steep birch-grown bent till suddenly we were on the Raven Rift, a most wild and strange

[1] i.e. Oxar-á, but usually spelt here Oxara. Ed.

189

place which we crossed by a sort of bridge or causeway—this rift is all tumbled together though it runs quite as straight as the Al[1]—I suppose because it is on the hillside.

Above this we came on to the bare lava again and then turning east came on to the most desolate Lyngdals Heiði that one can imagine on an afternoon grown cloudy and half-rainy now—rugged, torn and grey, the foreground all scattered with coal-black square stones of lava, on the south and east big flat-topped mountains showing, and on the west an awful empty gorge of black and grey between two hills, one all black like a huge cinder with rocks sticking out from it, the other a blunt-headed steep-sided mountain of small black lava stones, a few thin stripes of green running down its sides, where nevertheless some sheep were feeding: so nearer to this mountain, and going down hill round about its slopes that grew greener as we went and were quite covered with sheep and lambs—pretty to see them all running together to stare at us with timid eyes—so utterly different to our tallowy southland sheep, silky-haired with long crumpled horns all of them; some coal black, some sheeted [sic] or spotted, some a rich brown, and all most beautiful delicate little beasts. Next as we went there was a great plain of grass (Beitivellir) before us a little [raised] in the midst and the black mountains took a long sweep about it; amidst this plain we saw a many horses resting, and soon recognized them for the board-carriers; we met presently as we left Beitivellir and perforce rode with them some way: a strange and picturesque sight they made, the boards dragging on either side of the horses and other loads as well—barrels, stock-fish, skins, etc., all on the most primitive saddles; there were about 100 horses of them in all I should think: the drivers, some of whom got into talk with us, were as primitive as their saddles—altogether it was well worth seeing. Up again over other mountain spurs till we look into another wide plain, Laugardal, with two lakes in it—Apavatn, Laugarvatn—round the shores of the latter of which are many hot springs sending

[1] Almannagjá, the Great Rift. Ed.

their steam up into the air: it was getting very late by then we were in this valley, where we left the lake on our right and rode over rich pasture and marsh at the foot of the mountains, a drizzle of rain in our faces. It was nearly 12 when we drew rein at last at a little stead (not the one we were bound for) on the very slopes of the hills in a tun that was being mowed. We found with great looking a tolerably smooth place for our tent and pitched it with great expedition in face of the great hills. The stead seemed pitched down in a very pretty spot though it was a poor stead too, but there were two others close by. By the way, Jón is certainly an obstinate fellow and somewhat lazy to boot, though a good fellow too. Haldor is handy and cheerful, and quite a sweet-mannered little man, he also knows a few words of English and has the saga-lore at his fingers' ends. So to bed after a light supper of chocolate and cold bacon, I somewhat depressed, I suppose by an ungenial ending of a fine day and a cold I have got on me. I concealed it however.

Monday 21st. In camp in the tun of Scálholt.

I SLEPT well but woke up every now and then to hear the rain pouring down on the tent and the wind flapping it, but while we were at breakfast (chocolate and cold bacon) it cleared up for a little and we got away dry: we skirted the plain still by the mountain slopes and saw presently Miðdal and its little church, the stead we ought to have made last night; here the drizzling rain came down on us again and hid everything distant: it was charged too with fine dust that half blinded us and we seemed to be riding through a middling London fog.

Presently as we drew near a spur of the hills we had to cross, Jón went home to get us a guide across the ford of Bruará, and here the dust got a new and terrible significance, for the bonder told Jón there must have been an eruption somewhere as they never had sand storms in that part. As we turned up hill here the rain came on with a vengeance, and from here on to Scalholt I can tell you no more than my map

191

can, for we saw next to nothing. We came down to Bruará over a bog and crossed it, a fine clear deep river, into another bog, and in short rode through bogs till we came on to a little mound whence we could dimly see a wide water, the confluence of Tungufliot and White-water. Thence we got into another bog and over a ridge into a long valley all pure bog between two straight hillsides, along one of which we floundered till Jón showed us a mound on the other hillside which was Scalholt, so thither we turned by the least impassable way across the bogs, when lo, when we were halfway across, it cleared a bit and we could see the stead clear, a blue mountain rising in the distance over it, and below it a great bight of White-water, with a fine swelling mountain on the other side of it.

We were soon in the tún and pitched our tent in great haste, and just got it up before the rain came on again with wind enough to knock you down. This place once the seat of the South bishopric is now only a bonder's stead with a very big tún about it. As we got in here by 5 p.m., we determined to dine, so sent for a salmon down to the ferry and feasted off him and soup, trying our new cooking things which bore the trial (a severe one, my faith!) very well—the salmon, a twelve pounder, cost us about 1s. 4d. And now the rain set in again worse than ever but we shut up the tent and made ourselves snug and refused to be depressed, and so to bed and sound sleep.

Tuesday 22nd. In the church at Storuvellir.

IT rained hard all night, and we got up on a doubtful-looking morning expecting much such a day as yesterday, but were agreeably disappointed. Jón took us into the church to see the signs of the departed glories of Scalholt, the foundations of the Bishop's house, the school, the undercroft that led to the sacristy, the gravestones of bishops under the boarded floor of the present funny little church (not a bad building neither) or some of them out in the open air a long way west of the present church; finally two altar cloths with

a border of Icelandic silver to them, and a chasuble with fine
fourteenth century embroidery in good preservation. Then
we got to horse and away across that vile bog to the ferry over
Whitewater where it ran strong between two rocky knolls—
there was the usual long delay in ferrying, 1½ hours in this
case and then we set off again, the day ever bettering as we
went through sweet grassy meadows under a long down-like
hill on our right and on our left a tumbled mountain-country
dominated by Hecla, and Threecorner more in the foreground before us. Thence into a great sand waste dotted over
with knolls bound together by dwarf willow, and concealing
lava I suppose at no great depth. Thence past a stead on a
knoll in the midst of this on to more meadows again, where
we come presently on Thiorsá, up which we ride. Looking
from here some two miles over the plain is a mass of hill and
cliff quite indescribable but which strikes upon me as peculiarly Icelandic, though it is neither horrid nor grand, but
looks story-like—sharp slopes of grass rising from the plain
crowned with castle-like rocks, small peaks and house-roof
hills with long sweeps of valley between go to make it up.
Going on a while we come to the front of this where two
steads stand prettily on the slopes under steep basalt-crowned
hills for all the world like castle walls. The first of these is
Thrandarholt erst the house of a Landnamsman, Thrand
the Much-sailing. We are now getting near the place where
we intended to ford Thiorsá, and Jón goes up the stead to
get a man to show us the way to a waterfall on Thiorsa, and
the thingstead of the Arness Thing. We can soon hear the
roar of the fall, and are presently at the Thingstead, a pretty
grassy little valley nearly round, with the marks of the booth-
tofts all round it: indeed, it is certain that they did always
pick out an impressive place for their Thingsteads—the
riverward boundary of this runs up into a sharp cliff over
the river, looking down from whence you can see half of
Thiorsa tumbling its turbid white waters over a great wide
ledge of rocks of no great height certainly, say twelve feet.
Going down from this cliff one comes on a green bank by the

side of the fall, and can see the place thence (Hestaholt)
where Gunnar dreamed; by the waterside too is a big stone
traditionally called the sacrificial stone of this Thing. So on
over wide grassy plain, and queer to see a little two year old
bull how he came up to our train and bellowed at the horses,
to their great discomfiture, one after another as they passed;
close by him two ravens were making a sad noise. We were
now gotten to the ford[1] which Jón trying declares passable
though swollen by the late rain, but not good for the boxes
or milksops like me; so on we go to the ferry of Thiorsar-
holt which I have crossed before. The horses had a long way
to swim here and it was great fun to see them, and how much
cleverer some were than others to find their feet on the shoal.
So we all across with our luggage in the little boat, and off
presently to Storuvellir by the way I left it two years ago:
the old priest met us as we came into his yard and begged us
to come into the church as his house was being altered; so in
we came and found the chancel set out with a table and chairs,
and visible preparations for beds also: then he shook hands
again and thanked us for coming to see him, saying also that
his son would soon come in: the old gentleman had not
learned much English these two years to judge by his very
queer talk: but his son, who came in presently, talks English very well, and is a very modest nice young fellow: so
after a while supper in the chancel of the church, then bed in
the same and very sound sleep.

Wednesday 23rd. In camp at Breiða[bólsstaðr].

UP not over early and a great to do in lightening the
boxes as we have to come back here again before we
try the adventure of the Sand, and we want to have as
many horses as we can to fill their bellies till we come back:
the priest took us to see his new rooms; I was glad to see he
was like to have a snug house; by the way, the carpenter who
was at work there was named Kiartan Olafson.[2] At about
twelve we got to horse and away, the priest and his son go-

[1] Say half a mile wide.   [2] Laxdale Saga. Ed.

ing with us; we rode through the lava till it ended in a wall above soft green meadows along Ytri Ranga, which we crossed a little below where I crossed last time—neither are we going the same road as I went then. We rode first to a farm where the bonder could tell us of a trusty guide across the Sand, and went in, when there ensued a long talk on the probable man between the two Guðmunds, [the parson and his son] the bonder, Jón and Haldor, of which I understood about a quarter, the principal point being that the likeliest man in other respects was a drunkard. So thence we rode away over the same meadowy country: low rises away from the river and the flats about it broken by holts each crowned with its stead, till riding up a low mound we came to the stead of Thingskalar, where in a hollow on the hillside amid the tún are the tofts of the Thingbooths—again it is a beautiful place: a deep gill on one side cuts it off from a sandy wilderness on the other, when the lip of the vale rises up, it is level with a slope leading down to the river and its wide grassy meadows—the booths seem to have made an irregular street ending with a round mound, presumably the doom-ring, and a big booth for the Godi. We stepped one of the biggest and made it eighteen paces. They show you here two booths side by side with only one wall between them and call them the booths of G[unnar] and N[jal],[1] a thing not hard to believe. Here our hosts left us and we rode at once on to a desolate sand waste flat for a long time till it grew broken by hills of lava, a most wild and horrid place though the sun shone bright on it, and the dark masses of the mountain from Heckla to Threecorner were striped with sun amidst the clouds. So on we rode till we came on to short grass just where a queer round knoll stood crowned with a sheep-fold and with other sheep-folds about it—more in the foreground than Th[reecorner] now I can see the well remembered hills about Vollr: and a short ride brings us to Reyðarvatn, a stead lying [on a] little lake of that name prettily enough, with a little stream coming out of the hillside and running into the lake.

[1] "The Story of Burnt Njal."

We go into the house here and have coffee, Jón and Haldor lying upon the beds in great comfort. However, Jón falls to talk with the goodman, and presently in comes a man whom Jón introduces to me as the brother of the bonder and a man who knows Sprengissand full well. So we engage him on the spot and I write in my best hand to Síra Guðmund to tell him not to trouble himself about a guide, and well pleased we are not to be stopped on this score. I note here that I am nothing like so anxious about our journey as last time. Well, we leave the stead behind us and come again on to bare sand and mounting up a slope of it have all the great plain before us on our right, all away to Eyrarbakki, while on our left Threecorner is getting more on our side and we can see Vollr under the hill. The sandy slope we are on is extra desolate I think, and our fine day is somewhat clouded over and threatening here; now we can see East-Ranga winding along before us, and a long way up it the falls of a small stream running into it that I remember crossing when we went from Vollr; soon we come to the edge of the sand and looking down can see a wide grassy and marshy valley with Ranga cutting it in two; high up on our side of the valley are two steads both called Hof; and as we come to the wall of the first Jón sings out "here Skamkel[1] dwelt, and Mord at the other stead." So we ride on across the plain and down the riverside, and cross by the ford where Gunnar fought thrice, and so on again to the rising ground which running down the hills from Threecorner is really the Lithe, though another side of it than what is called so; once upon this we are on the same road I went from Lithend to Vollr, and I wonder how familiar all seems to me—all save one place, which touched me very much on this evening now grown very fine again, whereas our last ride hereby was on a dull ungenial day: this where we, going among the slopes of the Lithe, are getting toward the corner, and can look into a long valley with a

[1] Skamkell, who lived at Lesser Hof. See "The Story of Burnt Njal." E.M.

stead or two in it sloping upward between two horns of hills
to a low green ridge over which Threecorner towers grey
and majestic in the clear evening with its three peaks, while
over the further corner of the near hills the ice of Eyafell
comes in sight. It was about half-past eight and the evening
sun cast long shadows of us across the green slopes and it
was [a] warm and serene evening. I had felt much moved all
day by the remembrances of Njala and as I looked up toward
Threecorner I suddenly asked Jón where it was the H
and the B   [1] met before they went on their unlucky errand. Jón pointed up to Threecorner and said there between
the three horns is called Flosidal: that made me feel quite
queer for I had quite made up my mind it must be there. I
wish you could see it, and what a fit place it is for such a plot,
the most marked mountain in all the south, grey among the
green, steep among the easy slopes, no house near it, like a
piece of another world it looked that evening among the wide
green pastures.

    Half an hour more and we came on to the enormous plain
of the Njala and so to the stead of B[reiðabólsstaðr] where we
were hospitably received by the lady, whose husband was out
at first but came in presently, a tall young fellow with a large
family of funny white-headed children. So after a good Icelandic supper, to bed in the tent in the churchyard, after a
very pleasant ride on a fine day.

Breiða-
bólsstaðr

Thursday, 24th, same place.

I WOKE towards morning by hearing such a row, three
dogs (as far as I could make out) careering round and
barking violently, with a raven for fugleman somewhere
amidst them making all sorts of queer noises; they went away
and came again nearer apparently, for this time two or three
of them went bump against a tent rope, shaking the tent and
howling dismally at his fall, while the raven croaked as if to
mock him. I was very warm in bed but curiosity fought a

[1] So in orig. See note. Ed.

197

long time in me with laziness till just as I was making up my mind to go and see what it was all about I went to sleep.

There had been a little rain in the night but it was a fine morning when we got up, and as it wore got both sunny and hot: a thermometer on the church wall marked 67 in the shade at 2 p.m. This was a day of rest which I spent in writing up diary, sewing on again ten buttons on my breeches, and for the rest idling not unmixed with eating, for they treated us very well at the priest's, who, by the way, must be a rather rich man, for this morning I saw them milking the cows and counted eighteen in milk, besides twenty other neat, so you can imagine that it rained milk and cream in his house. I note here that the other day after we had stopped at a little stead and drank between us four some two quarts of milk, the people, poor enough, did positively refuse with loud laughter to have a penny for it. So the day wore pleasantly enough, but in the evening the great Eyafialla mountains were quite hidden by low clouds and all looked to an English eye like very bad weather. So to bed.

Friday, 25th. In the tún of Eyvindarmúli.

AGAIN about four the concert between the dogs and the raven, only this time taught by misfortune they did not tumble over the tent ropes; again also I fell asleep before I could go out, so their performances are shrouded in mystery for ever.

The morning was bright and hot even, at least to us in our winter clothes. We set off at about half past eleven up the Lithe, only we went by a lower road than last time—[? we toiled] along the road as tame as barn door fowls. At last as we rode I remembered the place where we crossed Thverá from B[arkarstaðir] and Haldor pointing up the hillside said, "What's that stead called?" and I knew—Hlið[arendi], where, by the way, Haldor was born. However, we passed it for this time and made on for the cot where Jón lives: he had gone to Eyafjalla[1] yesterday to bring up horses and we were

[1] Jón had gone east to the Eyjafjalla country to purchase the horses. E.M.

to meet him at his own house; however, he had gone on to
Ey[vindarmúli], where Haldor's father is bonder and where
we were to stay the night, so a young fellow, a horse-couper,
who had had some dealings with Jón (and cheated him) rode
on to fetch him and after a while we, riding on quietly, met
him coming with the horse-couper. He seemed excited and
unhappy, for the fact was he had let the said horse-couper
cheat him (and us) about a horse; however, he prayed us to
go back to his house, and we rode along the sweet green
meadows again and to the very hill's foot to look at Mer-
kiáfoss, which we found a very beautiful place, the water
falling sheer from the last hole some seventy feet in a deep
hole in the sunshine, yet bright though the clouds were
gathering over the sea for a shower; so thence with Jón and
the horse-couper to Jón's own lodging at L[ithend] C[ot].
He lodges upstairs now in a queer little den marked off but
by a principal [1] unboarded from the bað stofa in which latter
were two women and two lads, one a remarkable looking boy
enough who lies on the bed combing his hair; one of the women has a queer little baby on her lap and when it begins to
howl she take a little bag (of sugar) and gags it with said bag
leaving the ends thereof sticking out of its mouth: a fine way
for it can't howl and is well content then. Jón, very unhappy
about the horse, sends for dinner for us, which comes presently and is set on a deal table which *must* have been made by
our firm. Jón won't sit down with us, to my great discomfort,
and so to eat, I and Charley sitting on two funny little chairs
and the horse-couper (damn him) on the bed. First we have
a kind of rice milk with plums in it and then boiled smoked
mutton, very good of its kind; this latter Jón consents at last
to eat. Then the things are taken away and ensues a wrangle
about a horse that no human being can understand, which
ends of course in our being cheated and the horse-couper
going to go off with two of our horses for one of his. Jón says
he is ill with sorrow at this and visibly is very downcast, but
recovers a little over reading some Sturlunga to me. Mean-

[1] A principal rafter; any one of the rafters upon which rest the pur-
lins which support the common rafters.—Oxford Dictionary. Ed.

while a boy has been sent to Eyvindar Muli to bring the other horse for our enemy, but comes back without him, for Haldor would not let him go without a written order from us; so we had all to set off at once thither, and found Haldor at home there and our tent seen far off neatly pitched in the tún for us. Haldor was very kind and hospitable but in a great rage about our bargain, so that it was with some difficulty I could persuade him to let the horse go, which at last he did, and took it out in chaffing all concerned, Jón, the horse-couper and us, me in special, nor do I think he will ever forget it and I was fain for the nonce to chaff him in return, advising [him] to take our axe and settle the matter *more majorum.* There had been a longish shower while we were sitting in Jón's room but it cleared off before we went away and was a very fine quiet evening while we stood about in this pretty place talking to the people. The bonder, Haldor's father, remembered me very well, and his second son (Haldor was away at the time) remembered that Magnússon and his father had talked about the decay of the wood in Thorsmörk. To bed.

Saturday 26th. In camp in Steppafil in Thorsmörk.
I WAS woke at about 4 a.m. by hearing the haymowers at work in the tun, and so went out of the tent into a flood of bright white sunshine without a cloud in the sky, the Westmanneyiar as clear as if they were but a mile off; then I went to sleep again till Haldor woke us with coffee at eight. It was a very fine sunny morning still with scarcely a cloud in the sky yet and very warm or hot even.

We went up in the ghyll near the house and bathed in the clear water as well as we could, considering it wouldn't quite cover us lying down, and so dressed and into the house to breakfast of roast mutton presently, and so about eleven were under way for Thorsmörk where we were to sleep for two nights: Haldor's brother and sister accompanied us—the latter a very good-tempered but, alack, a very plain Icelandic damsel, not a bit like Haldor, who is a good-looking fellow enough albeit a little man. I was very much excited about the

expedition, especially as the day was so fine: we rode up the
valley some little way and down to the side of Markarfljot,
but Jón, after a look at the river, thought ill of it there, and
turning, led us down stream till we were opposite Ey[vin-
darmuli]; there the river looked a fearful waste of waters indeed, and including all its sand-banks could not have been
less than half a mile broad. As we went along two huge sea
birds brown with white tips to their wings swept over our
heads to and fro, sometimes coming within a few feet of us,
and flying in the most lovely way.

Well, at this wide place, which was good for us because it
was wide, both Haldor and Jón tried the water, Jón setting
off first, and when he was in the thick of it Haldor going upstream instead of down as Jón went—in fact, I could see there
was a kind of rivalry between them as water-folk. Jón came
back first saying that it was pretty good, not much above belly
deep, but meantime we, watching Haldor as [he] went from
shoal to shoal and at last came out on the further bank, could
see pretty plainly that he had the best of it, so Jón led us off
that way; the young lady was set astride her horse, Bersteinn
her brother led her by the rein and Haldor, who was back
presently, led me, C. J. F. refusing that aid. However, even
this first time I had little of my old nervousness left about
this river work, except that the *horses* would seem to be backing when we went down stream; so safe and unwet we all
came across.

Markarfljót: the day got a little cloudier as we rode along
the awful wastes of Laugarness: the road was bad and we
didn't [get] on fast, especially as one horse ran away, being
frightened at his burden getting loose, for I must tell you
that only one thing frightens an Icelandic pony and that
is this; and a frightful-looking thing it is to see him (as he
invariably does) gallopping over stock and stone with the
loose box or bundle banging about his heels and two or three
fellows after him on foot if they can. This time it was our
blanket-bearer who had also got the guides' coffee-pot and

Markfleet cream-bottle, and he had soon banged off both bundles and then gallopped away as hard as he could split, up toward the Jokul, where he turned perforce and down the valley, the three chaps after him as hard as they could, we staying behind to look after the other horses; they came back in about half an hour with him, having lost their coffee-kettle lid and broken their cream bottle; and so off we set again, and after two hours very rough ride including the venomous little Steinholtsá came to the smooth grass of Goðaland just where [a] ridge divided the two valleys of Markfleet and Crossá, and presently we were in that awful place; all along we had had before us of course that terrible ice-capped wall I have told you of before: though I remembered it so well from last time my wonder at it had lost none of its freshness. We were however not to go the same way as before quite, even here, for when we came about opposite to where we mounted up before to that glacier-tail, having crossed Krossá once, Jón declared it would be impassable higher up, and we turned perforce into a little green valley on the lower or left side mountains and so scaled a strange height of mixed sand and rock round a peak named Vala Merkr, and fell a-riding over a most tumbled set of hills and dales of sand with huge masses of conglomerate stone making monstrous caves every here, then and there; now and again were patches of deep grass sprinkled with white clover, and the beautiful horned sheep were feeding everywhere. So up so high that we could look into one end of Thorsmörk which I can now see is a valley sweeping round from the Crossá to the Markfleet valleys. This way, though neither so terrible nor so beautiful as the valley way, was at least new to me—and moreover, when one was fairly up the hillside one could see how the whole place really went and the great glaciers above the rugged wall of rock running up in one place into the flat cone of Eyjafell: but first where the glaciers did not come low down was a great table-land at the top of the cliffs with peaks of its own and its own plain below them, and from that the buttresses of the higher dreadful ice-crowned mountains went up, and

202

most marvellous all this was to see, a world of mountains, like, Markfleet
above the mountains, all utterly inaccessible apparently,
for no sheep were to be seen there, and above it all, as aforesaid, Eyafell's ice in one part running right down into the
valley, and that dreadful ice-crowned wall with its caves and
trickling waterfalls—ah, what an awful place!

Coming about to the top of the ridge we had to cross, Jón
stopped us and would show us a cave, so we went with him
to the top of a very deep descent and he pointed out where
the cave lay into a mass of rock at the bottom, but the climbing up would have been impossible to me in my boots so I
said no; however, from here we could see all down the waste
of Markfleet, and also its course from up the valley, where it
came winding down from the Jokuls, but no longer going
manifold and level with the shingle but having cut for itself
a way between low steep cliffs in the stony table-land; beyond
this rise desolate black peaks from which a lowish bare ridge
broken with strange shaped cliffs runs, nor is any of the country high till you come to the Jokuls which even do not rise
so high on this side—but so barren and dreadful it looks and
yet has a kind of beauty about it. Now we go down a bit and
find Jón lying in wait for us with another cave, which not being so steep up to we manage to see; it is a little hole in an
enormous mass of rock that overhangs the narrow path below, there are three or four rough footholes cut in the face of
the rock by which Jón, being in skin shoes, manages to scramble up, and crawls into the cave where he sits like a reel in a
bottle some twelve feet above the path; the face of the rock is
all cut about with initials, and there are runes also cut in it but
whether these last are old I don't know. Now we go down a
very steep gorge...and we came into one of the Thorsmörk
valleys, Laugadal by name, little low grassy hills shutting [it]
in with a little brushwood on them and a clear brook running
amidst it; but we didn't stop there, Jón being intent on our
camping in a more remarkable place, and I wanting to camp
in the same place as I was in last time. However, when we
were now come into the main valley we saw the said place

203

called Stafaness, and Haldor said there was no water so we had better camp elsewhere; Jón got into a great rage at this (though it proved true enough in the end) as he was very anxious that we should camp in the pearl of the valley, but in spite of him we turned aside into this little valley much like Laugadal only shorter, and with more wood on the hillsides; there we pitched our tents upon very soft mossy grass on a rock's edge from two to three feet wide, the redwings twittering (they don't exactly sing) in the birch wood above us: the door of our tent fronted the main valley and looked right on Eyjafell where the great glacier comes lowest into the valley split by a ridge of black rock on whose flank was a rock just like a real castle to look at—here I fell to cooking dinner, and so to eat it and a pipe and bed.

Sunday 27th, the same.

WE lay abed till past nine, when we got up and bathed in a pool of the gill, which might take us up to the knees maybe, and then after breakfast mounted and rode into the main valley and down it toward the glaciers— passing by the wooded hillside where we were two years ago; crossed Krossá again and then yet again on the other side of the valley, and so went on till we were close under the huge wall of the glacier mountains where the whole valley really seems to end, Krossá coming from one glacier-tail and a little river from another, the two subvalleys being divided by sharp spiky tongues of ridges that run up to the huge sides of the Jokul; here we came on to a bit of green grass under another of those prodigious cliffs or stones of conglomerate, called Búðar Hamar, which rises rather more than perpendicular above the grassy knoll below it, a queer little cave is in the face of it rather than round the corner: the near cliffs give back from the valley here, and there are low slopes covered with birch scrub through which we walked, and lay down a little in the fine day; and so presently to our horses and back again to the side of Krossá which Jón declares to be unfordable but Haldor says is the same as earlier; however, Jón

wants to walk over Stampanef, the hill to which we came last
year, and so we make no opposition and go his way, getting
off our horses at the foot of the steep birch-covered hill and
letting them go over a lower sandy spur of it; it is heavy work
climbing up among the birch bushes, but Jón's enthusiasm
is very much excited by the place, and when we sit down
among the boughs high up the hill he says he would like to
live there always: indeed it is a beautiful place if a terrible, as
I told you before. So we are soon down the other side and
getting to our horses ride on and into our valley where we
have left the tents—just opposite this, by the way, but not
visible from our camp is one of the very strangest of those
Robinson Crusoe caves often mentioned. I forgot to say that
just before we left Búðar Hamar Jón took us to another cave
in the side of a rock with a very small entrance to it; into this
we all got by creeping and could stand upright in it easily
enough; it might have been twelve feet over all. Jón said it
was one of those caves they use when they go to get in their
sheep in autumn time; his imagination seemed queerly excited by being in it. The little valley looked very sweet and
quiet after the horrors of the big one, and we set ourselves to
making ourselves comfortable, cooked dinner, eat it, and
then drank a bottle of Madeira in solemn conclave in honour
of the occasion, after which the others went to bed and C.J.F.
and I spent half an hour in damming up the little stream to
make our bathing-place better, and so to bed (a very fine day
and evening).

Monday 28th. Eyvindar Muli.

GOT up and bathed and found our bathing-place decidedly deeper, and then presently breakfast and de-
camping—it was no use trying Crossá, so we had to
go the same way we came, up Laugadal in and over the hills.
The clouds began to come down on Eyjafell as we were about
this, and by then we were over Steinholtsá, were lying quite
low down on the hills, hiding the end of the Thorsmörk valley; but there was a bright line out to sea and the rain never

Markfleet came down: we came to Markfleet-side without any adventure except that C.J.F. crossing St[einholtsá] by himself, when we came up to him, we found him pouring the water out of his boots, for he had got into a deep place. When we came to Markfleet just opposite where we crossed two years ago, Haldor found us a ford by a very roundabout way. We were a long time in the water, and once Jón and I were very deep, being in quicksands, but I have quite lost all nervousness in the rivers now, and strange to say I can see the horses really going forward when the stream is running with them ; so over the black stone to Fliótsdal at a great pace, Haldor's brother and sister going on before us on what errand was obvious when we came there. It was a neat and pretty little house as I have mentioned before; there were cocks and hens strutting about and when I congratulated the bonder on them, he grinned and replied proudly that he had pigs also. After we had sat here a while dinner was obviously getting ready and in fact it was clearly a premeditated feast, and Jón and Haldor were taking us round in triumph: it was a very good dinner, only dashed by Faulkner complaining of toothache coming on, in despite of which he managed to stow away his share at table.

So the bonder led us out, and at the house door, lo, a pig which received nearly as much attention as we did, and many words of endearment from the goodwife, and seemed indeed quite conscious of his own importance: then over the meadows at a great rate to Barkarstaðir where we must needs go in and were welcomed by the bonder as before, the same awful idiot as before and the tall fellow (*nomine* Sigurd) who it seems was not the bonder's son but only a workman living in the house: he makes himself quite at home though, and Haldor introduces him as his dearest friend, and seems very proud of him. Thence away toward Eyvindarmúli where, however, we didn't get without another stoppage at the house of an old fellow who is blind, a very ill-favoured old gentleman whom Jón respects as being knowing in old lore, and so home to Eyvindarmúli where our tent is pitched in a minute or two and where we are very kindly welcomed again by the The day was rather sad but unrainy; we had had a very happy time of it up in Thorsmörk; and we should have been very comfortable indeed but that Charley was getting worse and was very gloomy as he well might be, and though I managed to keep up my spirits, somehow I had uncomfortable apprehensions about delay and sickness—which, however, I kept to myself. So to bed.

Tuesday 29th. Keldur.

TO bed but not to much sleep: poor Charley was so bad that he spent the night in groans, and I in consequence in trying not to notice them. I stole out of the tent about seven and left him to sleep if he could, and some time after I was dressed and had wandered about a bit, he declared himself awake; I pressed him to stop and rest a day but he would go on and so away about twelve, the bonder accompanying us who refused to take anything for his entertainment in spite of pressing. We picked Jón up at his own house where he had slept the night before (and let his horse run away to the place it came from). We were bound to go in again here and drink something (chocolate) but got away after a little delay and to Lithend once more. Here Charley who had picked up a bit at starting was so bad again that we left him on a bed in the dirty little parlour, while once more I went to Gunnar's howe. It was the same melancholy sort of day as yesterday and all looked somewhat drearier than before, two years ago on a bright evening, and it was not till I got back from the howe and wandered by myself about the said site of Gunnar's hall and looked out thence over the great grey plain that I could answer to the echoes of the beautiful story—but then at all events I did not fail.

So we turned away by a different road to that we went before—we are to go by the east of Three[corner], a place full of story, for thereabouts under Threecorner lived Starkad[1] and the others. Jón had to stay behind to look after the strayed

[1] " The Story of Burnt Njal."

horse and we went on with Haldor and his father still; the
latter talked so incessantly and with such a saw-sharpening
voice that I was ungrateful enough to wish him away in spite
of his kindness. We rode straight over the hill top above L[i-
thend] and over a downlike mostly grassy country whence
looking back once or twice I had the furthest possible view
of the great plain and could see the sea separate from the
land between it and the Westmanneyiar; this for a little till
the head of Th[reecorner] (double here) showed over the
lower land, and soon riding over a ghyll we came into the
great sweeping valley called Under Th[reecorner], a beautiful place, the lower part of the great mountain sweeping into
a long shallow valley that ran on all the way with it; so on till
in the distance we could see Jón coming with his captured
horse, and there we began to mount again a low ridge at the
valley's end, at top whereof we could see the great grey plain
that goes up to the spiked ridges that buttress the sides of
Hecla, and were come, just as we passed a small river (Fiská)
to the other end of Th[reecorner] beyond which at a lower
level were the fells above Vollr showing. This took us into
the lava again, a grey and old lava, till we came to another
strip of green through which runs East Rangá, and crossed
it just by the place where Gunnar retreated to when he
saw the ambush at Knafa[hólar]. The lava on the other side of
this, past a farm Á[rgilsstaðir] is new and bare amidst loose
sand, a most frightful place, but we rode over it at a good
pace, till at last we could see the green tún of Keldur and
presently rode into it out of the lava—a big tun of pretty undulating ground just above a clear stream that feeds Ranga
beyond which go great flat meadows right up to those Vollr
hills. We pitch the tent in the smoothest place we can find
here, while the old man, a funny old chap wanting no virtue
but soap and water apparently, comes out to us with many
welcomes. Charley is gotten very bad again, so I had all the
fun to myself this evening. They gave me a piece of half salt
ling at the stead which I cooked with great care in the midst
of about a dozen men, women and children, and then we

dined in no great comfort owing to toothache; after which I went out, and found Haldor and his father walking about, so
went out, and found Haldor and his father walking about, so
I went with them about the fields and over the stream to
where were a lot of ewes folded, and three girls milking
them, a thing I had never seen before: it wasn't a very pretty
sight, the poor wretches were so crowded; there also I tasted
ewe milk for the first time and thought it not bad being quite
new so. The bonder, Haldor told me, was a rich man, having
200 ewes but the grass was too thin to make much hay, as was
obvious from what [hay] was a-making in the tun. So back to
the tent, and another night much like the last.

Wednesday 30th. Storuvellir.

I LEFT Faulkner sleeping and went about a bit talking to
the folk, and down to a little stream where there was a sort
of water-mill, and close by a lot of springs bubbling out
of the sand that ran away in a wide shallow rivulet between
pretty grass banks. There were three or four more places
about the house where these springs come up. It was the same
sad kind of morning as the last few days. When I got back to
camp Charley was stirring and declared himself much better,
and refused to think of not setting off for Storuvellir; so off
we went, leaving Haldor to pick up two missing horses and
our guide across the Sand. We went identically the same way
to St[óruvellir] this time as I rode two years ago. It was raining at last when we came into the garth, but lightly. Faulkner
was tired with his ride and seemed ill, but I kept up heart as
well as I could and went out fishing with young Guðmundr.
When I came back after very good sport I found Charley still
queer, and Haldor also had come in without the guide, whose
brother he said had fallen ill of typhus and couldn't spare him,
so another had to be looked for. So to dinner after having
settled that we were to stop here to rest Faulkner to-morrow,
and bed a little after.

Thursday 31st. Same place.

FAULKNER better but not first-rate yet. The old priest took me a-fishing upstream this morning while he sent his son a ride after a Guðbrandr bible he wanted to show me. Dinner at four, G[uðmundr] having not come back: he came back just as we were finishing, the old G[uðmundr] having made a mistake about the bible. So presently to fish down the river where I had little luck but a very pleasant walk, the river clear and with smooth green banks running among smooth meadows at first and then amid old grass-grown lava all in little hills. As we turned to come back, the day, which had been doubtful hitherto with a thin drizzle falling, though always half to windward was a clear green space, bettered and the clouds broke overhead, the clear space to windward widening as the sun set bright and orange: the reflection from him was a wonder on the mountains opposite, brightening Burfell till one could see the structure of it plainly, slope and steep cliff and grass-grown top—reddening the sharp buttresses of Hecla, and brightening even the black sides of that, grown now all clear of cloud; presently we could see F   F [1] Jokull and E. even among the clouds, the snow all pink: so I came in [in] better spirits (I had never been in bad in spite of apprehensions) and supper and peaceful bed followed, for I was very tired with walking about all day, in the morning in my heavy boots.

Friday August 1st. Galtalœkr.

STARTED at three about from here: old G[uðmundr] informed me with excuses that he could not come with us as a widow had died and he had to make a sermon on her, so young G[uðmundr] rode with us alone. We rode over grassy meadows skirting the lava till Burfell on our left grew very plain, and Heckla (five thousand feet) on our right, with its buttressing hills; it had been rather rainy in the morning but cleared up into a very bright rather windy afternoon, under which the mountains looked very clear and bright except

[1] So in orig. See note. Ed.

for an obstinate cloud that hugged the top of H[ekla]; as Galtalœkr
we rode nearer this last, Threecorner showing still very clear,
we could see above and between grassy and birch-grown
slopes the new black-lava, one stream of which G[uðmundr]
pointed out to us as that of '45, the last eruption. So in two
hours to G[altalœkr] the last stead before the wilderness,
standing in a plain of grass with its brook at the back making
for Ranga, Burfell a fine mountain with ash gray slopes and
staff crown very near, and other low ranges showing north
among the wilderness. We speedily had up our tent and
asked G[uðmundr] to dinner in it and did our best in a hurry
to feed him: before he went away the evening had grown
very threatening at our back (north-west) but the cloud had
cleared off H[ekla] and showed all his huge flank and long
ridge at the top broken in four little peaks on this side. Gudmund took his leave about eight, and the rain came down
heavily about an hour and a half after he left, and everything
looked sad for to-morrow's first wilderness journey. Before
the rain came we walked down to the brook—a considerable
river in Scotland it would have been—and to a very pretty
waterfall on it where it split round a little grass-grown island
where the birch trees grew prettily overhanging the water,
and then taking a sharp turn east made its leap over a steep
slope into a great pool overtopped by great cliffs of sand and
lava. So to sleep with the rain rattling on the tent but a warm
night.

Saturday, August 2nd. Tungna-á.

WOKE at half past five by Haldor rattling ropes on
the back of the tent, and very unwilling to get up
but his friendly face in at the tent door and his
voice announcing a very fine day compelled me. Sure enough
when I turned out I found the sun ready to shine out among
the morning drizzle that wrapped Hecla about now. So to
breakfast in the tent and afterwards amid shower and sun to
a dish of *skyr* in the bonder's (Finnbogi) house—his bath-
stove, for he seems to have no parlour: 'tis a queer stuffy place

with beds on either side and children lying asleep in them. I asked him how many children he had and he told us he had had sixteen but eleven were dead. As we sat over our *skyr* a queer little head with tousselled yellow hair and a chubby red face came up and awoke, and I asked him its name which was Margret, in honour of which I chucked its chin as I went out. The bonder refused payment for everything but horsemeat and ropes bought, etc., and so we were off at half past nine for the wilderness on what I thought would be a long ride but turned out not to be. We rode at first over birch-grown and grassy ground till we had well turned the corner of Burfell and were in a long narrow valley between its long flank (for what we saw before was only the end of it) and steep slopes on the other side of Ranga, Thiorsa running alongside of Burfell. Here the ground was nothing but a waste of stones and sand nor Burfell neither, though on the other slopes was a little scanty green. We could not have been more than a mile from either river till Rangá now coming more from the east, its banks fell back and showed us high peaks and ridges, the north boundary of H[ekla]. Two of these, twin pyramids, were very remarkable in form—the snow lay in many places of them. We must have been getting high up now for Th[iórsá] is obviously running fast and we saw one biggish force sending a cloud of spray high up over the bank. Now we are come to where Burfell dies off into a great plain and Th[iórsá] falls back a long way from us; we also turning off from it over a little clear stream and into a space of lava, spiky, half covered with drift of sand in many knolls; we go up hill here, seeing Valafell, a long low hill besprinkled with green sheep-walks over it, and coming to the top can see a great plain of sand before us, all sprinkled over with stones of lava, the boundary of which on our right is the green striped Valafell and on our left low hills, the bank of Th[iórsá] looking faintly green from this distance, H[ekla], the very end of it, behind us, with the twin pyramid between. It had turned out a bright sunny day with some wind and many clouds about. Changing horses in this plain we make straight across it to where we

shall meet Th[iórsá] again, and soon have Valafell behind us, Tungna-á
and are getting near the river bank where our guide Asmund
points out a faint green patch which is the bank of T[ungna-á]
which comes from the east draining the Vatna[jökull] to
meet Th[iórsá], the drain of Arnarfell['s-jökull]; so at last
off the grisly lava and sand on to thin grass and heath plants
mixed with moss, a short ride over which brings us to T[ung-
na-á] near the tongue of the confluence which names the last
river. Asmund rides on to see after the boat which (such is
our virtue) we have got leave to use before, and we are soon
on the river bank: a very swift stream as wide as the Thames
at Maidenhead with low broken cliffs on our side and a slope
of grassy moss on the other. There had been a sharp shower
just when we left the lava e'en now, but now the sun is shining very bright and hot: it needs all that to light up a very
desolate-looking place I must say, the green is all yellow with
the moss and all is scanty and bare; nevertheless many sheep
manage to find their living there. We come down to a break
in the cliffs just opposite to where on the other side are the
ruins of a sheep-washer's hut, and drive the horses into a
stone-walled enclosure where we unpack and swim them at
once, after a ride of only six hours—but it was a long job in a
small boat ferrying everything across (in four trips), making
the boat snug, pitching tents (both ours on a bit of doubtfully
level black sand), cooking the dinner (boiled mutton) and
getting to table; and by the time all that was done the evening was spoilt and the rain was beginning to come down and
it soon fell very heavily. We were in good spirits, however,
shut up our tent and drank a bottle of madeira in honour of
the waste, and so to bed.

Sunday, August 3rd [at " Hvamgil "].

UP at six again on a morning still rainy and promising
to my eyes an evil day, nevertheless before we have
begun breakfast it clears up for a little and the sun
shines brightly: there are two swans cruising up and down in
the muddy water of this fierce river: over the cliff on the

other side shows a sea of confused dark peaks, the outer
wards of H[ekla], those two pyramids showing naked
among them; H[ekla] itself is clearly defined, though with
a veil of fine rain over it. So away at ten in good spirits for
Hvamgil, an oasis by the side of Th[iórsá]. We ride at first
over the dreary slopes of thin herbage along the river side,
which, however, are cleft here and there by little streams
down the gils of which the plants grow sweet and rich: the
other bank at first is mere desolation of black stony slopes
going right up to the further mountains, till it changes all at
once, and there is a quite green tableland on the other side,
most populous of sheep, whose bleating fills the air all about
us, while our bank is gotten stony and desolate, lava and sand
and ice-brought stone alternating. I noticed a bank of black
sand amidst the river hereabouts, all besprinkled with ere-
rose. Now away from the river slightly but definitely, and
across flats of lava into a space under high slopes which is
grown over with ground-willow and heath plants; and thence
mounting always till we are some way above the river and can
see the gorge of Kaldaquisl, a feeder of it, and have left Valafell and the H[ekla] mountains clean behind us. Here the
slopes which are of deep ochry sand are all cleft with gorges of
small streams very steep which give us both time and trouble
to get across. From here we can see a bit of green pasture on
the side of Kald[akvísl called] Klifshagi, but now we leave
it all and make up rising grounds of quite bare sand covered
over with small stones so closely and neatly laid together that
it looks quite like a pavement. The day here by about four
o'clock has quite changed: it had been doubtful with shower
and sunshine, but now the clouds break up everywhere in the
most beautiful way and the sun shines hot and bright as we
mount up ever—only black clouds (so black) hang about
H[ekla] which nevertheless [is] easy to see with all its snow
patches beneath his mist veil, the other mountains gradually
getting lighter but all the H[ekla] range being under this
cloud. So on till over the slope before us rise first a sharp
black peak, and then a long line of glacier going west from it

214

and the other black peaks about which the clouds yet hang,
an exciting sight, for these are the north Jokuls, Arnafell and
Kerlingafioll. A little more and we are on the other side of
the slope and H[ekla] with all his mystery of peak and slope
and ridge under the black clouds is gone. I suppose I shall
never see that side of them again. The sun shines bright still
though the clouds seem coming up from the west now, and
presently on our right a piece of glacier and black rock, a flank
of the Vatna-[jökull]: on and on over those strange stone-
covered sands under a bright sun toward the bank of Th[iórs-
á], low and faintly green as before, for over there are
famous sheep pastures. At last we get near the ragged mossy
willowy grassy land again which gets a little greener in one
place—our camp. We cross a little gill and are on it, more
willow than anything else. We can see before us a big waterfall of T[hiórsá] and two or three brooks trickle off toward
the big river, ever cutting for themselves deep gorges; on
the side of one of these on the willow and grass we pitch our
tents. The evening has clouded over so that we can only see
the Jokul and fells dimly: it is cold but not cold for the place.
So to bed after about seven hours' slow riding and waiting.

Monday, August 4th, at Eyvindarver.

UP at six again, Haldor inviting us to come and see the
sun shining on the Jokul, and going out found it a
bright morning though the sun was not actually shining overhead and it was rather cold. The mountains we had
seen but dimly yesterday seemed all clear, they were a collection of black cones and pyramids and I see by the map are full
of hot springs: the Jokul away from them was indeed bright
with the sun: it does not rise very high above the level of this
plain for we are high up now; it is nearly a straight ridge very
long, rising in the middle a little and then falling till the cone
of Arnar[fell] rises from it on the east. We were in the saddle
by nine and rode away under a very bright sun that fairly
scorched one: we rode over this broken herbage-ground
along Th[iórsá] side at first, coming on to its very ledge here

and there and making slow way because of the many gills;
leaving this at last we were on the bare sand and stones again
and mounting somewhat saw several peaks rising over the
flatter ground which seemed very wide indeed. These were
first on the right a flank of the Vatna-jokul and black peak,
then after a long gap a strange mountain Thóris T[indr] like
a cone cut in half vertically, then another gap and at big inter-
vals two huge truncated cones Hagamyn, south and north,[1]
and soon dimly, much further north, a black mass whitened
here and there, Tungna-jokul; it is between this latter and
Arnarfell that our night's lodging lies. A raven greeted us in
the last gil by the river side, and now will fly on with us as
we go: Asmundr's dog keeps running after him, and the
raven lets him come within a yard and then goes off with a
queer noise. There were a lot of sheep on this waste when we
first came on to it; when they see us they all set off at a great
pace before us stringing out in regular file. So on we go till
we get nearer the river again and come on to another scanty
patch of grass; here we have to pull up at the side of a deep
gil with quite vertical sides, a most wild and awful looking
place, no regular stream running through it, just a few pools
here and there and a few wells running down into them. The
raven flies about here making noises like winding up a big
clock—and we have to go up it a good way to get across—
which done we are still on the same black plain and ride over
slope after slope of it. We were getting on now long ago
among the Kerlingafioll; higher peaks burnt brown had
shaken the clouds half off them and rose up into them in a
fashion that I have seen time and again in Iceland and that
always excites and exhilarates me. This was a very beautiful
set of mountains. But now big black clouds had been coming
up from the east and it soon began to rain, and presently came
down in a heavy shower. Meanwhile we had edged away from
the river along the wastes ever driving those sheep before
us—how strange they looked! at one time all going one

[1] This should be Haganga en nyðri, en syðri (High-walk the
northernmost, the southernmost). E.M.

216

after another along the top of a hill against the sky. But now
we turned from them heading towards Th[iórsá] again still
over the same bare ground till riding over a knoll we come
on a shallow tarn with a border of most wretched green to it.
Here we stop and eat for half an hour in the very front of the
great Jokul and shift horses, and then on again through a
confused heap of small hills alternating with sandy streams
and tarns. It is hard work across the sands here, as in many
places the horses go in over their knees and we have to wind
about a good deal, always, however, edging toward the Jokul
and leaving Kerlingafioll behind: the Hagamyn[1] have come
up now so that we have seen them to their feet and lost them,
and Tungnafells Jokul is clear before us. At one place we got
free of the sands for a little and came on to a mossy willowy
space just by Thiórsá side where it spreads out very wide
and makes a ford (Sóleyarhöfði)[2] and then rode a space
with a long low hill on our right and Th[iórsá] winding
ing in and out of its pools on our left dotted about with many
swans. The day had quite cleared up again and the sunshine
was glorious if the wind was a little cold. Again out of the
sandy valley into a region of grassy bogs where at last was a
regular track of the sheep gatherers, and so to a halt in a little
nook where the grass grew rank about a stream and the ruins
of a hut were left—Thufuver. Here sitting while the horses
feed a bit we hold counsel and agree to stop at Eyvindarko-
verver all to-morrow to rest the horses before we try the adventure of the Sand. It was very hot in the sun as we sat on a
bank in the very face of the great Jokul and the dark peak of
Arnarfell: so on again over a low sandy hill to a river side
with a wide sandy bank amidst a marsh where swans were
swimming in the pools: the river came in a waterfall from out
of a gorge up which we could see T[ungnafells] Jokul among
black clouds, the foot of a very bright rainbow against it.
Again over a stony hill still nearer the Jokul and along the
bank of a most solitary stony tarn—a most wild strange place
down from that to a little river running into it, and over an-

[1] Hagöngur.   [2] Buttercuphead. E.M.

other neck, half stony, half sandy, and there down below us is a space of boggy greenish land toward which the guide rides at a sharp pace: my heart tells me that this is Eyvindrkoverver, though I had rather it shouldn't be, for 'tis a dreary-looking place with its sloppy pools and brook going right up to the Jokul side. Down into it we ride, however, on the brightest of all evenings at about half past six and Asmundr welcomes us to Eyvindrkoverver; it is just opposite Ar[narfell], a great cone that rises out of a deep black hole where the Jokul splits and pours round it on either side; opposite on the north-east is Tungnafell['s-jokul], a big mass rising into three small waves amidst of it, and the Hagöngur are still high up further south: low rises block up the pass north—a most desolate solitary spot it is. Amidst it by the brook side are the ruins of a hut where Eyvind lived: the whole place is little better than a bog, and on such spongy sloppy ground had we to pitch our tent as well as we could for lumps and wet. However, the glorious evening mended all, and by then we got our dinner the day ended in a wonderful sunset, faint green with crimson stripes over the great mass of the Jokul,[1] and the east hills fiery red or bright rose with the reflexion according as to whether they were snow-clad or not. So to bed.

Tuesday, August 5th. Same place.

A BRIGHT morning (we up at nine) with a strong wind blowing from south-east, and heavy clouds in that region: the guides say, however, that is not bad for the Jokul country. I notice in the morning sun that there is a great patch of green, be it moss or grass. So the day goes on in writing journal, cooking dinner, eating it, and four games of cribbage. The rain duly coming down at about five o'clock and raining hard to make us uncomfortable for to-morrow's journey—for we are to get up at one in the morning for our last day across the wilderness. So to sleep at about ten.

[1] i.e. Hofsjökull. E.M.

Wednesday, August 6th, [at Fliótsdalr].   The Sand

I DULY woke at one and found the wind blowing very
hard, apparently from the north-east, and the rain just beginning after a short lull. No one came to disturb me so I
thought I would be quiet for though I could feel it was cold
I was warm enough in my blankets bating the draught in my
face: so I gently let myself go to sleep again, and woke at last
at half past four, to find the rain ceased and the wind a little
lulled, so I ran out of the tent in a hurry to call the guides
and found them awake and eating their breakfast, and then
went back to finish dressing and help C.J.F. pack. Lord!
how cold it was, and the rain looked only staved off a little,
and in short I hardened my heart against the counterpart of
just such a day as we rode over Grimstunguheiði. However,
we packed and decamped without any rain and set off from
the dismal place about seven, to my great joy, for I began to
be afraid we might be weather-bound there, and presently
found that the day was not like to turn out so bad as seemed
likely at first, though most bitter cold it was.

We rode away from our swamp along the side of the great
glacier, and for about an hour, the clouds almost hiding
T[ungnafell's-jökull] and lying on the tops of the Hag[ön-
gur] below, as for about an hour was a scantier continuation of
the same boggy moss and grass as we slept on last night; and
we passed over two little brooks on the sides of which were
a few stalks of angelica; and I noticed a tuft or two of cranesbill, and tried my horse at some dandelions that grew in the
black sand. Over the first of these brooks, by the way, hung
a few terns looking after worms, and a little past the second
a stone-bunting flew up into the air, and that was the last
living thing except ourselves and horses that I saw for many
hours, and after that we were on the wilderness indeed.

It is not a flat but is in great waves, not like hills, not high
enough for that and especially having no stability about the
look of them; as to the ground you go over, it is all sand indeed but varies as to what lies on the sand. Sometimes it is
little pebbles, looking before your horse's hoofs sink into the

sand, as if the whole place were neatly paved, and most strange it is to go over this and see no track till your horse makes one, and most strange when you are travelling in the shadow of a cloud to watch the sunlight brightening some wave of this into such a wan ghastly colour, for the colour else is a not very dark grey. Sometimes there were big stones and rocks even strewed about the pebble-covered sand: and these sometimes ran together into boulders and shaly flags heaped up together: with one exception to be spoken of presently this was the near landscape everywhere; for the rest we went as I said parallel to the long line of A[rnarfell's] Jokul a long while, gradually leaving behind us the black peaks of the big A[rnarfell] till at last we were alongside of a great black tableland of cliffs that, sticking out at a corner of the Jokul, are called A[rnarfell] the Little. On the other side we soon had the H[agöngur] behind us and were alongside of the big rather shapeless mass of T[ungnafells-jökull], whose lower flanks are striped with green—and folk say that there are valleys about them that are green and snowless while the lower lying sand is covered with snow. Jón firmly believes in outlaws living among these still—for which the others chaffed him much. The day soon grew quite bright, for as cold as it was, and when after six hours' ride we got off our horses to eat, sitting with our backs against a big stone, we found the sun quite hot and summery—still it *was* a cold day.

For a long time there was little change of any kind about us, for the mountains were so big you may ride hours without changing them, at last as we came to the top of a wave, Asmundr pointed out to us a low blue ridge ahead and told us it was Fiorðingir: it seemed to be right across our path and some two hours' ride brought us close under it with Ar[narfell] behind us and the corner of T[ungnafell's-jökull] turned that ran back in lower reaches of Jokul till it was joined by lower un-iced mountains to the Vatna[-jökull]. We rode over a couple of miles of pure black sand here which brought us down to the banks of a long lake lying under F[iórðungs-]A[lda] and there we stopped to change horses

while a light shower came on amid the sunshine, throwing a
rainbow from the lake across a great waste of more black sand
· on to a stony brent that bounded it. Through that we rode
presently, a most [1]   place to see; then up a brent on our right,
on the brow of which Asmundr showed me Ar[narfell] now
far behind and told me we should lose it when we were over
the brow and before me showed me the Vatna-[jökull] again
with two low mountains, one running out from it and the
other from T[ungnafell's-jökull], the space betwixt which
was the Vonarskarð, the pass which the way takes that leads
(if it can be said to lead) round the back of the Vatna-[jö-
kull]: all waters now, he said, ran north, and that the change
was just where we stopped by the lake side. On a little higher,
and a huge table-like mountain comes up, Kistufell, just
north of the Vatna-[jökull], and beyond it a great flat cone
just like Sk[jaldbreið] in the West and called indeed so but
more commonly Troll.[2] We can soon see all the country between us and the Vatna-[jökull], mysterious, with dark
ridges and waves, and a little pyramid or two thrusting up at
whiles. All this is the Ód[aðahraun] [3] along the flank of which
we go now till the journey's end.

Still on over much the same land as before we came to the
black sand except that the sand is wetter, and often we seem
to ride through an under sand stream, for our horses will
sink up to their knees in it. At last we come down on to a
little stream fair and clear which is running north, and the first
we have actually come on which does: about this grows a little, very little, scanty grass and willow, and we rest there a
few minutes; then on for about an hour when the low hills to
right and left of us are gathering more a look of stability and
a swift river (white) turning a corner of them runs through a
little valley with something more of grass in it, and over the
low boundary of which nearly meeting together one can see
blue mountains in the distance. I know this is where we are
going to stop, because the guide gallops into it and up on to

[1] Word omitted.   [2] Trölladyngia (Troll's Bower). E.M.
[3] i.e. Misdeedlava. E.M.

Fliótsdalr the grass-grown brent, takes off his saddle and stands there awaiting us, and presently we are camped and our horses are enjoying themselves in the first grass after a twelve hours' ride: it was not so long as we had expected which rather disappointed me. It was a fine sunny evening though cold enough still: the river is one of the great northern rivers and is called Ski[álfandafliót], the little valley is Fliotsdal, called after it. So to bed (warm and sunny at first, [wind] southwest).

Thursday, August 7. At Miofidal.

UP at eight and after breakfast a walk down to where Sk[iálfandafliót] runs in rapids out of the little valley: away at eleven o'clock: for though we are off the sand proper we have still a goodish ride before us to the peopled parts. So up over the hillside on to very rough broken ground differing little from the last of yesterday, except that on our right Sk[iálfandafliót] runs through a deep gorge of perpendicular rocks: so on till we look from the top of our hill into a long valley that Sk[iálfandafliót] flows into, all full of lava, with high down-like hills on either side, while another small stream, cutting for itself another deep gorge and running green at the bottom of it, comes to meet Sk[iálfandafliót]. This is Kið[a-gil] [1] where folk mostly stop who come from the wastes because a little grass is on a patch that overhangs the gill, but our place was better for so many horses. Out of this valley we mount directly a very steep and high hillside from the top of which is a glorious view of all the big mountains. T[ungnafel] and the Vona-skarð, the long mass of the Vatna, Kistufell['s-jökull] and Troll[adyngia], and finally far to the east Herðubreið, the second highest mountain in Iceland, a huge solitary stack rising into three points icecovered. So over the brow on to a very rough Heiði not quite grassless but a most abominable road—where also the weather changes and gets cold and falls to raining very hard about two o'clock, about which time we see the head of the valley

[1] i.e. Kidgill. E.M.

222

we are bound for with faintly green sides. The rain goes on
till we are fairly in the valley by the side of a swift clear
stream, coming from time to time on patches of real grass
which looks most sweet and fresh after the waste, and there
are very many sheep. At last crossing the river for the last
time we are fairly on a regular grassy hill-side of a long
down-enclosed valley shut in apparently at either end and
full of sheep, and presently we come on a neatly-built sheep-
house and then by the river-side see the bright patch of green
that means a tun, and then the many sheep-cots and the gables
of the stead, and are soon there and pitching our tents in a
smooth-shaven pretty and big tun sloping down to the river:
most sweet and clean it looked after the waste. This was an
eight hours' ride after all, the road being so bad. So to *skyr* in
the house, chocolate afterwards in our tent, and bed.

Friday, August 8th. Haldorstaðir.

UP at eight, the morning cold, grey and uproarious,
though it bettered soon; to coffee in the house; the
people I thought seemed depressed and poor, the last
tenant has emigrated to Am[erica]—perhaps this cast an air
of gloom on the place, but there was something beautiful
about the valley, long, green-sided, shut in at either end. We
clomb the hillside just above it, & over a rugged bit of ground
into another valley where was a stead called Isholl at the head
of a small tarn. The day had got very bright now though it was
still somewhat cold: we rode by a stony hillside along the lake,
till near the other end we crossed a marsh, and came into a
narrow valley through which the lake stream ran clear with
bright green banks widening ever with the mountain streams
till it fell over a highish force and ran down a deep gil from
which ran a steep grassy hill on one side, with a cliff sticking
out of bare basalt some way down, and on our side lower
slopes grassy also: the whole place seemed very sweet and
pretty to our eyes after the bare waste. But presently we found
ourselves looking into the great dale of B[arðardalr] that this
runs into, and Skiálfandafliót winding through it. The other

side of it looked brown and bare with lava right down to the bottom which disappointed me because I had been expecting more and more greenness as I went on. So we were come to the little valley's end and could see across it the house of Myri[1] lying green on the opposite hillside. We had to ask our way across the steep gil at a little stead on this side: and so over the clear river just where it joined Sk[iálfandafliót] all coloured with the Jokul water still, and into a big tún all dotted about with sheep-houses sloping down the hillside, and Jón welcomed us to Barðardalr.

The bonder here was a spoonsmith and we were after spoons so we accepted hospitality of coffee in the house and went into a very neat parlour where sat the bonder, a little old man of eighty, who fell a-talking eagerly with the guides, and took out a bit and stirrup he had just made with some pride, to their great admiration; he told us also that the G[reenland] ice was lying only sixty miles out to sea at the north; also that two hundred folk had been minded for America by the "Queen" which could take only half of them; and again I confess it saddened me to hear of it; but it seems the people here have had many bad years together and it has sickened them of it. Then the spoons were brought out and bought, and a great big horn, too big for us to carry, and we started off again through the great green tún, the valley narrowing before us. Looking back when we had gone a little way we could see the tail of the gorge out of which Sk[iálfandafliót] runs, just like before at Fliótsdalr. So on over low birch scrub soon, with the other side of the valley getting green too, till on the other side the river, we could see the church and stead of Lundabrekka, and presently on ours the parson's house of H[aldórsstaðir] lying pleasantly, it, too, in a wide tún. There we drew rein and camp on a very fine night. I thought the valley beautiful—long, narrow, winding, down-enclosed, a great snowy mountain (Liosa) blocking up the north end, and the Jokul mountain black-blue and white showing above the sheer gorge of Sk[iálfandafliót] at the south. The priest

[1] i.e. Mere. E.M.

224

new-appointed here was away ill, so we only saw a workman.
So to bed after a rather elaborate cooking which, or something else, depressed me and made me homesick.

Saturday, August 9th. Gautlönd.

A MOST lovely morning when I got up at eight, still depressed and homesick, which depression I had to throw off in getting breakfast, so that by then I was in the saddle I was excited and in good frame for travelling; moreover, there was something eminently touching about the valley and its nearness to the waste that gave me that momentary insight into what the whole thing means that blesses us sometimes and is gone again. We rode down under guidance of the workman between the staring haymakers, men and women, to Skiálfandi, where Jón and he tried the direct ford to Lundarbrekka first and found it over-deep for the boxes, so we had to go down the river a bit before we could cross: even there it was the deepest river we have forded in Iceland, wide too and the bottom not very good. Nevertheless the whole thing had got unfrightful to me now and I crossed it pipe in mouth, not troubling myself at all: and so all safe across. This river, though a Jokul river, is very little coloured and looks very nearly clear at the sides where the water is shallow and the stream not strong. So up to the stead,[1] where was a regular hive of men women and children (such a lot of the latter). We wanted to buy spoons and a guide across the marshes, so went into the parlour of one bonder and had coffee. It was a neat room with quite a pretty shut bed in it— a shelf for books inside said bed and all. This is the stead of the Lund. Thence the bonder guided us up a very steep stony hillside which he told me had once been the Lund[2] which gave its name to the house. Thence over rough ground whence, the day being serene and cloudless with a very hot sun, one can see a great ring of mountains—the Jokuls farthest southwest, a long shining line almost mixing with the light blue horizon: then all the others above-named, Hekla quite clear

[1] i.e. Lundarbrekka. E.M.   [2] lundr, i.e. grove. E.M.

Gautlönd now with its glittering tent-shaped Jokul; behind us to the north a long scarped gorged range snowy and black about L S [1] and presently rising up above the tableland the strange mountains of the Myvatn-side, a long table mountain first, then running up from it a long and stupendous range of cliffs—Blá[fiall], then the peak of Námafiáll, the sulphur mountain, and then again another sharp peak amidst a gap, till we meet those on the north again. So on and over some frightful bogs and round a little tarn at the end of which our guide leaves us, and after one or two ups and downs the lake of Myvatn with its many islands lies before us underneath long grey brents broken by strange shaped cones, a raw ugly patch of drab blotching the grey under N[ámafiáll] which is H   lith.[2] For the rest the ground all about is changed here, being very old lava mostly grown over with birch-scrub grass and heath plants, and very populous of birds. We ride a good way down this till we see a wide túned stead lying in a scoop of the slope that ends in a marshy valley with a tarn in it, and crossing a steep gil through which a bright stream runs, are presently at the rich house of G[autlönd] whose owner is away at the Althing at present. The tun is hilly and we have a very pretty camp here just by the brookside, where there is a little flat piece under a knoll just big enough for our tent. We wander about till late, eat *skyr* in the house, and so at last to bed on the calmest if not the hottest day I have known in Iceland (moon over Blafell).

Sunday, August 10th [at Grímsstaðir].

UP at before seven and down the brook to fish on a beautiful morning, where, after much patience, I caught breakfast in the form of two orange-bellied char; so back to Faulkner and breakfast: which done we see a riding of men from the north-east, and presently come into the tún two English men with their train, and Gisli for one guide. Talking with them kept us rather late, but at last

---

[1] Dyngiufiöll long far away.   [2] H—lith or Hlith in the text. Ed.

they departed west and south and we north. We rode over ^{Fishing} lumpy ground round the marshy tarn, and came from that on to a very old lava, grass-grown except where the great rocks thrust up. So on a few hundred yards till we came to the arm of a swift clear river running among the lava with grass-grown banks and holms amongst it, quite luxuriant with small shrubs and hvam:[1] then again the river tumbling over rapids by many arms, bright blue in the sun, with castle-like walls of lava broken above and the grass growing every-where to the water's edge and more holms (some like castles and some flat fertile holms) and the big mountains about the lake-side for a background—the most beautiful river I have seen in Iceland.[2] Here the train went over a shallow ford while Charley and I stayed behind to fish according to agree-ment, and so spent the afternoon happily enough in the bright sun, I catching big trout enough for us all to live upon for two days: the only drawback was the midges that swarmed incredibly. We left the river about six, and so on over more branches of it (it runs out of the lake here to a little stead called Geirastadir); going over some grassy lumpy ground we come on to the lake shore, a wide sheet of water cut up by innumerable islands and with many ins and outs to it: some of the islands are flat, some strange-looking cinder heaps and craters; these last are repeated again on the lake shore as we ride (on our right; on our left the ground is flat and boggy) till we come on one of the two pyramidal horns we saw from Gautlönð; this, running up from the boggy ground into a steep horn, thrusts out into the lake and is called Vindbelgr.[3] We skirted the base of it and could see another marshy lake again between us and the strand. (Then over a down, where a shepherd and his sheep stood as we came up, to look at us, and on to a somewhat dis-

[1] Probably hvönn=angelica. Ed.

[2] This is Laxá, running through Laxár-dal and Aðalreykjadal into Skiálfandi. E.M.

[3] i.e. Windbag. E.M.

^{Q2}   227

mal bog). But the ground all about us was old lava, broken by the blowing up of its bubbles into caves and holes full of water and grown about with plants and shrubs, from whence one could see on a slope our home of Grímsstaðir whereto a short trot brought us and we found our tent pitched by Haldor up in a big tún where the haymakers were at work in front of the gabled house. So to cook a bit of trout for dinner (at nine) cribbage and bed: moon again.

Monday, August 11th [at Grímsstaðir].

A BRIGHT day again: the lake lay below us with its many islands; at our sides rose the great burnt pyramid of Náma[fiall], on the other side of the lake were a small pyramid and teeth of lava, that led up to a great low flat crater of grey sand some mile across; then came more teeth of lava and grey-green slopes that led up to the wretched drab waste of the sulphur fields tossed up into little cones: and so slopes of grey and burnt up to N[ámafiall] again. Back over the crater rose up Burfell, a big house-roof mountain and south of it Blafell again, more of a stack here and less of a cliff as we are passing from the flank to the end of it. We borrowed the bonder's boat to go a fishing expedition on the lake—a most queer little tub like half a boat. Jón and Haldor rowed exceeding ill beneath our jeers and we didn't get fast or far: the lake turned out to be quite shallow, and fishless at this end; so we disembarked at a little island on which was a stead called Hrauntún. It was a curious collection of small cinder hills and lava, grown about with sweet grass, on which it was pleasant to lie in the sun. Here we had out the map and arranged for going on to Dettifoss the next day; then away slowly back again, I sculling at first and then Faulkner, and so up on to a little island very pretty, all grown over with birch and willow, two or three quite big birches standing above the others, a little deep round pond in the middle from which flew out three little ducks and swam about with their tails up: a little bay quite full of young ducks just able to fly—angelica all round the borders. So away home to

228

Grìms[staðir], and diary writing and dinner, by when the day was got colder, and clouds were gathering in the leeward which I thought betokened rain. To bed early because we were to start to-morrow at four for Dettifoss, come back thence to a deserted stead called Littahagi, rest there four hours which we hope will bring us back to-morrow about midnight.

Tuesday, August 12th [at Hliðarhæli].

ALL this was upset though: we did wake at half past three and Charley went into the house to wake Jón and came back in a rage (justifiable) because Jón said that the farmer would not let his horse and man get up earlier than six the usual time: however, we got off without the pack and with a shepherd named Joachim at about seven on a grey morning not rainy nor cold but threatening I thought.

Turning out of the tún we soon came on to a patch of lava which somehow I hadn't ever noticed before as it lay a little sunk: this was quite new being the tail end of a stream that flowed from Krabla one hundred and thirty years ago. It was terrible-looking enough—all in great flakes at this latter end, otherwhere with great waves tossed up sometimes, or broken all into rough fragments, or the familiar regular flowing stream: young as it is, it is beginning to be grown over with moss. Off the lava again through a little grassy valley spotted with marshy tarns, and again on to it where it seems to have been stopped by the soft ground; then round the foot of a grassy down to a pretty little nook once, where the lava flowing down the valley between the two downs, has made an island of grass where stand yet the foundations of three houses that it surrounded without destroying, then again another stream of lava that passes by us and breaks on the lake-strand stopping short of the stead of Reykjalið, where however the church (the same as then) yet stands in an island surrounded by it along with a big sheep-house. A few rods further on and we are among the black sand, and huge clinker rocks of lava at the foot of the sulphur hills, an ugly place:

a valley sloping up into a narrow pass among steep sand-heaps of hills burned red and buff and yellow by the sulphur, grassless of course; and every here and there the reek of a sulphur kettle with the earth about it stained bright yellow and white. So up the pass, going past a cloven sand peak with a kettle at the foot of it, and winding along the path till on the hill's brow we can look across a wide open country, lava-covered, grey and dismal, walled by a sweep of ink-black peaks and saw ridges: close under us on our right goes up a great cloud of reek from the great mud kettle, and two or three other kettles amidst some six acres of sulphurous de-posit: we turned from this intending to look at it closer on our way back; and so between the lava rising into a steep wall head-high on our right, and a pretty flowery shrub-grown steep hillside, to the bight of a valley where heathy and sandy hills rose again east of us; that way we turn, with hills of sand and stone on our left not over remarkable saving one peak whose castle-like rocks crown the sand, great masses of which lie tumbled about our path. These seem to be of the same conglomerate as that of the hills, mixed with black lava stones. On our right the hills having died away show us still the big lava plain with the black ridges and peaks (Burfell) bounding them. Before our way lies a mass of sand hills on whose flank we soon are, one rising higher than the others we ride along the side of; it is bronzed with sprinkling of sulphur. Now again on the brow of its slopes a big plain comes into sight, it is faintly green and is bounded by far-away mountains low and ridgy; amidst it a white smoke is seen which the guide points out as the spray of the foss; the whole view dismays one beyond measure for its emptiness and dolefulness. Down now over lava stones on to lumpy heathy ground (of a plain), most troublesome to get the horses over, we keeping the force steam in sight; the hills we have come through give back and form a wall to this great waved plain of steep greenish brent and black ridge till some miles to the north rises a steep cone, Eilífr, over a small lake of the same name, then they run (lower) east.

230

Now came the threatened bad weather—mist and drizzle, so that our guide was at fault after we having left the grassy lumpy land came first on to sand and stones and then into a long lava valley with low walls, a most dreary place. However, we crossed over a defect in this and into another valley of this waste of stone when Jón dismounting went on further through the mist and said that he could hear the river. So on a little further into another dismal valley, where dismounting we left our horses tied nose and tail, grassless, on a patch of sand, and went up a steep bank on to a tableland scattered about with big stones, and on till we heard the river indeed, and presently came to the brink of a great rift wherein I doubted not the river ran. But, lo no river but a wide rift some furlong across regularly walled, almost regularly paved with flat lava stones up to the dry bed of a river running through, the mist creeping through it. Down into this we went by broken stairs in the wall and along it to where we thought the river was. Some way down we came on a transverse break crescent-shaped in the river-bed, visibly an old fall, made of the hugest blocks of rock, and then all the rift floor sank into confusion together, and turned into a sharp tumbled heap of slopes that led down to a gully amidst which we could see a black stream running at right angles to the other and seeming small enough for our ideas of Jokulsá. Round this we went to find the force: came across rocks like organ pipes with wool atop at end of rift. Force higher up across rift, down a low rock on to a flat space of wet moss; there foss say one hundred feet coming down from a channel like the rift, more or less a crescent, into a very deep gully quite wallsided of lightish grey built-up rocks—say one hundred and fifty feet. So back home at four in morning, day still grey—not much rain after Liðarhagi.

Wednesday, August 13th. At Greniaðar[staðir].

OFF at two: day greyish and cold but not bad: over a valley or two, one wooded, on to a waved sand high up from which on right we saw a group of pyramid mountains fine and sharp: then heathy ground into Laxardal, very steep descent: down-like hill opposite, clear river running amidst stead just below us, among lava—the lava like a wall. So we go down and along the river and into the lava-wall on to a space of smooth green turf—horses frightened at foam: hillside above tremendously steep, otherwise green banks (holms in river) grassy grown lava. Neat stead in big tún—coffee: dale fine from here (big lumpy hill just before us), lava wall cutting valley in two: very cold, mist coming down: ride round lumpy hill away from river at first, skirting dismal bog country and so till we came across the valley again, turning rather west now: over dreary bog to G.[1] our valley opening out into main valley, say the west wall failing here (Thegiandidal), G.[1] stead rather above marshes at tongue of north wall of Th[egiandadal]. Old priest there and his ways. (Six hours).

Thursday, August 14th. At Halsi.

OFF at about eleven, round the tongue into a widish valley[2] and along its hillside: valley marshy with marshy lakes in it: past these on to their feeding river, and across to north wall of valley: by stead, Helgastaðir in the middle. Inner end of valley fair from here, with smooth hills tumbled about, our side bettering as we go on: fair hard meadows, people haymaking: many steads on a long green lithe. So to Einars[staðir]—man with coffin lid: up hill thence, very steep, by turf beacons. Think it wrong—a long way across heath (day cold and grey, getting worse and mistier). From brow Barðardal again, long valley with brown barren hillsides and Skialfandi with many streams: our side very steep and high. Found we had gone wrong—too high up; down again along hillside till this side died away, and a plain before us running up into another valley: high table mountain at the

[1] Greniaðarstaðir.　　　[2] Reykia-dal (Reek-dale). E.M.

tongue and great screens of mountains pushed out from the Háls other side to meet: other side of Barð[ardalr] steep but green: clouds on very top of it—reek of G[oða] foss a little way over the plain. So past the foss, I just seeing it and a lower one smaller, in deep gorge, strange spiky roofs half pierced with caves all about: across river by a little stead and down it to foss—heathy ground—several streams of river, two hot, coming over foss: foss not high, moonshaped, a big rock splitting into two (Grettir's-rock)—most character about that—not much just below foss till it got into rapids again, then a very narrow gorge all eddies, below which great rocks stuck out into the stream all mined into caves till it came to the little fall and rocks above-said. Away towards hillside (cloudy) over flat ground grown over with half dead very small birch-scrub; on lower slopes of hill Thorkel Foulmouth (Oxara) (green valley running up into hills here); green meadows and rising a little—Liosavatn visible and stead on low spur of green just in the jaws of pass,[1] pretty but wet (Faulkner on house).[2] Getting late, raining now, mountains much hidden —Haldorstaðir man for guide—along lake shores [Liósa-vatn], black sand at lake end and swift stream through it. Lake close to hillside green, mountains on other side very fine, great ridge ends pushing forward: all the road a very visible pass. We going up—at Hals at last, half past ten, raining hard—seems to be at pass end, can half see valley beyond; hard to get in (ten and a half hours from straying).

Friday, August 15th. Saurbœr.

OFF at half past eleven; fast ride; sun and cloud; are indeed on the very neck of the pass and high up: south of house high mountain running up into a peak, great sloping mountains opposite (all not very like Iceland but fine) long valley high bounded running at right angles to this—Fnjoskadal[3]—down into this and along fine birch wood, then up steep hillside on to a heath Vaðlaheiði, from

[1] Liósavatn-skarð.
[2] C.J.F. mistakes the grassy house-roof for a slope. Ed.
[3] i.e. Touchwood-dale. E.M.

brow of which Eyafiorð, a huge slope down to it; then a great flat valley, many streams of river running into narrow firth: line of shallow little town under hillsides: barque, three or four schooners: Akreyri—towards other end valley widish with steep hillsides breaking into mountains at whiles; other side quite high mountains broken into gaps at whiles and showing valley and mountain among them; leave horses at Ellifsta; over bogs on to riverside, great wide meadows somewhat marshy between us and hill-slopes on our side, on other hill-slopes quite by river, so away from river to M[unka] Th[verá]: important-looking stead on a little rise under mountains, deep ghyll in the hillside: foss there—very cold and raining now: nice parlour: Espihol on other side of river a round cindery knoll, above it the mountains rising into sloped roof-like peaks—very grand. Amidst the plain before the house a small knoll—Glum's thingstead: across the river by Espihol (and by many steads, for there are many on both sides) on to a piece of lava with big stones, a great cleft valley of the mountains behind it: scene of the sorb trees: end of valley closed in by tent-shaped mountains standing free mostly. Moðruvellir on slope of opposite side. Ways of priest.

Saturday, August 16th. Akreyri.

OFF at eleven with priest and across river to Moð-[ruvellir]; shows us one stead, south was Glum's sheep cot, another north his calf-cot; one hundred men in the house: great stone with ring handles in front of house: pretty parlour with carved furniture in it: (church). So away again, priest leaving us at Litlaholt, halfway to Akreyri: other priest and his dull library: ride beyond where we came before: haymakers with tents on swampy holms. A[kreyri]—busy—merchant, sorb trees: chaffer—hotel—me like Wapping—dull day, cold, no rain.

Sunday, August 17th. Moðruvellir.

BRIGHT and cold—a fine mountain at firth end, much
striped with snow; loiter away day; off at six after much
drinking: alongside of firth: great mountains opening
up at back of town very snowy (Jokul): stopped at little house
by very firth side; wonderful sunset, north sky all red, flat-
topped crinkled snow-mountain reddened by it. Away from
firth thence—Horgardalr over brow: impressed me much:
river down below, then a flat and slopes going up unbroken
in very steep mountains, regular tents in shape: north-west
the great firth-side, south-east the valley narrowing and shut
up by pyramids and ridge ends foreshadowing higher mountains behind Fiðriksgáfa. Governor and his ways.

Monday, August 18th. Steinstaðir [in Öxnadalr.]

A BRIGHT warm sunny morning; up the valley the cha-
raćter of it continuing much the same, but further up
it visibly splits atwo, our way Öxna[dalr], lying to the
east; stead on little knoll with grass garth on one side and in
front four trees, birch and sorb in one, six in other, quite trees.
So across river making for Oxnadal (Bægisa, poet's place)
where valley forks; very narrow valley, flat at bottom, grassy
going up on east in one long steep slope into mountains topped and crested with pillar and gable rocks and much cloven
by ghylls; on the other side a very steep high lithe that gradually gets lower as it goes south, but behind it is slipped a screen
of mountains high and precipitous, a thin saw ridge thinnest
at north, and splintered into broken palings, one very marked
and excessive, widening and heightening into a dragon's back
peak at the south end. St[einstaðir],[1] a house on a green slope
on the west side.

[1] Goodwife and sister of poet, fifty years at Steinstaðir.

Norðardal Tuesday, August 19th. Ytrakot Norðardal.

OFF at twelve, with bonder, over an intricate group of stony hills that half block the valley just here; beyond the great grass slopes again the west mountains higher running more west into another valley; the east screen is now the valley boundary, a most wild set of rocks and hills running up at its highest into a mountain cleft right atwain by a ghyll: thence dropping off into quite a low ridge which is our pass. From just this we can see looking north the whole length of the valley unbroken save as above and bounded only by the Eyafirth hills. Looking back from the first of the pass we can see the very tail end of the valley winding into an apparent cul-de-sac: the mountain behind us is very steep, stepped half way up, flat-topped, except for a peak rising up far at one end: mountain of cul-de-sac snowy (Jokul?). Pass rough, road not very stony: other side mountains visible near by from first: haymakers in marshes at first: gets very narrow in one place, then we go down hill alongside a tremendous chasm, met by another chasm that cleaves the hills into grim and enormous lumps of sand, and so presently look into north of Sk[aga-fiördr]: a grey barren hill opposite for boundary, a small stream at bottom among a grey wilderness of stones, and the tongue of another valley, two stepped pyramids rising out of a table cliff. Looking back we can see the last of Oxnadalr.

236

NOTES BY EIRÍKR MAGNÚSSON

I. THE JOURNAL OF 1871.

PAGE 21, l. 2. By mistake this is located a little west of Swinefell. But Hall o' Side lived at Hof in Swanfirth, the bay next to Berufirth on the south, a long way *east* of Swinefell.

P. 29, l. 1. The name of the river is Elliðaá, an historic river deriving its name from the ship 'Elliði,' in which Ketilbjörn the Old, a famous settler, landed at the river-mouth perhaps as early as c. 890 A.D.

P. 41, l. 15. Sœmund 1056-1133, Ari 1067-1148, Snorri 1178-1241. That Ari was ever an inmate of Oddi is not on record, though it may be possible. That he and Sœmund had literary converse together is certain.

P. 47, l. 25. The sentence 'except that ... the east wall is,' etc., has gone out of gear somehow, and I am not absolutely certain how. I know the place well, and the likeliest meaning of the passage seems to be 'except that over this western corner of the wall you can see the summit of Eyja-fell, and somewhere in advance of the east [you see naught but the] wall [which] is,' etc.

P. 56, l. 8. The whereabouts of Biorn's homestead, 'Mark,' is probably to be sought further east than Thorsmark, in the country-side under Eyja-fell, where to this day there are clustered three homesteads of the name of Mark (Stóra, Mið-, Syðsta-Mörk).

P. 56, l. 11. Kari married Helga the daughter of Nial, and had house at Dyrholmar east in Mýdal (Midgedale), but lived with his parents-in-law until their death. Where the homestead of Thorolf's-fell exactly was is not known, but it must have been somewhere on the sunny side under the mountain of the same name at the east end of Fleet-Lithe range as shown on the map.

P. 81, l. 17. Kalmanstunga derives its name from Kalman who came from Sodor (Sudr-eyjar, Hebrides) and set up house here probably before the close of the ninth century.

P. 94, l. 1. Published 1584 in folio by Bishop Guðbrandr Thorlaksson (1542-1627), the second protestant Bishop of Holar (1571-1627), the northern diocese of Iceland, abolished 1797, since when the whole island (some 40,000 odd square miles in extent) has formed one diocese.

P. 94, l. 19. Viðidalr—Willowdale, is historically a very interesting countryside. From the settlement period it formed for a long time an important link between the west and the north of the country, and plays a conspicuous part in many of the most interesting stories such as Grettis, Heath-slayings, Vatnsdœla and other sagas. It will interest English readers to know, that according to Landnáma, the first settler of the valley was Audun Skokul, the grandson of an English lord, Hunda (Hounds'-) Steinar, who himself was married to Alof daughter to Ragnar Lodbrok. Audun had a daughter, Thora Mossneck, mother of Ulfhild whose daughter was Asta, mother of Olaf the Holy. His daughter by Astrid daughter of King Olaf of Sweden (†1022) was Ulfhild, married to duke Ordulf of Brunswick (before 1043), ancestress of the Hanoverian line of English sovereigns.

P. 97, l. 32. Viðidalstunga seems to have been a homestead of importance since the 14th century at least. In 1385 it came, together with the farms of Swalastead, Littlebank and Peaklava (Tindahraun), into the possession of the magnate Jón Hákonarson (1350-1398), the earliest owner on record of the famous Flateybook, which is the largest existing vellum from Iceland; now in the royal library at Copenhagen. The most famous owner of the place in later times was Páll Vídalín (1667-1727) a justiciary and the most learned commentator of the Code of Icelandic law—'Jóns bók' from 1281.

P. 119, l. 4 from bottom. Holy Fell has been a place of note ever since the tenth century. Snorri Goði (the Priest) as a youth of eighteen first set up a house here by A.D. 963, and after an occupancy of 45 years exchanged it (1008) for Sælingsdale-Tongue, the home of Gudrun, then Bodli's widow. Up to the middle of the twelfth century this house seems to

238

have been in the possession of the descendants of Gudrun and her fourth (last) husband Thorkel Eyolfsson, Gellir, Thorgils and Ari the Learned who died in 1148. A house of Augustinian monks was established at Holy Fell in 1172 by Thorlak Thorhallson, Bishop of Skálholt and the national saint. After a useful existence of 371 years it was dissolved in 1543.

P. 125, l. 7. In a dissertation on local names in Thorsness-Thing (Safn II, 277-298), Thorlacius says that a narrow tongue of land called Orrustunes (Fight-ness) runs into the firth on its northern side; he also mentions the skerry, but gives no name to it—in Eyrbyggia it has none. However, it is quite possible that Thorlacius may have told Mr. Morris that it was called Vigra- (Swords'-) or Orrustu- (Fight's-) Skerry, for in Collingwood's map of Thorsness (Sagasteads of Iceland, p. 85) both Orrustunes and Vigrasker are given presumably on the authority of local antiquaries; but though appropriate, the names rest on no ancient warrant.

P. 133, l. 27. The spot in front of us was the Thralls'-scree (þrælaskriða), where blind terror drove Thorarin the Black's slaves over the precipice some four hundred feet high. Eyrbyggia, ch. 18, p. 37.

P. 139, l. 20. Here Morris omits mentioning an incident unique in this journey. When he was "settled in his blankets," he offered to tell us the Saga of Biorn, the Champion of the men of Hitdale. The offer was accepted readily enough; and he told the whole saga in abridgement with remarkably few slips, winding up with the old rhyme:

> And here the Saga comes to an end;
> May all who heard, to the good God wend.

And the audience was still awake when he finished!

P. 139, l. 21. The full name is Arnar-stapi (Erne's = Eagle's-Needle or Pillar) and the name is derived, says Kålund, from an isolated rock pillar outside the coast, presumably haunted by fish-eagles. In the days of Eric the Red (the discoverer and first settler of Greenland, 983), it seems to have been a place of some importance. In modern times it has been a trading station, and from 1821-56 (?) it was the seat of the governor of the West of Iceland.

P. 144, l. 5. They grow on sea-covered rocks off the coast and are torn away by the violent surf and washed ashore.

P. 144, l. 14. The same place that in Eyrbyggia occurs so frequently under the name of Lavahaven (Hraunhöfn).

P. 145, l. 24. Otherwise called Staðr á Ölduhrygg (the Stead on Wave-Ridge) counted among the best livings in Iceland. In the twelfth century it was a property belonging to the kindred of Ari the Learned, and from them passed to Thord Sturluson, Snorri's eldest brother. It has always been a house of note, more or less.

P. 154, l. 16. Borg is about the most famous of the Saga-steads of Iceland. Kveldúlfr, a sworn foe of Harald Fairhair, fled, together with Skallagrim, his son, before the power of the King to Iceland about A.D. 878. He died on the voyage, but left the will that Skallagrim should take up a fixed abode where his (Kveldúlfr's) coffin should happen to drift ashore. At a spot nearest to the point where the coffin was found Skallagrim laid the foundations of the famous house in 879. It remained for a long time the chief seat of the goðar of the Mýramenn, Skallagrim's descendants. It was Snorri Sturluson's residence from 1202 till, perhaps, 1206. It has been a church-stead ever since Thorstein Egilsson built a church there directly Christianity had been made the law of the land —under lay patrons till 1849, when by a royal decree it was made a 'benefice.'

P. 154, l. 19. 'Odd of the Tongue' did not live at Deildar-Tongue but, as Landnáma and the saga of Hen-Thorir say, at Broadlair-stead (Breiðabólstaðr), the house set up by his father, the 'landnáms'-man Önund Broadbeard. Out of that house disused grew in later times the manorial home of Reykholt. Thverar-lithe lies to the north of White-water-side separated from it by 'Örnolf's' or 'Kiarra'-dale. White-water-side is the northern slope of the White-water valley.

On the southern side of the river rise the hill-ranges that form the northern bound of Reykja-dale (Reykholtsdale).

P. 156, l. 6. The house of Stafaholt (as the old spelling is) was already in the tenth century one of note, when the goði, Einar Teitsson, as Egil's saga relates, backed Steinar Önundsson, the quarrelsome tenant of Anabrekka, against Thorstein Egilsson of Borg, an affair with which Gunnlaug Wormtongue chaffed Thorstein (ch. 5 of Gunnlaug's saga). In the thirteenth century this place was famous as the dwelling of Olaf White-skald, the son of Thord, Snorri Sturluson's eldest brother; Olaf was born ab. 1210, died 1259, a poet, and a writer on rhetoric. For the last fourteen years of his life he kept a private school here for the instruction of theological students.

P. 161, l. 13. This is the same force as Biarni's-force in the Heath-slayings' story, which indeed states that 'There was in those days' (10th century) 'and long after, a bridge over the river beside Biarni's-force.'

P. 163, l. 7. He was born 1178, at Hvamm in Hvammfirth; he was fostered by the mighty goði Jón Loptson of Oddi from 1181 to 1197. He married the heiress Herdis of Borg 1199; left Borg for Reykholt, acquired by purchase ab. 1206; was murdered at the instigation of Hákon the Old, King of Norway, 1217-1263, by a band of assassins commanded by his own son-in-law, Gizzur Thorvaldsson, in the night of 22nd–23rd September, 1241. Tradition knows nothing about his grave or burial place. For further information about Snorri see Saga Library, VI, pp. xvij ff.

P. 163, l. 21. For 'bitumen' read silicious sinter (islandice 'hveragrjót') (bitumen does not exist in the country and was not an article of import in Snorri's time).

P. 166, l. 2 from bottom. The pass is misnamed here; possibly Goðaskörð is meant, a name given to a road which from the pass branches off to the north-east. The name Jóruskörð does not exist; but Jórukleif, an excessively difficult lava pass, is found on the opposite, i.e. the south-western shore of the Lake of Thingvellir, and to that the legend alluded to in the text refers. Probably the guides or some person at Thingvellir told the author the legend and localized it at Goðaskörð, at the north-east of the Thingvellir *valley*, instead of at Jórukleif on the south-western coast of the Thingvellir *lake*.

P. 170, l. 15. The site of the Lögberg here defined is the traditional one. The latest researches go to show that the Rock (berg) of the Law had its place on the nether (southern) wall of the Almannagjá, a little to the east of the gap through which the road goes from Thingvellir to Mosfells-heath and further to Reykjavík.—See Kålund Bidrag til en historisk-topografisk Beskrivelse af Island, I, 131 ff.

P. 170, l. 21. From a law which was sanctioned by the Althing in A.D. 1200 at the instance of Páll Jónsson (Bp. of Skálholt 1195-1211) and several of the mightiest men of the country, we learn that in order to facilitate trade intercourse between Icelanders and foreigners (Englishmen) it was provided that the length-measure (stika: measuring rod) used in measuring 'wadmal' (Icel. homespun) 'linen and cloth' should be twice as long as that standard of length (kvarði) which was marked on the wall of the church of Thingvellir. This standard was the ancient Icelandic ell-measure of 18 inches and a fraction. The new length measure of the country was therefore to equal an English yard (36 in.). How important the reform was considered may be gathered from the further provision of this law that the yard measure should be marked on the wall of every church that possessed the right of burial (parish church). This law is a very interesting piece of evidence as to the overwhelming importance the Icelanders attached to British trade in the twelfth century. It is quite possible that the stone in the churchyard of Thingvellir may have some traditional connection with this law. But the law does not say that the new measure should be marked on a *stone* in the church wall. The church of Thingvellir was built of timber in the eleventh century. Snorri (Heimskringla [Saga Library], II, 241), who mentions that the church of Thingvellir had been built of timber given by Olaf the Holy, says nothing about its having been pulled down or rebuilt of

242

other materials when he wrote Olaf's Saga. The learned Páll Vídalín (cf. p. 238 above), in discoursing on the length of the Icel. ell, says that in his day no one knew anything about any stone on which the yard measure was marked. How the present yard-stone has come to be where it is is unknown; but according to Dr. Kålund it was there in 1820. But the measure cut on it does not seem to tally with the old law with which it is probably safe to say that it stands in no direct historical relation. What the parson took for a Bremen ell is more likely to be the Hamburg 'Elle.'

P. 170, l. 32. The Speaker (Lögsögumaðr) was the highest office-bearer in the land and the central figure in the life of the Althing. The Althing, to begin with, was a term that covered not only in a narrower sense an assembly of legislators (Lögrétta, Lawrighter) and judges (four Quarter Courts and the Fifth Court), but also the whole gathering of unofficial people, men and women, who from all parts of the country crowded hither for business, show and pleasure.

The Speaker's business was wide and varied. He was elected by the Legislative Assembly already mentioned for three years. He must recite from the Hill of Laws to the assembled people every year the whole of the section of the law that related to the judicial procedure, and, in addition, one-third of the rest of the body of the law. If he found his memory at fault, he could summon to his aid, before beginning his recital, five experts to put him right. He was the guide and director of the deliberations of the Lögretta and thus, in a way, the guardian of the logical consistency of the law. In this assembly sat, besides him and the two bishops, the thirty-nine goðar of the land and nine chosen 'lawrighting' men so as to make forty-eight in all, or twelve representatives for each of the four quarters into which legislatively and judicially the land was divided. Each of the forty-eight principal members of the Lögretta was provided with two counselling assessors, one of whom sat in front the other at the back of him; so the whole legislative body consisted altogether of 147 persons. They sat on three rows of benches

R2   243 (stones) in the open, at various spots at various times, during the fortnightly term of the Thing. The Speaker appointed the spot where the four Quarter Courts, each consisting of nine judges, should hold their session. His duty was also to inform inquirers what was the right interpretation of the law in this or that disputed point.

The Althing of Iceland was held here (at Thingvellir) from A.D. 930 to 1800. After a suspension of forty-four years it was revived at Reykjavík 1845 as a biennial consultative assembly, and is, since 1874, a legislative (biennial) Diet.

P. 185, l. 22.

Æ man lifa	Ever will live
Nema öld fariz	Unless mankind perish
Bragna lof	The praise of men
Eða bili heimar	Or the worlds give way

The original is found in Snorri Sturluson's Háttatal, 96th strophe, and reads :

þat mun æ lifa	That praise of the princes will
nema öld farist	ever live unless mankind per-
Bragninga lof	ish or the worlds give way.
eða bili heimar.	

Bragnar (of Morris's reading) is masc. pl., properly used of the body-guard of the legendary king *Bragningr;* and then, as a kenning : *men* in general. But Bragningr was the dynastic name given to the kings descended from Bragi, son of Half-dan the Old (Sn. Edda I, 520-22). In Snorri's poem, Bragningar refers, of course, to the two princely persons he is praising, King Hakon the Old and his father-in-law, Duke Skúli.

II. THE DIARY OF 1873

P. 189, l. 14. The veritable battle-holm : the holm on which judicial single-fights used to be waged until 1006, when Gunnlaug and Raven fought there, and the legislature put a stop to any further duelling in Iceland. See Gunnlaugs-saga.

P. 192, l. 18. The South bishopric. The Bishop of Skálholt

244

was sole bishop over Iceland 1056-1106. From 1106-1807 he was bishop over the southern diocese. From the latter date the whole island has formed one bishopric. As the most interesting of the historical memorials connected with Skálholt is shown the spot where the last Roman Catholic bishop, Jón Arason, together with two of his sons, was decapitated on November 6th, 1550.

P. 197, l. 10. What H— & B— are meant for I cannot say. The event alluded to is obviously the meeting 'under Three-corner,' which took place between Flosi and his band of B[urners], from the East, with the party of Höskuld or Huldigunn, represented by the sons of Sigfus, from the South (Burnt Nial, II, 164-165).

P. 199, l. 17. baðstofa: the *baðstofa* was of old the 'bath' of the homestead ; in modern times it is the general sitting-room and dormitory of the household. Here, in the long winter evenings, the people read out their sagas and sing their *rimur* (heroic ballads). This chamber is the special home of the domestic industries of the country, except weaving, which, when the people can afford to have a loom, proceeds in a separate room.

P. 208, l. 24. This is a mistake. They came to Keldur, past Árgilsstaðir some distance off on the left, up from the South. But Knafahólar is a spot some distance to the north of Keldur and was not touched till the train left Keldur on the route for Stóruvellir the next day.

P. 210, l. 21. What the initials F— F— may mean I cannot say. There is no jokul, so far as I know, known under the names thus initialled. Whether Eírik's jokul is visible from Stóruvellir I cannot say, nor, for that matter, is it at all certain that that name is intended.

P. 211, l. 9. A staff-crown, i.e. made of standing basaltic columns rising sheer out of the 'ash-grey slopes,' somewhat like this— Of course, never having seen the mountain, I cannot be sure that I give a correct outline of the appearance of Búrfell to the eye. But this type of mountain formation is extremely common in Iceland. To describe such a mountain as one with 'ash-grey slopes and staff-crown' brings its image vividly home to one's mind.

P.211,l.35. *Skyr:* Persian *shir,* sour milk; sour curds, milk curdled when lukewarm by means of rennet; a very common article of nutriment in summer.

P. 212, l.27. A little clear stream: called Helliskvisl, which, running north-west, joins Tungna-á at Mosa-tunga.

P. 212, l. 33. Still further to the left (west) than Valafell.

P. 213, l. 5. Arnarfell's jökull: it is the name of the south-eastern portion of the huge Hofsjökull.

P. 213, l.8. The tongue of the confluence: the name of the narrowest part of the tongue right at the confluence of the rivers is Mosa-tunga, Moss-tongue, which soon runs into the impassable Buðarháls (Booth's-neck) which takes up a considerable space of the tongue formed by the two rivers.

P. 214, l. 5. Hvamgil, an oasis by the side of Thiórsá: Arriving at the day's destination, Morris does not mention the name of the camping-stead, but says it is where, before them, Thiórsá forms a big waterfall, and 'brooks trickle off toward the big river' through 'deep gorges' (gills). 'On this [i.e. the southern] side of one of these, on the willows and grass, we pitch our tents.' This must be the spot which on page 214 is called Hvam (should be Hvamm) gil (Comb-gill). But my impression is that the place goes by the name of Hvanna-gil, (Angelica's gill—gorge of angelica). The name is not marked on the map.

P. 214, l.15. Ere-rose: Icel. eyra-ros (gravel-rose, sand-rose), *epilobium montanum* L.

P. 216, l.6. Thoris Tindr (Thorir's peak). East of Kalda-kvísl flows into Tungna-á the Vatnakvisl, and far up the the Tongue formed by these confluents of Tungna-á stands, on the western side of Vatnakvisl, the isolated Thóris-Tindr.

P. 216, l. 26. We were getting on now long ago among the Kerlingafiöll: there is some mistake here. Kerlingafiöll are at a very considerable distance, about twenty miles, west of Thiórsá, rising under that south-westerly skirt of Hofsiökull

246

which is called Blágnýpuiökull; but the travellers were *east* of Thiórsá on their way to Eyvindarkofaver, their camping-stead, under the western brow of Tungna-fells-jökull to the north-east. They were still more or less, according to the condition of the ground, on the Thiórsá, some little distance south of Soleyarhofði; before coming up as far as that ford, they baited 'in the very front of the great Jokul,' i.e. the Hofsiökull or, more accurately, the Arnarfell, i.e. the south-eastern section of it. They were, therefore, at a spot near Thiórsá, due south of the said fell and south-east of Kerlinga-fiöll. When the caravan has been under way for some time after baiting as above, Morris notices that they were 'edging toward the Jokul [i.e. Hofsiökull] and leaving Kerlingafiöll behind.'

P. 217, l. 10. edging toward the Jokul: this must refer to Hofsiökull, under the southern brow of which Kerlingafiöll were gradually vanishing as the travellers proceeded further north round the south-eastern protuberance (Arnarfell) of Hofsiökull.

P. 218, l. 15. Eyvindr, generally called Fialla-Eyvindr (Fell-Eyvind), is one of the most famous modern outlaws in Iceland. He was the son of goodman Jón and his wife Margret, who kept house at Hlið (Lithe) in the commune of the men of Hrune in the shrievalty of Arness. He seems to have been born in the very early years of the eighteenth century. With his wife Halla, he spent, as the tale goes, some twenty years of an outlaw's life in the wildernesses of Iceland, or in captivity. Handsome, good-natured, exceedingly handy at all craft, swift of foot, an unrivalled climber and runner, he out-lived somehow the penalties of the law and got into favour with the governor of the country then residing at Bessastaðir in the South, and is said (by some) to be buried in the church-yard there. Espólin, Arbækr, IX, c. 50-51. Islenzkar Þjoð-sögur II, 243-51. Maurer, Isländ. Volkssagen, 242.

P. 220, l. 30. Fiórðungar is meant, but that is not the name; it is Fiórðungs-Alda (Quarter-wave, i.e. Quarter-hillrise), a little north of where the plateau of the wilderness reaches its greatest height (2200 ft.). The name of the hillrise is probably connected with the fact that it was taken as dividing-mark between the south and the north quarters of the country in olden times.

P. 221, l. 10. Vona-skarð: Vonarskarð (Hope's-pass) is the opening between Tungna-fells-iökull to the west and Vatna-iökull to the east. It was passed for the first time in the history of Iceland by Bard, the settler of upper Bard-dale, in the ninth century, who went south over Sprengisand with his whole household, cattle and all, making every animal draw a sledge laden with its fodder of hay. The journey, though undertaken perhaps as early as February, seems to have been quite successful, for Bard became a settler of great note at Gnúpar in the south-east country.

P. 221, l. 13. by the lake side: as a matter of fact the line of the watershed is the northern root of Tungna-fells-iökull, where we have the fountain-head of Thiórsá and of Skiálfandafliót in proximity to each other.

P. 222, l. 7. Skiálfandafliót, the Fleet of Skiálfandi, which is the name of the bay into which this long river flows.

P. 224, l. 30. Lundabrekka: the statement that Lundarbrekka (Grove-brent), on the eastern side of the valley, is the church-stead, but Haldórsstaðir on the western side of it was the parson's house, might seem odd on the face of it; such, however, is the actual case. By a royal decree, April 17, 1857, it was settled that instead of two churches which heretofore had existed, at Eyjardalsá and Lundarbrekka, for the future the only church of the parish should be at Lundarbrekka, but the parson's residence should be at Haldórsstaðir.

P. 224, l. 34. (Liosá): the meaning must be that some snowy mountain north by Liósavatn (Lightwater) closed the view of the valley from Haldorsstaðir.

P. 225, l. 29. This is the stead of the Lund: i.e. Lundarbrekka, which, a few lines further, the goodman explains originally took its name from the *lundr*, grove, which was found on the hillside above this homestead.

P. 226, l. 3. L— S— must mean Látra Strönd, the northwesternmost coastal part part of Thingeyarsýsla on the Eya-firth side, the inland mountain formation of the tract corre-sponding closely to the description here given of it.

P. 226, l. 14. H— lithe can hardly be meant for anything but Reykiahlið (Reeklithe), although it could not be said exactly to be 'under' Námafiall. But perhaps some other place may be meant; I do not feel quite sure of the text here.

P. 227, l. 20. Geirastaðir: a place which has been in exist-ence ever since the 'landnáma' period. The great number of grottoes (*skútar*) in the lava around this stead serve cattle for asylum from the ravages of midges on warm summer days.

P. 229, l. 5. a deserted stead called Littahagi: Littahagi is an impossible form and would seem to stand for Litlihagi (Little-haw), but it is the same spot which at the end of this section is called Liðarhagi (for Hliðarhagi). Neither name is marked on the map nor known by Kålund. But Lock (Guide to Iceland, p. 48) says: 'travellers' (in quest of reindeer) should 'strike due west from Dettifoss for a lake near a moun-tain called Eilífr (the Eternal). South-west of this lake is an abandoned ruinous farmhouse, known as Hliðarhæli, wherein the author has frequently passed a night...' This Hliðarhæli (Lithe-shelter) would seem to be the spot where our travel-lers put up their tents on the night of August 12. But the Journal is not very clear here.

P. 231, l. 28. Dettifoss is due east from the mountain Eilífr, the river forming it being called Jökulsá a Fiöllum (on the Mountains, in the Wilds), which is one of the greatest rivers in Iceland, 115 miles long.

P. 232, l. 5. Laxardal: the valley formed by Laxá (Salmon-river) which the travellers crossed, passing round the western shore of Mývatn to Grímsstaðir.

P. 233, l. 9. In Grettir's rock, unknown in the Saga, there is possibly the nucleus of a legend current in the country-side.

P. 233, l. 15. Thorkel Foulmouth: see The Story of Burnt Nial, II, 138 ff, and the Saga of Gudmund the Mighty in Islenzkar Fornsögur, 1880, p. 182 ff.

P. 234, l.8. Ellifsta: this must be Leifsstaðir, a farmhouse in the northern part of the Rape of Aungulstaðir, near to the point where the road from Háls strikes the head of Eyafirth. On the Eyafirth side of Vaðlaheiði there is no local name that suits better or anything like so well.

P. 234, l.11. M— Th—: Monks' Thverá, a place of great note both in heathen and Christian times. In heathen days it was the manorial residence of the descendants of Ingiald, the son of Helgi the Lean, the original lord of the whole of Eya-firth. From Glum (Slaughter-Glum) it passed into the pos-session of his kinsman the stateman Einar Eyólfsson, brother of Gudmund the Mighty of Madder-vales, and it remained in the possession of his descendants till 1155, when Biörn Gilsson, bishop of Hólar (1147-1162) acquired it and turned it into a foundation of a Benedictine monastery; like the rest of the religious houses, it was dissolved in the middle of the sixteenth century and its property taken in charge by the crown of Denmark.

P. 234, l. 13. Espihol: otherwise called Stórholl, a house famous as the birthplace of Jón Jónsson Espólín, the most distinguished modern annalist and genealogist of Iceland (1769-1836) whose Islands Abækr, Annals of Iceland, in ten sections, from 1262 to his own lifetime, are an inexhaustible mine of information, remarkably faultless, considering the vast period they cover.

P. 234, l. 16. See Víga-Glum-saga, ch. 27.

P. 234, l. 19. Scene of the sorb trees: what is meant by this is uncertain. On his left, as he rode down the main valley from Saurbœr, just opposite to the house of Grund, is the farmstead of Möðrufell, in the neighbourhood of which is a lava, and in that lava a sorb grove which, tradition will have it, grew up from the cairn of a brother and sister who had been executed for incest. From this stock of sorb trees, the story goes, are derived many of the sorbs which are met with in various places throughout the countrysides of Eya-firth. Possibly the 'scene' mentioned in the text refers to some other locality. For the tradition about the Möðrufell sorb,

250

Gisli Bryniúlfsson's poem in Ny Félagsrit, 1847, pp. 196-8, may be consulted with advantage.

P. 235, l.13. Friðriksgáfar: Moðruvellir, on the western bank of Hörgsá, towards the mouth of Hörgárdalr, is an historical homestead, having been a house of Augustinian canons regular, from 1296 till 1547. In the year 1783, the King fixed Möðruvellir as residence for the Governor of the North-country. In 1826 the place was burnt down, and King Frederic VI caused a stone house to be erected to serve the northern Governor as official seat. The house was named by the first occupier, Grímr Jónsson, Friðriksgáfa, i.e. Frederick's-gift, but was burnt down the year after Mr. Morris visited the place.

P. 235, l. 20. Bægisa, poet's place: the meaning of the curt note is somehow this: Jón Thorláksson (born 1744), one of the greatest poets that Iceland has ever produced, was priest at Bægis-á in Öxna-dale from 1788 to 1819. He translated Milton's 'Paradise Lost' and Pope's 'Essay on Man.' He was much befriended by the Rev. Ebenezer Henderson, a learned Englishman, in whose Journal in Iceland there is a very appreciative estimate of the great gifts of Sira Jón.

P. 235, footnote. The poet alluded to is Jónas Hallgrímsson, born at Steinstaðir in Öxna-dale in 1807, died in 1844.

PRINTED BY W. H. SMITH AND SON AT
THE ARDEN PRESS LETCHWORTH